Sex and violence

How do we recognize and identify sex and violence in our own and other cultures? How do anthropologists and feminists differ in their analysis of the relationship between sexuality and violence? The contributors to *Sex and Violence* are established anthropologists and committed feminists, personally involved in the paradoxes and contradictions inherent in the answers to these questions. They look closely at the relationship between social anthropology and its political effect, particularly in terms of the theory and ethnography of gender relations.

The range of case studies – from Bolivia, Brazil, Britain, Colombia, Fiji, Peru, Japan and the USA – challenges what constitutes violence and sexuality in other cultures and questions the appropriateness of these culturally loaded terms for the analysis of other societies. The chapters examine the distinctive ways in which human relationships are realized and expressed through idioms which we in the west recognize and identify as both sexual and violent. They also take up the question of objectification in the study of others by focusing specifically on sex and violence – a topic which, in the west and in feminist politics, epitomizes the hierarchical relation between those who look and those who are looked at.

This collection of rich and varied ethnographic case studies is an important and original contribution to the debate between feminism and anthropology. Its exploration of gender difference and gender hierarchy is of central concern to both anthropologists and feminists, and the book's multi-cultural approach will appeal to a wide readership, including students and teachers of social anthropology, cultural studies and gender studies.

Penelope Harvey and **Peter Gow** are both Lecturers in Social Anthropology at the University of Manchester.

Sex and violence

Issues in representation and experience

Edited by
Penelope Harvey and Peter Gow

London and New York

First published 1994
by Routledge
11 New Fetter Lane, London EC4P 4EE

Simultaneously published in the USA and Canada
by Routledge
29 West 35th Street, New York, NY 10001

Typeset in Times by LaserScript, Mitcham, Surrey
Printed and bound in Great Britain by
TJ Press (Padstow) Ltd, Padstow, Cornwall

British Library Cataloguing in Publication Data
A catalogue record for this book is available from the British Library

Library of Congress Cataloging in Publication Data
A catalogue for this book is available from the Library of Congress

ISBN 0–415–05733–7 (hbk)
ISBN 0–415–05734–5 (pbk)

Contents

List of contributors

Deborah Cameron is Senior Lecturer in Literary Linguistics at Strathclyde University.

Sophie Day is Lecturer in Social Anthropology at Goldsmiths' College, London and Research Fellow in the Academic Department of Public Health, St Mary's Hospital Medical School.

Elizabeth Frazer is Fellow, Tutor and University Lecturer in Politics at New College, Oxford.

Peter Gow is Lecturer in Social Anthropology at the University of Manchester.

Olivia Harris is Senior Lecturer in Social Anthropology at Goldsmiths' College, London.

Penelope Harvey is Lecturer in Social Anthropology at the University of Manchester.

Cecilia McCallum is a Post-doctoral Research Associate in the Department of Social Anthropology, London School of Economics.

Henrietta Moore is Reader in Social Anthropology at the London School of Economics.

Christina Toren is Senior Lecturer in Social Anthropology at Brunel University.

Peter Wade is Lecturer in Latin American Studies and Geography at Liverpool University.

Editors' acknowledgements

We would like first to thank all the contributors, and Heather Gibson of Routledge, who were long suffering in what became a lengthy editing process. We are also grateful to all those who participated in the conference for their comments and support: Shirley Ardener, Joan Burke, Helen Callaway, Deborah Des Jardins, Harriet Evans, Pat Holden, Stephen Hugh-Jones, Nicola Lacey, Julia Leslie, Francesca Lewis, Joanna Overing, Maria Phylactou, Frances Pine, Kay Richardson, Peter Rivière, Anne Tatham, Megan Vaughan, Ann Whitehead and Sue Wright. The Cherwell Centre, Oxford and the Centre for Cross Cultural Research on Women gave us much appreciated help in the organization of the event. Finally, especial thanks are due to Joanna Overing, who provoked us into proposing a conference on this topic, to Shirley Ardener, who took up the challenge when we would have let it go, and to Marilyn Strathern, who refused to write a conclusion to this volume and explained why it was not needed.

Introduction

Penelope Harvey and Peter Gow

This volume is a collection of papers written by people working in anthropology and cultural studies on the common theme of sex and violence. The papers were all presented at a conference in May 1989 in Oxford, with the help of the Centre for Cross Cultural Research on Women. It has the failings and virtues of such an origin. It makes no claims to being an authoritative statement on these issues. The problems, and the ways in which they are approached in this book, do not call out for authoritative statement. Instead, it presents a set of approaches, unified by the common focus on the issues in question. It has the virtue that all the contributors were present at the original conference, and thus heard the original papers and participated in the discussions which motivated this introductory chapter.

In line with the nature of the papers herein collected, this introduction is neither an overview of the general literature, nor an attempt to give the background to the internal debate of the volume, nor yet an attempt to provide a succinct summary of that debate. This is not a derogation of editorial duty. The literature on the subject is vast, and the debate has been carried on in so many diverse times and places as to defy summary. But, more importantly, the issues raised by our title, *Sex and Violence*, are so close to our common, everyday experiences that any attempt at summary of debate or background would be both impossible and pointless. And distasteful, for how could we claim to know what anyone brings to their thinking on these issues?

This introduction is just that, a way in to the reading of the separate papers in the volume. It is our own reading, and it is designed as an invitation to readers to make their own.

The title of this book, *Sex and Violence*, refers to a certain interface between anthropological studies of cultural difference, feminist concerns with the politics of western gender relations and their social effects, and an acknowledgement of a genre of mass appeal, the commodification of persons and bodies, the desire for participation without responsibility that sells so many newspapers, magazines, and novels. Why might people buy a book on sex and violence, or flick through it surreptitiously? Why might such a title draw people's attention to the work?

Anthropological studies of sexuality and violence apparently hold out the promise of delving into two central western fantasies – the eroticization of domination and the eroticization of 'the (dominated) Other'.[1] To read and to write about sexuality and violence in other cultures might in itself be an activity that affords pleasure.

Violence, a self-evident and everyday occurrence in Britain, is nevertheless legislated, controlled, and studied as outside or beyond normal, constructive human practice. Violence is by definition unacceptable, out of control, beyond reason. Furthermore, it is transgressive; transgressive of our sense of bodily integrity and the spirit enclosed therein which enables the notion of violation to apply to more than physical hurt. It is in this sense that the concept of violence is so closely associated with western understandings of human sexuality. Despite what Foucault had to say on the matter,[2] sexuality is also associated in Anglo-American cultures with the transgressive individual, that aspect of self that emerges through lack of control, that exists and finds expression against reason enabling the momentary transcendence of individuating boundaries.

Western cultures have constituted and responded to sexuality and violence by discourses and policies of exclusion, expulsion, and repression. Violence is excluded by its defining anti-social nature, sexuality by its location in an intensely personal space of embodiment. A volume on violence and sex promises to look at things that we usually confine to our private fantasy worlds, associated with the erotic danger of that which we keep on the edge. Once put in this way, however, it is also important to point out that our familiarity with such material and the experience of it as pleasurable, crucially depends on the distance which exists between our own lived personal experiences and the experiences of those who have become the object of the voyeuristic gaze. Distance is essential if the fantasy is to maintain its ability to please.

Is this the field of interpretation into which the anthropological texts will be read/interpreted? If so, should we remain silent on these issues? And in addition to a concern with how these texts might be interpreted, should we not also address a concern about how such texts are produced? Is the objectification of highly charged emotional events itself a form of violence? Does writing, representational practice, not involve us in a process of effacing social relations between people in order to produce the text as cultural artefact? How, in other words, does a book on sex and violence speak to the current moral crisis in contemporary ethnography where representation of otherness is seen to imply both disassociation and objectification?

In the process of western colonial expansion out over the globe, the other cultures contacted and dominated came increasingly to work as fantasy images of the metropolitan culture. From Montaigne and Voltaire on native South American cultures through Gauguin and R. L. Stevenson on the South Pacific to Freud on Australia and Picasso on Africa, these other human cultural worlds came to provide the basis for a critique of all that was bad about the world of the western writer or artist. Increasingly, alternative images of social possibility required the backup of concrete exemplars. Depictions of the Tupinamba as acephalous cannibals gave added authority to a critique of absolutist monarchy, while the rampant primitive sexuality of the Tahitians or Samoans gave added authority to a critique of European sexual repression. By the same token, these actually existing others provided equally powerful support for reactionary critiques, as fantasy images of the social results of weak or absent states or of uncontrolled sexuality in a dark world of cannibalism, insecurity, and, especially, inadequate technical control over nature. Images of the other are inherently polyvalent (Torgovnick 1990).

Anthropology developed as a scientific extension of this enquiry into those human cultural worlds which were most other to the lived worlds of the agents of western expansion. As with these older uses of images of other cultures, anthropology has always been a more or less explicit critique of the home culture, whether affirmative or oppositional. But anthropology added a new dimension to the issue, for it made explicit its role of critical reflection on the images of other cultures operating in the home culture itself. Accounts of these other cultures ceased to be the starting point of a critique of the home culture, and became an end itself. Ethnography as the accurate and objective description of other cultural worlds became a central activity of anthropology, the groundwork on which analysis was built. Ethnographies are true representations of the other. But, because they are images of the other, they are also polyvalent. Ethnographic texts therefore occupy an uneasy place in imagery of the other because they claim, at some level, to be true. Far from solving the problem of the unscientific uses of this imagery, ethnographies extend it in novel ways and with unforeseen effects. Each ethnography, as it sets out to challenge some previous erroneous image of the people described, produces a new and more potent image of the other.

A good example of the problem is provided by Gregor's account of sexuality and institutionalized gang rape among the Mehinaku of the Alto Xingu of Central Brazil (discussed further by McCallum in Chapter 4 of this volume) (Gregor 1985). Starting from the premise that the very cultural otherness of these people will provide an important perspective on western sexuality, he produces an ethnographic account of them that provides an image of a culture at once very similar to western culture, but in very important senses different from it. Gregor clearly hopes that these differences and similarities will shed important light on aspects of his home culture which remain opaque or confusing to its members. In particular, gang rape is one of the most shocking and dramatic forms of sexual violence by men against women, but western people have no clear and overt language in which to discuss the motivations of the aggressors or the implications for the victims. The Mehinaku by contrast, in Gregor's account, have institutionalized gang rape, and provide an open and public discourse about why it occurs. Because the Mehinaku, who seem to talk about sex with remarkable frankness, can openly discuss this act and why it happens, they provide an important perspective for our own culture, by openly revealing what we conceal.

But, as a produced image of the other, Gregor's ethnography of the Mehinaku provides the point of attachment for other images of alterity. What kind of culture institutionalizes gang rape as a public activity, indeed as a religious one? Gregor's attractive image of the Mehinaku, a people at ease with talk of their sexual desire and activity, conjures up a deeply unattractive image of the Mehinaku, a culture in which the collective domination by men of women is supported by religiously sanctioned acts of collective male violence against any woman who challenges their power. Both images provide the grounds for action, but the actions diverge in the extreme. Gregor's overt image suggests that we western people should do something about our inability to talk openly about sexuality and sexual violence, and by doing so learn more about its motives. We should, in short, become more like them. But the other image, equally overt in Gregor's text even if never intended by him, suggests that we should continue to repress and exclude the other. We should, in short, become as different from the Mehinaku as possible.

This problem runs deeper, for imagery of other cultural possibilities has always functioned for western people as the source of another type of action: changing the other. Western culture is intrinsically bound up with doing something about the other. An image of the other has no sooner been invoked as a call to do something about ourselves, than it inverts its valency, and becomes a call to do something about them. Times have changed, and we might be reluctant to send missionaries to clear away the gross moral darkness of their religions, but we would not be reluctant to insist that development projects must address the position and interests of women, even when these conflict with those of men or of traditional cultural practices. Western people, often uneasy about the domination intrinsic to their modes of action, are happiest when domination is done to empower the dominated.

And the problem runs deeper yet. The image of the other is a call to action, and action requires some sort of change in the parameters of our relationship with the actually existent other. Our unease about the actions which result from our images of the other reaches its fullest form in the suspicion that the truth of our relationship to the other is purely that of the domination of the image of the other. This is the suspicion that all representations of the other are pornographic (Kappeler 1987). This problem assails all of anthropological endeavour. Perhaps the interest that anthropologists take in Gregor's *Anxious Pleasures*, or Mead's *Coming of Age in Samoa*, or Malinowski's *The Sexual Life of Savages* is really not that different to the interest taken by 'other people' (never explicitly identified) in 'snuff movies' or other forms of hard-core pornography. Certainly, the popularity of ethnographies of sex or violence among non-anthropologists suggests that this is so. Is anthropology simply the representational domination of the other for the gratification of the self? Should anthropologists stop doing it? Does the harm it carries outweigh the good? This is a question that constantly assails most politically concerned practitioners, and makes anthropological politics among the most nervous of all academic politics.

FEMINISM AND ANTHROPOLOGY

The very issue that has caused a crisis in anthropological representation is the explicit starting point for feminist analyses of the relationship between violence and sexuality. Here the analyst seeks both to name/objectify/reveal the violence of particular social relations, and to disassociate themselves, and hopefully their readers, from engagement or collusion in such relations. Feminist scholarship is thus problematic for the ethnographer. The objectification and disassociation involved in the politics of naming and revealing requires the imposition of absolute values on particular practices regardless of how these are understood by those involved. What are the political and theoretical consequences of relativizing or not relativizing violent acts and their motivations?

Discussion of the relationship between feminist scholarship and anthropological treatments of gender was a strong sub-text to the conference proceedings – perhaps less evident in the papers themselves than in the motivations for participation. While the conference did the usual anthropological task of relativizing the concepts 'sex' and 'violence' and questioning the basis for any kind of cross-cultural comparison through these terms, it also revealed very strongly held and opposing views among the conference participants about the relationship between gender difference as an anthropological issue and gender politics in a more general sense. Beyond the topics of specific papers, the conference itself produced a series of debates/confrontations which were not so much to do with the possibility of cultural difference, a position which all participants would have upheld, but had more to do with the extent to which anthropology can sustain/contain any kind of political commitment and if so what kind? Can an anthropological commitment to incommensurability which acknowledges that cultural difference is not merely the difference of political interest, simultaneously address such issues?

The relationship between anthropological and feminist understandings of gender has occurred in a sequence where previous traces are never entirely covered over.[3] We are thus not at a moment of consensual plurality – both the politics and the anthropological concerns that various writers are addressing are of their own times and circumstances. Gender emerged with force into anthropological debate in the 1970s. The context of the 1990s into which the anthropology of gender is now produced has changed. Anthropological knowledge is no longer self-evident. Researchers are increasingly aware of the extent to which the relationships in which they come to know things are themselves integral to the resulting knowledge. The accumulation of comparative data on gender has removed certainties about gender as a category of comparison. At the same time 'gender' is no longer the 'issue' it was twenty years ago. Gender is mainstream, an aspect of research of quite varied political and theoretical approaches, a central component of all undergraduate courses, generally accepted to form an integral aspect of economic, political, and ritual practice.[4]

Anthropologists have always had an interest in what both men and women do, particularly in the field of kinship.[5] However, early analyses, concerned with the structure and function of social life, were highly normative; indeed it was the norms that scholars sought to reveal. Men and women were understood to act as 'men' and 'women', maleness and femaleness were thought about in terms of what men and women *are* and *do*. Socialization was essentially the acquisition of normative sex roles, the internalization of the rules through which children came to behave as adult men and women.

This focus was not antithetical to feminist interests in exploring and explaining the extent of male domination in contemporary societies. In fact anthropology, the comparative study of human social practice, entered a phase of very direct dialogue with feminist scholarship. During this phase powerful meta-narratives were produced to explain this apparent cultural universal in which the concept of gender was articulated to various theoretical interests within anthropology. Ortner's (1974; Ortner and Whitehead 1981a) consideration of prestige and value identified the construction of sex and gender as essentially symbolic practice through which the value of female association with nature was systematically undermined by virtue of men's additional access to the symbolic domains of culture; Rosaldo (1974, 1980) articulated a more sociological approach in her identification of the private/domestic sphere of female practice as universally encompassed by the public sphere of largely male concerns; and Chodorow (1978) drew on psychological theory to establish that male domination of women was related to the differences in male and female experiences of the mother as a figure of attachment and authority in childhood.

These studies had an impact, not least in the important work that was immediately produced in refutation of the universalist assumptions on which they were based. A clear tension emerged between anthropological and feminist projects in the deconstruction of the nature/culture, public/ private dichotomies. These studies drew attention to the fact that this emergent consciousness of the symbolic domain had produced a theory of the 'natural' that failed to identify central concepts such as nature/culture, public/private, man/woman as culturally specific not merely in their uni-versal salience but also in their dichotomized relationships of opposition.[6]

The cross-cultural comparison of gender-related issues became an amazingly powerful heuristic within many different fields of anthropology, making visible the ways in which analytic connections and categories that had previously been deemed natural and thus neutral were in fact em-bedded in western practices and understandings. There was extensive investigation of what it meant to be a woman and how cultural under-standings of this category varied through space and time. There was also considerable emphasis on the nature of women's experience which gener-ated discussion concerning the cultural specificity of central concepts such as production, reproduction, household, family, marriage, and the concepts of property which systems such as bridewealth and dowry entailed. Within these studies the focus was both on women's experience and on culturally specific understandings of a sexual division of labour and particularly the value of gendered activity.[7]

This work, which sought to undermine universalizing tendencies and to reveal western cultural categories, took up and developed the central notion that gender was concerned with social/cultural constructions and was thus firmly situated in the domain of symbolic practice. Gender existed everywhere and, in those studies where the focus shifted from looking at expressions of gender difference as instances of male domination, scholars found that attention to idioms of gender enabled powerful connections to be revealed between apparently discrete domains of social practice. Studies of how women operated as cultural signifiers revealed how, in many cases, cultural practice which operated through the articulation of gendered identities was in fact directed towards the production of androgynous non-gendered social realities.[8] Gender symbolism was complex, its values contextual, its cultural purpose frequently not about the activities of men and women at all. In this vein it became quite straightforward within anthropology to carry out studies of gender with no reference to feminist agendas. The interest which particular symbolic 'systems' were identified as serving were not necessarily gendered ones.

A subsequent/parallel point of common interest emerged in the interest in studies of agency and subjectivity. Feminists were concerned to reveal women's practice as active and to undermine models which only attribute agency to men's activities. In a reversal of the data offered by anthropologists to confirm theories of universal domination, anthropology was now offering evidence of effective gendered agency. One of the implications of these studies was that gender difference was not necessarily indicative of gender hierarchy.[9] The difference again in focus between anthropological and feminist versions of this issue was the extent to which gendered agencies were held to be commensurate with the agencies of men and women. From within anthropology it was argued that men and women did not always act as 'men' and 'women', that identities were not coherent and prior to the interactions through which they were constituted. Persons are gendered in and through their daily practice. Gender is thus a process of becoming rather than a state of being. To insist *a priori* that women be treated as social actors is to ignore the complexity and variability of indigenous notions of the person.[10] For example, it has been argued that in Melanesia persons are regarded as objectifications (personifications) of relationships.

> In Melanesian culture, people are imagined in contrasting modes – male and female, same-sex and cross-sex, a person always one of a pair of interrelated forms. As persons women and men are equally the objects of the regard of others, and thus objectify their relationships. Since persons are the objective form of relationships, the outcomes of their acts are held to originate in and thus belong to those relationships.
>
> (Strathern 1988: 338)

Strathern has paid particular attention to the ways in which western models of the active subject pervade both anthropological and feminist scholarship, and she seeks in her work to reveal how western models of exploitation and male domination depend on notions of the possessive individual, on commodity logics, and on a particular relationship between experience and identity.

When we look at gender concepts we are not necessarily looking at how people construct identities but rather at how they constitute relationships. The critique is thus not simply directed at essentialist notions of gender but also at the implications of models in which gender is unproblematically produced as a social construction. The problem with social constructionism is that it depends on a cultural concern with symbolic analysis and representational practice, a concern which cannot be taken as a cultural universal.

Such disagreements within anthropology were also articulated as incompatibilities between anthropological and feminist scholarship. The real difference lies in 'the nature of investigators' *relationship* to their subject matter' (Strathern 1987a: 284). Feminism operates on the basis of a common identity among women while anthropology builds on the premise of difference and the possibility of incommensurability. The radical aspect of feminist scholarship is the concern to challenge the misrepresentation of women's experiences brought about by the totalizing discourses of male-dominated disciplines. The radical aspect of anthropology is of a different kind, as anthropologists attempt to construct knowledge in relation to, rather than in antagonistic separation from, an other. The antagonistic relationship is with that part of oneself that embodies habitual practice and anthropologists attempt to reveal that side of themselves in order to maintain an awareness of it. The relationship between anthropology and feminism is one of mutual mockery in which feminists laugh at anthropological pretensions to joint authorship, a delusion which they say overlooks asymmetrical power relations and the politics of how the world is structured, and anthropologists in turn laugh at the feminist pretensions of achieving separation from their antithetical other. Feminists point out that dialogic texts cannot represent the voice of the other when their interests are not convergent with those of the anthropologist, and anthropologists reply that feminists are inevitably trapped within their own ethnocentrism which produces male and female antagonism through particular understandings of personhood and relationships which condemn women to collude in their own oppression. The terms of this paradoxical relationship between the feminist and the anthropologist are, of course, often embodied in one scholar (Strathern 1987a).

However this particular formulation of the 'awkward relationship' is more complexly located within feminist scholarship than Strathern's dichotomy proposes. The deconstruction of the category 'woman' was also, indeed originally, associated with the realization that feminist politics had become a politics of exclusion for many women. Both essentialism and the explanation of women's domination in terms of particular western notions of women's practice, particularly the associations with motherhood, child-bearing and domestic labour, were located by feminist scholars as stemming from modernist philosophy. Postmodernism, as a method, with its anti-totalizing approach and awareness of both the complex nature of human subjectivity and the contingency of historical fact, made visible the tendency within modernist feminisms to generalize from the experiences of western, white, heterosexual, middle-class women.[11]

> There is nothing about being 'female' that naturally binds women. There is not even such a state of 'being' female, itself a highly complex category constructed in contested sexual scientific discourses and other social practice. Gender, race, or class consciousness is an achievement forced on us by the terrible historical experience of the contradictory social realities of patriarchy, colonialism, and capitalism.
>
> (Haraway 1991: 155)

It is clear that gender is epistemologically central to our attempts to understand the dynamics of human sociality. It is clear that gender is no longer taken simply as the 'add women and stir' approach, but its centrality, the success of earlier generations of feminist scholars, has gone hand in hand with diminishing heuristic effect. It is also clear that the works of writers such as Strathern and Haraway are producing new awkward relationships – an awkwardness that still revolves around the possibilities for an effective political practice. Their work is scientific, directed to specific specialist audiences. Their deconstructionism is one of ever receding horizons in which subject positions are continually removed. Strathern reveals that the expression of an awareness of cultural constructions is itself a cultural construct. Moving beyond gender has produced the essentially androgynous relational persons of Melanesia. These are mirrored by the cyborgs of Haraway's work, science-fiction's amalgam of humans and machines, hybrids that work against totalization and its concomitant exclusions. Haraway works against 'the dream of a common language' (Rich 1978). Both Strathern and Haraway practise a politics of destabilization and disruption. This politics provokes reaction from those who feel excluded on other grounds: on grounds of accessibility, on grounds of isolation, objections which are easily exploited by reactionary writers, such as the ubiquitous Camille Paglia, who can offer recognizable stereotypical fixities. Attempts to reject common language can all too easily have the effect of privileging a particular critical horizon.

Cameron (1992) has argued that 'communication is about the attempt to create intelligible realities . . . there must be something between the totalising code of the (feminist) dream and the untrammelled heteroglossia of the cyborg, both equally Utopian in the nature of language'. She suggests the creole as the new icon for feminist politics, an icon that allows for 'the interplay of the body and history, the fact that language is embedded both in the generality of our human inheritance and in the particularities of our social relations. Creoles are precisely communication systems developed by people without a common language.'

It should be clear from this brief review of the relationships between anthropological and feminist understandings of gender that there is no consensus within anthropology on how gender should or could be used as an analytical tool. The concept of gender has been brought into anthropology in relation to particular and varied theoretical concerns, which co-exist, in tension, in debate, sometimes in ignorance of each other. The concept of gender is effortlessly evoked in relation to discussion of social structure, symbolism, the relationship of structure and practice, and of representation and experience, the nature of difference and even the contemporary concern to reveal the rhetorical practices through which anthropologists produce texts and through them their objects of study.

The contributions to this volume reflect this diversity of theoretical approach. Such theoretical diversity also implies contrasting understandings of political effect. Each of the authors has dealt with this aspect of analysing sex and violence from different perspectives.

Four of the papers focus on the politics of ethnography. Toren is concerned with the experiential reality of violence in Fiji (both against children and against women) as a constitutive part of Fijian notions of kinship. Here, violence (including sexual violence) is fully integrated within the production of kinship as an overarching value. Politically the contrast is with those older studies which tend to see violence as 'collapse of social order'. Toren shows how violence is intrinsic to the Fijian social order, and implicitly critiques a tradition in ethnography which would mask that centrality. Harris operates in a similar frame, but within a different tradition of ethnographic writing which has sought to underplay the role of violence in Andean cultures in order to subvert the racist images which have stressed that violence. Without undermining the ethnographic project of subverting those images, Harris seeks to address her field experience of violence. Like Harris, McCallum is concerned to challenge unanalysed and pernicious popular images of the cultures described, in this case indigenous Amazonian people. She shows the fit between religious gang rape and the emphasis on peaceful relations between men and women in the Alto Xingu by showing how the former does *not* stand for what it would in the west. Harvey, by contrast, is concerned to reveal the complexity of meaning in acts of violence in another Andean context. Certain forms of violence may be celebratory of community and regeneration, but others are not.

Wade and Moore address the politics of theory in ethnography. Wade starts with an account of personally unattractive aspects of relations between men and women in his field site, and then shows how they 'make sense'. Here the stress is on making sure the theoretical frame is right. This concern is revealed even more clearly in Moore's paper, where the focus is on getting the theory right as a political act. For Moore, the problems of ethnographic description are the effects of ideological prejudices or of inadequate theorization. She proposes a general theory of sexual violence in order to reveal the hidden logic of particular ethnographic cases.

For the other two papers, the political issue is representation. For Cameron and Frazer, representation is first and foremost an issue of politics, and theory is a branch of politics. The gender of the representers matters, and women making representations are intrinsically challenging to the dominant representational and theoretical codes. As they challenge these codes, they reveal new and unexpected connections within them, as the Serial Sex Murderer is opened out as hero of post-Enlightenment philosophy. For Day, the problem is one of ethnographic representation. In addressing the lives of London sex workers, Day shows how these women can most easily expose the problems of representation and experience, but how they are simultaneously least able to do so. They are the subjects with the best evidence of rape as personal violation (the breaking of a formally agreed contract governing intimacy), but are the least able to defend themselves in public (because their profession is illegal, precisely because the contracts they draw up violate the category-divisions of English society). This ethnography, coming as it does from the home culture of the ethnographer, is able to speak for itself. As a representation, it stands in vivid contrast to the lived experience of those described.

VIOLENCE AND SEXUALITY

As was mentioned above, participants to the conference were all open to the idea that both violence and sexuality are culturally embedded concepts which do not necessarily have commensurable salience cross-culturally. This was one of the issues which the conference set out to discuss. Contributors were given no specific brief or definitions to work to. Discussion of violence, limited by the association with sexuality, thus ranges beyond Riches's minimal cross-culturally valid definition of violence as the 'contestable rendering of physical hurt' (1991: 295). The particular substantive categories of violence are generally recognizable in terms of this frame; murder, sex-murder, warfare, torture, beating, chastisement, and physical violation, but also include less visible categories of broken contract and the notion of threat. Contributors also reveal particular understandings of violence as associated with contestation, by discussing the celebratory, life-affirming, positively transformative effects of rendering physical hurt. The incommensurability of these non-western practices with the transcendental self-affirmation of a post-Enlightenment western context is well illustrated in Chapter 7 by Cameron and Frazer.

The connections drawn between violence and sexuality also vary considerably across the contributions but in all cases that connection is understood as an effect of social relations rather than of individual pathology and it is these relations which then are the subject of enquiry. Eroticized violence, violence for sexual pleasure, is discussed explicitly by Cameron and Frazer and addressed more tangentially by Harvey and McCallum. Violence motivated by the sexual relationship and particularly if contested, and notions of appropriate behaviour within such relationships are the subject of the chapters by Day, Harvey, Toren and Wade. Finally, Day and McCallum discuss the relationship between violence and sexuality with reference to acts directed towards the private, sexual body.[12]

It seems likely that a dominant western discourse which constitutes violence as explicit and public and sexuality as private and subjective has made it easier for us to be more open about violence than we have been about sexuality.[13] Furthermore there is an implicit ambiguity in the volume concerning the relationship between sex and gender. Gender, concerned with sexual difference as cultural signifier, is easier to talk/write about than sex, articulations of desire that cannot necessarily be reduced to gendered bodies, particularly in the psychoanalytic tradition which insists on the inherent bisexuality of the subject.[14] This point reveals a link between the papers which concerns the effects of sexuality and violence in the achievement and expression of inter-relatedness. We tend to think of sexuality and violence as contrasting modes of relating, sexuality associated with attraction, violence with separation. When the two come together in western cultures the paradox that lies behind our sense of transgression is produced. It is also this view that enables some to argue that sexual intercourse is inherently violent, involving penetration and the transgression of bodily boundaries. Torture, shown again and again to be a highly sexualized activity, dwells on this notion of bodily autonomy, on attempts to rupture the boundaries of the self.[15]

This brings us back to the beginning of this chapter. Bodily excess has long been used as a western technique through which to reveal the self. Europe's others have long been thought of in terms of bodily inversions, displacements and duplications which, as Mason (1990) has shown, are modes of excess. As Cameron and Frazer (Chapter 7) show, sexual violence has also been used as an excessive means of reclaiming self from society, revealing self by individuated opposition. Taken collectively the articles that comprise this volume reveal the partial nature of these western concepts while nevertheless addressing the social relations in which they are produced.

NOTES

1 Benjamin (1983); Graziano (1992); Hulme (1986); Montrose (1991); Mason (1990); Theweleit (1987).
2 Foucault's position that sexuality is constituted discursively and is an effect of the ways in which 'the apparatuses of power are directly articulated on the body' (1976: 200), does not pre-empt this other, recognizable discourse on sexuality described further by Cameron and Frazer (Chapter 7).
3 Conversations with Sarah Franklin have been extremely helpful for clarifying this debate and providing much of the vocabulary with which to discuss it.
4 The integration of gender into studies of politics, economics and ritual began in the 1970s. The following are some of the more influential review articles and edited texts: Rosaldo and Lamphere (eds) 1974; Reiter 1975; Quinn 1977; Caplan and Bujra (eds) 1979; Rapp 1979; Etienne and Leacock (eds) 1980; MacCormack and Strathern (eds) 1980; Ortner and Whitehead (eds) 1981; Young *et al.* 1981; Atkinson 1982; Collier and Yanagisako (eds) 1987; Strathern 1987b. For the most recent overviews see Moore (1991) and di Leonardo (1991).
5 See, for example, Malinowski (1929); Evans-Pritchard (1940); Radcliffe-Brown and Forde (1950). In famous husband and wife teams there was also frequently a division of labour in which women wrote about aspects of women's lives. For further references on this topic see di Leonardo (1991: 6).
6 A key text in this regard was MacCormack and Strathern (1980). Critiques of the domestic/public dichotomy were made by Rapp (1979); Yanagisako (1979); Rosaldo (1980); Strathern (1984). For Marxist analyses which entailed an evolutionary understanding of male domination see Leacock (1972; 1978); Etienne and Leacock (1980); Sacks (1974).
7 Again there is a vast literature on these topics. For a good overview see Moore (1991, Chapters 3 and 4). Central texts are: Strathern (1972); Reiter (ed.) (1975); Sharma (1980); Croll (1981); Hirschon (1984); Caplan (1985).
8 See, for example, Bloch (1987).
9 See Harris (1980); Strathern (1987b); Harvey (this volume).
10 Gow (1991); McCallum (1989); Strathern (1988).
11 See, for example, Fraser and Nicholson (eds) (1990).
12 An evident gap in this discussion of sex and violence is any reference to the motivating force of sexuality in western institutions and the consequent importance of sexual difference in the 'violence' of social inequality. Prominent theorists in this field include: de Lauretis (1987); Martin (1987); Pateman (1988); Haraway (1989, 1991).
13 Psychoanalytic theory, a privileged and salient domain of western discourse on violence and sexuality, posits a contrast between a social public self and an inward private self. Analysis is the process through which the patient narrates the links between these conscious and unconscious dimensions of self. Although it is not necessary to psychoanalytic theories that the unconscious self is privileged as more real, this was the effect of some of the ways in which feminist scholars engaged with this model. For obvious political reasons the notion of an unconscious/repressed self became a powerful analogue of an authentic oppositional self which liberationist politics could work to redeem.
14 This issue points out another missing dimension to our discussion at the conference, that of the association between politics and sexuality as discussed in the literature which challenges the normative heterosexual perspective.
15 Scarry (1985); Graziano (1992).

BIBLIOGRAPHY

Atkinson, Jane (1982) 'Anthropology: review essay', *Signs* 8: 236–58.

Benjamin, Jessica (1983) 'Master and Slave: the fantasy of erotic domination', in Snitow, A., Stansell, C. and Thompson, S. (eds) *Powers of Desire: the politics of sexuality*, New York: Monthly Review Press, 280–99.

Bloch, Maurice (1987) 'Descent and Sources of Contradiction in Representations of Women and Kinship', in Collier, J. F. and Yanagisako, S. J. (eds) *Gender and Kinship: Essays Toward a Unified Analysis*, Stanford: Stanford University Press.

Cameron, Deborah (1992) 'Why the Cyborg Doesn't Dream of a Common Language', Unpublished paper, Glasgow University.

Caplan, Patricia (1985) *Class and Gender in India: women and their organisations in a South Indian city*, London: Tavistock.

Caplan, Patricia and Bujra, Janet (eds) (1979) *Women United, Women Divided: Comparative studies of ten contemporary cultures*, Bloomington: Indiana University Press.

Chodorow, Nancy (1978) *The Reproduction of Mothering: psychoanalysis and the sociology of gender*, Berkeley: University of California Press.

Collier, Jane and Yanagisako, Sylvia (eds) (1987) *Gender and Kinship: essays toward a unified analysis*, Stanford: Stanford University Press.

Croll, Elizabeth (1981) *The Politics of Marriage in Contemporary China*, Cambridge: Cambridge University Press.

de Lauretis, Teresa (1987) *Technologies of Gender: essays on theory, film and fiction*, Bloomington: Indiana University Press.

di Leonardo, Micaela (ed.) (1991) *Gender at the Crossroads of Knowledge: feminist anthropology in the postmodern era*, Berkeley: University of California Press.

Etienne, Mona and Leacock, Eleanor (eds) (1980) *Women and Colonization*, New York: Praeger.

Evans-Pritchard, E. E. (1940) *The Nuer: a description of the modes of livelihood and political institutions of a Nilotic people*, Oxford: Clarendon Press.

Foucault, Michel (1976) *Histoire de la Sexualité*, Paris: Gallimard.

Fraser, Nancy and Nicholson, Linda (eds) (1990) *Feminism/Postmodernism*, London: Routledge.

Gow, Peter (1991) *Of Mixed Blood: kinship and history in Peruvian Amazonia*, Oxford: Clarendon Press.

Graziano, Frank (1992) *Divine Violence: spectacle, psychosexuality, and radical Christianity in the Argentine 'dirty war'*, Boulder: Westview Press.

Gregor, Thomas (1985) *Anxious Pleasures: the sexual lives of an Amazonian people*, Chicago: Chicago University Press.

Haraway, Donna (1989) *Primate Visions: gender, race and nature in the world of modern science*, London: Routledge.

Haraway, Donna (1991) *Simians, Cyborgs and Women: the reinvention of nature*, London: Free Association Books.

Haraway, Donna (1992) 'The promises of monsters: a regenerative politics for inappropriate/d others', in Grossberg, Lawrence, Nelson, Cary and Treichler, Paula (eds) *Cultural Studies*, London: Routledge, 295–337.

Harris, Olivia (1980) 'The Power of Signs: gender, culture and the wild in the Bolivian Andes', in MacCormack, Carol and Strathern, Marilyn (eds) *Nature, Culture and Gender*, Cambridge: Cambridge University Press, 70–94.

Hirschon, Renée (ed.) (1984) *Women and Property, Women as Property*, London: Croom Helm.

Hulme, Peter (1986) *Colonial Encounters: Europe and the Native American*, London: Routledge.

Kappeler, S. (1986) *The Pornography of Representation*, Oxford: Polity Press.

Leacock, Eleanor (1972) 'Introduction' to F. Engels' *The Origin of the Family, Private Property and the State*, New York: International Publishers.

Leacock, Eleanor (1978) 'Women's Status in Egalitarian Society: implications for social evolution', *Current Anthropology* 19 (2): 247–75.

McCallum, Cecilia (1989) 'Gender, Personhood and Social Organization among the Cashinahua of Western Amazonia', PhD Dissertation, London School of Economics.

MacCormack, C. and Strathern, M. (eds) (1980) *Nature, Culture and Gender*, Cambridge: Cambridge University Press.

Malinowski, Bronislaw (1929) *The Sexual Life of Savages*, London: Geo. Routledge and Sons.

Martin, Emily (1987) *The Woman in the Body: a cultural analysis of reproduction*, Boston: Beacon Press.

Mason, Peter (1990) *Deconstructing America*, London: Routledge.

Mead, Margaret (1928) *Coming of Age in Samoa*, Harmondsworth: Penguin.

Montrose, Louis (1991) 'The Work of Gender in the Discourse of Discovery', *Representations* 33: 1–41.

Moore, Henrietta (1991) *Feminism and Anthropology*, Oxford: Polity Press.

Ortner, Sherry (1974) 'Is Female to Male as Nature is to Culture?', in Rosaldo, Michelle and Lamphere, Louise (eds) *Woman, Culture and Society*, Stanford: Stanford University Press, 67–88.

Ortner, Sherry and Whitehead, Harriet (1981a) 'Introduction: accounting for sexual meanings', in Ortner, Sherry and Whitehead, Harriet (eds) *Sexual Meanings: the cultural construction of gender and sexuality*, Cambridge: Cambridge University Press, 1–27.

Ortner, Sherry and Whitehead, Harriet (eds) (1981b) *Sexual Meanings: the cultural construction of gender and sexuality*, Cambridge: Cambridge University Press.

Pateman, Carole (1988) *The Sexual Contract*, Oxford: Polity Press.

Quinn, Naomi (1977) 'Anthropological Studies on Women's Status', *Annual Review of Anthropology* 6: 181–225.

Radcliffe-Brown, A. R. and Forde, D. (eds) (1950) *African Systems of Kinship and Marriage*, Oxford: Oxford University Press.

Rapp, Rayna (1979) 'Anthropology: a review essay', *Signs* 4(3): 497–513.

Reiter, Rayna Rapp (ed.) (1975) *Toward an Anthropology of Women*, New York: Monthly Review Press.

Rich, Adrienne (1978) *The Dream of a Common Language*, New York: Norton.

Riches, David (1991) 'Aggression, War, Violence: space/time and paradigm', *Man* 26(2): 281–97.

Rosaldo, Michelle (1974) 'Woman, Culture and Society: a theoretical overview', in Rosaldo, Michelle and Lamphere, Louise (eds), *Woman, Culture and Society*, Stanford: Stanford University Press, 17–42.

Rosaldo, Michelle (1980) 'The Use and Abuse of Anthropology: reflections on feminism and cross-cultural understanding', *Signs* 5(3): 389–417.

Sacks, Karen (1974) 'Engels Revisited: women, the organization of production, and private property', in Rosaldo, Michelle and Lamphere, Louise (eds), *Woman, Culture and Society,* Stanford: Stanford University Press, 207–22.

Scarry, Elaine (1985) *The Body in Pain: the making and unmaking of the world,* Oxford: Oxford University Press.

Sharma, Ursula (1980) *Women, Work and Property in North-west India,* London: Tavistock.

Strathern, Marilyn (1972) *Women in Between: female roles in a male world,* Mount Hagen, New Guinea; London: Seminar Press.

Strathern, Marilyn (1984) 'Domesticity and the Denigration of Women', in O'Brien, D. and Tiffany, S. (eds) *Rethinking Women's Roles: perspectives from the Pacific,* Berkeley: University of California Press, 13–31.

Strathern, Marilyn (1987a) 'An Awkward Relationship: the case of feminism and anthropology', *Signs* 12(2): 276–92.

Strathern, Marilyn (ed.) (1987b) *Dealing with Inequality: analysing gender relations in Melanesia and beyond,* Cambridge: Cambridge University Press.

Strathern, Marilyn (1988) *The Gender of the Gift,* Berkeley: University of California Press.

Theweleit, Klaus (1987) *Male Fantasies,* Minneapolis: University of Minnesota Press.

Torgovnick, M. (1990) *Gone Primitive: savage intellects, modern lives,* Chicago: Chicago University Press.

Yanagisako, Sylvia (1979) 'Family and Household: the analysis of domestic groups', *Annual Review of Anthropology* 8: 161–205.

Young, Kate, Wolkowitz, Carol and McCullagh, Roslyn (eds) (1981) *Of Marriage and the Market,* London: CSE Books.

1 Transforming love

Representing Fijian hierarchy

Christina Toren

The following story – a Fijian man's account of how he came to fall in love with his wife – was told me during the wedding celebrations for a young couple in Sawaieke, the village on the island of Gau in Fiji where I spent 18 months, from July 1981 to February 1983. The man who told me this story was in his early forties – gentle and humorous, a thoughtful husband and father; his wife was a witty and lively woman, understanding and kind, the mother of many children. Their marriage appeared to be contented and successful; they were clearly fond of one another.

My friend began his tale by saying that as a young man he had desired his wife's sister; she was prettier, he said, and more lively; but one of his classificatory fathers had advised him differently. Look, he had said, at the other one. *She* would make a good wife; watch her, you will see that she is skilful at women's work, knows how to look after a family. So my friend had changed the focus of his attention and had found that all his father said was true. It didn't matter to him, he said, that she was 'no longer a girl' – not a virgin, indeed already a mother – he asked his father to ask for her in marriage. Then they got married and he took her home and at first all went well, though perhaps they were rather shy with each other, not quite at ease. Then one night he stayed out late drinking kava and woke up bad tempered the next morning. He went to breakfast, but it was late, already past ten, the others had eaten and the tea was cold; his wife served it to him cold. He had thrown the tea back at her, right in her face and then he had hit her hard, punched her with his fists and when she fell to the floor he kicked her and then he left the house.

I looked at him dismayed; his voice and expression were amused, fondly reminiscent. This was terrible, I said, how could he have done such a thing? But he lifted his hand, gesturing that he had not yet finished. Wait, he said, you will understand it all soon. Three days had passed and he and his wife did not speak to one another. The first day or two she spent at her mother's house; when she returned each went about the daily duties – his wife with her eyes downcast and a sorrowful face, she cried a lot and would not look at him, and he felt grim and angry. Then on the fourth morning he got up, bathed, brushed his teeth; then he dressed and sat down at the cloth for breakfast. His wife was in her place *i ra*, below, her eyes downcast and her face turned away from him – he mimed the posture for me, the corners of his mouth turned down, his whole person expressive of injury – but as she handed him his glass of hot tea their eyes had met. And at once, he said, they began to laugh. She began to laugh and he began to laugh and they could not stop. They laughed and laughed, recalling details of the previous events, how he had thrown the tea and punched her, how she had screamed and run off to her mother, how they had gone about unspeaking. He looked at me then, smiling, sure that I would understand; *sa qai tekivu na veilomani dina*, he said, 'and thus began true love'.

At the time I did not, as he had said I would, understand this story. This paper is an attempt to do so, to show how in Fijian thought and practice sexual love or desire is constituted in opposition to compassionate or familial love and how compassionate love is wrested violently out of desire, which is thus transformed and apparently contained by the hierarchy thought proper to social order.

From the analyst's point of view, there are no acts that are *symbolic* of love, for love is constituted out of those acts that are supposed to stand for it. From cradle to grave each one of us is inevitably situated in relation to love via the manifold interactions which love encompasses and in which it is inscribed. This is not to say that everywhere 'love' is made to take the same forms, but rather that, whatever forms it is made to take are constituted in and through social relations, and that because we are each born into and can only become who we are in relations with others, we willy-nilly constitute ourselves in relation to love, to its presence or absence, and we submit to the meanings others have made of love and to those meanings we make in response to theirs. So one cannot signify love in any simple way because any dyadic relationship in which love enters (wife–husband, parent–child, sister–sister, brother–sister, lovers, cousins, friends, etc.) inevitably informs the others and so each new relationship in some sense contains those that precede it and/or coincide.[1] So in any person's experience, 'love' undergoes a kind of developmental cycle that itself implies specific power relations both within and across households, domestic groups, families. So it is that for any people, the acts that at once constitute and express love within dyadic relationships are an integral part of the political and economic processes that describe social relations at large.

In this essay I attempt to uncover something of the interacting processes through which certain Fijian villagers come to be at once subjects and objects of love. The analysis of this developmental experience is intended to show how suitable a vehicle is love for the playing out of power relations, how central and fundamental it is to those other social processes with whose nature anthropologists are more usually concerned. My other, less obvious, purpose lies in an attempt at once to preserve the particularity of my own and others' personal experience in so far as this is contained in what I was told and what I saw and heard, and to show how this proceeding itself makes possible a revealing analysis of Fijian social relations. I am not so much concerned with 'reflexivity' as with the analytical insights that emerge from an attempt to preserve the insights of Fijian villagers on their own experience. I begin with some information on the Fijian categories within whose terms 'love' may be spoken of.

Veilomani, the term used by my friend to speak of true love, is the mutual compassionate love that helps to constitute kinship. One's kin in the widest sense are all other Fijians; 'loving each other' is part of what it means to be Fijian. The root *loma* denotes the inside of a thing and in many compounds the mind or the will, e.g. *loma ca*, lit. 'evil-minded' denotes malice; *loma donu*, lit. 'straight-minded' denotes sincerity. The verbal form *lomana* means to love, pity or have mercy on; *kauwaitaka* – to care or to be concerned – was given me as a synonym. The reduplicative form *loloma* translates as love, pity or mercy, while *i loloma* is a gift or a token of love. It is the 'free gift' as distinct from the gift – *i soli* – that manifests obligation and implies exchange. But the gift out of love coerces recognition of the love that gave it and the form taken by this recognition denotes the status relations entailed. For, while the love denoted by *veilomani* is reciprocal, such that the will of each party to the relationship is in harmony with the other, it is also – with the important exception of cross-cousins – a function of unequal relationships. The nature of this inequality varies according to the interaction between rank, gender and seniority that governs any particular hierarchical relation between kin.[2] In marriage, it is axiomatic that the husband holds sway over his wife. This relationship is crucial for the continuity of Fijian hierarchy for it transforms a relation of competitive equality between cross-cousins – by definition one always marries a cross-cousin – into the hierarchical relation between husband and wife. Cross-cousins are kin to one another but the competitive and equal relations between them make them a special kind of kin, as does the potential for sexual relations.

Here I must emphasize that in Fijian village life *all* one's relations with others are encompassed by *veilomani* – mutual compassionate love – and where these relations are hierarchical are, for people older than 14 or so, characterized by respect and avoidance. With one's cross-cousins one is familiar and asserts equality, both within and across-sex, so in day-to-day friendly relations with them, *veilomani* takes on an aspect of equality.

Elsewhere I have shown how marriage seems to contain and overcome the implicit threat that cross-cousinship and balanced reciprocity pose to chieftainship and tributary relations, and how this apparent 'overcoming' is played out at every meal in every household and every kava-drinking. At the same time, marriage as process transforms sexual love or desire between equals into love that is proper to hierarchical kin relations.[3] It is only in marriage that equal and hierarchical behaviours and the representations to which they contribute confront one another within the confines of the one dyadic relationship. In other words, in a lifetime in which *all* one's relationships prescribe either hierarchy or competitive equality, only marriage makes it clear that each form contains the possibility of the other. The challenge of this conjunction erupts into personal experience when *veilomani* – mutual compassionate love – is confronted by *veidomoni* – passionate and mutual sexual love.

Veidomoni has connotations of desperation, for the root word *domo* figures in terms for obstinacy and courage – *veidomomatuataki*, *domodomoqa* – and for terrifying or frightening – *vakadomobula*, lit. arousing a lust for life. As a homonym, *domo* means throat, or the sound of a thing. So a woman who laughs loud and high is said to be sexually promiscuous – a notion that connects with a nineteenth-century one that women called their lovers by laughing.[4] Fijians are fond of suggestive puns, so a throat infection I had gave rise to innumerable jokes suggesting that a sore and swollen throat meant that I needed a man. In both these examples female desire is represented as unspoken – so women's feelings are denied even while they are acknowledged. In my own case, sexual frustration was attributed to me *because* I could not speak; joking apart, it was proper that thwarted desire in a married woman be manifest in an inability to express itself. Even a woman who is said to be sexually promiscuous does not express her desires in speech but in provocative laughter. By contrast, male desire is allowed to be spoken and its association with the throat lies in an analogy between sex and eating. A man's wife – especially while still young and pretty – is often jokingly referred to as *na kena*, 'his to eat'. And uxoriousness in a husband is not referred to as *dodomo*, 'passionate love', which would make him appear faintly ludicrous – one does not fittingly *domona* one's wife – but rather as the desire to eat what is his, *sa via kania na kena*. So far as I know this term is *not* used reciprocally, i.e. to describe a woman's desire for her husband.

As wife and sex object, a woman is under her husband's command. As an object of desire outside marriage she disposes of herself as she wishes: it is up to her whether or not she assents to a sexual relationship with one of her cross-cousins. But such a relationship is illegitimate, so she cannot *freely* dispose of herself; a girl's sexuality should be under the guardianship of her father and brothers, held in trust for her husband. On her wedding night her mother formally asks if she is 'truly a girl' (a virgin). If she says she is and fails to prove herself so when the bedding of the wedding night is examined by senior women, then she and her side may be publicly shamed by the presentation of the feast foods that follows consummation – the belly of the cooked pig given to the 'side of the woman' is left gaping open, or a banana thrust into it; had she been a virgin it would have been modestly closed and concealed with leaves.[5] However, this ritual can occur only for marriages arranged by senior kin – those that over the preceding months involve a series of exchanges between both sides and where the wedding ceremony takes place in church.

The usual form of marriage is elopement (*veidrotaki*). This is accomplished when the girl is discovered to have spent the night with the young man in the house of his parents or other close kin. The rituals that follow are to placate the girl's kin and, later, to celebrate the new couple. A church wedding may or may not follow. Couples who elope are usually already lovers; their feeling for one another before marriage is that of *veidomoni*, i.e. 'mutual sexual love' or 'mutual desire'. The term is used reciprocally, but it is noticeable that it is usually the young man who is said to *domona* – desire – the young woman; in other words, both desire and responsibility for the elopement are represented as the young man's. The image one has of the girl in these affairs is that she passively accepts his urgent suit.

Young men are generally assumed to have sexual liaisons; at the same time, girls are assumed by their elders to be chaste. Men compose and sing most Fijian love songs; they often represent desire as a helpless yearning for the woman – *au dodomo ki na nomu vinivo*, 'I love/desire even your pinafore'; or themselves as dependent on a woman's whims – *bogi koya, bogi koya, au a oca na wawa*, 'that night, that night I was tired out with waiting'. Male sexuality is understood to be urgent, difficult to control; so a girl who goes alone to meet a man is said to be culpable if he forces himself upon her. But such an action is considered to be rape and, so far as I know, it is up to the girl herself to decide what she wants. If the young man making the tryst is serious about a girl he will say that he just wants to meet her and enjoy her company, *veitalanoa*, 'telling stories'. However, if a girl allows herself to be alone with a man or men who are drunk on alcohol then she may be raped. A man drunk on alcohol is thought to be in a state of uncontrollable desire, he *has* to have a woman. A man who is drunk on *yaqona* (kava, the ground root of *piper methysticum* infused in water) is not said to be so aroused; rather, untroubled by desire, he will sleep a dreamless sleep.

Alcohol is understood to embolden a man so that he can approach the desired woman with sufficient *kaukauwa* – lit. strength, but here meaning sexual magnetism and/or self-confidence – either to gain his end or retire with dignity if refused. The convention is that a man doesn't know what he is doing when drunk and so asking and refusal can be forgotten while asking and acceptance can form the foundation for future meetings. This brings me to the subject of dancing and its connection with sexuality.

During my first months in Sawaieke the girls (*gone yalewa*, those who are unmarried, but over 16 or so) often told me how much fun we would have when there was dancing. At last the time came; the chiefs said we might 'stand up' in the hall to the music of the young men. The convention is that a girl or woman gets up, goes to 'touch' a man and returns to the lower part of the room, well below the *tanoa* holding the *yaqona* and at the polar extreme from the area 'above' where chiefs sit. There the man joins her and, side by side, they put their arms about each other's waists and proceed in gentle rhythm back and forth across the floor; this is *taralala*. One can also dance a sedate form of rock 'n roll, or waltz – provided one holds one's partner at a distance of ten inches or so. I was stunned by the degree of reserve and circumspection that dancing entailed. So far as I could tell only the spectators enjoyed themselves. The dancers remained impassive, gazing over each other's shoulders or into the middle distance. The next day I listened to the girls discussing what a good time we'd had and wasn't it fun, Christina? I agreed, but it was only several dances later that I began to discover *why* dancing is so much fun and even, from certain points of view, dangerous.

Seating arrangements in any gathering effectively segregate men and women of similar ages. But during dances subtle messages may be sent from one person to another – by brief and careful eye contact or a squeeze of the hand or even, if the lighting is not too good, a rapid verbal exchange. Young men and women expect dancing to lead to sexual liaisons; so do adults and especially church leaders who cannot countenance dancing and must leave the room where it takes place.[6] From a chiefly perspective, dancing is improper because people are standing up in the presence of chiefs.[7] So when dances *do* occur (and this is rare on Gau) one must not show too much enthusiasm, let alone smile or talk with one's partner. I was often cautioned by elderly men to be careful, for when my husband came to visit me and was told about my dancing I should certainly be punched. My assertion that my husband had never hit me in the previous thirteen years of our life together was considered frankly incredible.

The heavy sexuality that is attributed to dancing finds its truest expression in dances that take place in *na rubbish hall*, lit. 'a rubbish hall'. This is a temporary shelter outside a village; its sides are open, its roof made of unfixed sheets of corrugated iron; the floor is earth and there are no mats to sit on, but planks of wood are fixed to form rough benches along two sides. The dances are to raise money, for example to send the sports teams to Suva for the annual games. No chiefs are present, but two or three married men and women attend as chaperones.

Dancing in the rubbish hall is associated with drunkenness and thus with untrammelled male desire. Sawaieke was 'dry' and 'homebrew' was strictly forbidden; even so, young men managed sometimes to drink alcohol. My first rubbish hall dance was wildly exciting. Nearly all the young men were drunk; the few who were not were playing guitars and singing or looking after the *yaqona*. The latter were doing their best to observe the proper ritual form – a difficult task in the free-for-all fights that erupted among the others during any pause in the dancing. Young men asked girls to dance, slow songs were the most desirable and waltzing *de rigueur*. Then the dancing became a battle to interpose some little distance between one's own body and the man's. Some girls pushed their partners away, and were most derisive with 'little young men' (*cauravou lalai*, aged up to 19 or so), preferring young men (*cauravou*) in their twenties. Men took the chance to ask for assignations whose object was sometimes implicit but more usually obvious: 'Could we perhaps go together?' to which the standard response is '*Isa*! go together where?'[8]

The sexual implications of dancing are a corollary of the fact that only those who can call each other cross-cousin may dance together; only they may joke and flirt, challenging one another with remarks heavy with sexual innuendo; only they may tease or confront or ridicule. All other categories of relation (ideally, all Fijians are kin to one another) demand varying degrees of avoidance and respect; they are all incest categories – *veitabui*, 'forbidden to each other'. Cross-cousins are potential spouses or siblings-in-law; their relationship is inherently mediated by sexuality.[9] A young person making a tryst always goes with a cross-cousin of the same sex. A girl's female cross-cousin protects her from the suspicions of adults; a young man's male cross-cousin gives moral support or comfort if his suit fails. Girl or boy may ask the cross-cousin to speak for them, if they are shy or want reassurance; sometimes 'double dates' are made.

Flirting – *vosa vakawedewede*, lit. attention-getting talk, joking (*veiwali*) and teasing (*veisamei*) are not only the prerogative of cross-cousins, but even their duty. All the fun of any village gathering depends on the way that those who call each other cross-cousin excite amusement and enjoyment by their jokes and liveliness with one another. The equal relation between them is at once constituted and expressed in these activities and in the competitive and ulti-mately balanced reciprocity that characterizes exchange between them.

The contrast between *dodomo* and *loloma*, between sexual love or desire and compassionate or familial love, is assimilated to an ideal contrast between 'the European way' and 'the Fijian way'. The language of *dodomo* is often English: a young man obsessed by a girl is 'lovesick', his regular girl is his 'dame', a sexually promiscuous girl is a 'bitch', sexual desire is uncontrollable under the influence of alcohol (*yaqona ni vavalagi*, 'European kava'), and both alcohol and sex are linked to European-style dancing in 'rubbish halls' outside the village where one pays money to get in. Here 'the European way' is amoral, without kinship or moral obligations, and implies a wild, uncontrolled, incestuous sexuality. By contrast, the language of *loloma* is Fijian and the behaviour that constitutes it is proper to kinship; contained and legitimate desire is manifest in sedate dances in the village hall where men can be drunk only on *yaqona*, which does not arouse desire and which when presented in its root form is paradigmatic of tribute to chiefs. The ideal contrast between the European and the Fijian ways here refers to an earlier contrast between bush (*veikau*) and house (*vale*).[10] Indeed, illegitimate sex between young people often perforce takes place in garden shelters or temporarily deserted bush houses or school outhouses – all of which lie outside the village proper.

Uncontrolled sexual desire poses a threat to ordered hierarchy, so the ultimate triumph of the Fijian way over the European way is made possible by the mediation of cross-cousins. Between them *loloma* has an aspect of equality, but when cross-cousins become lovers or when first they marry they discover and submit to the passion of *dodomo*. In time, marriage as process will transform their passion into *loloma* – now become the love proper to hierarchical relations, the love whose very constitution reproduces 'the Fijian way'. With respect to *dodomo* a man seems helpless, the victim of his own desires, but this is represented as the fault of the girl who arouses his passion. A young man resents feeling strongly for a girl; being 'lovesick' is a condition to be avoided if sexual desire is to be thought of as a hunger best satisfied by a wide variety of foods. This notion is common among young men, one of whom – aged 21 and already repenting of his recent marriage – said, 'I have been eating only cassava everyday – today it no longer tastes good to me.'[11] If a young man feels strongly for a woman, his own sexuality is called into question. A man who, when sober, urges his suit so hard that others realize his predicament and his frustration at refusal, is publicly humiliated by his own feelings and blames the woman who aroused them. Young men hold it best to appear indifferent; only when married can a man afford to let his feelings show, for then they can manifest as jealous anger. It is said that girls spurn a man who reveals his love. So women as well as men were appalled to see the explicit devotion displayed by a young Australian visitor for his half-Fijian wife; several elderly women laughed at his desire to be with her all the time and declared his little kisses disgusting; other younger women said he showed a foolish and unmanly fondness for the girl.[12]

Men are understood to be depleted by sexual intercourse. During the football season, young men are strictly forbidden to 'go with' girls lest they lose their strength; this is manifest as heat, and football practice is often referred to as *vakatakata*, lit. 'making hot'. That a man can be reduced or humiliated by desire is implicit in notions about sexual liaisons between young men and older women. A young man whose lover is perhaps six to ten years older than he is, is likely to fall ill with *dogai*. He cannot work or do anything but sits at home all day staring into space. Very small things look large to him and if an insect flies his way he ducks to avoid it. He does not know he is sick but one of his close older female kin recognizes the illness and cures him with a herbal medicine; the cure, it seems, brings the liaison to an end. *Dogai* is caused by the strength (*kaukauwa*), here implicitly the sexual strength, of the woman; an older woman is more sexually powerful than a young man.[13] This implies that the sexuality of young men and women is of equal strength, but when I asked if this was so, my informant (a young man in his early twenties) said decidedly that it was not; if they are the same age then the man's sexuality is stronger. Fijians of both sexes would, I think, agree with this but while the strength of his sexuality is a young man's boast, it is also his undoing. It puts him at a disadvantage with any girl for whom he feels a powerful attraction, because it makes possible the potential triumph of the girl in refusal.

This accords with the competitive equality that characterizes relations between cross-cousins outside marriage, both within and across sex. A male cross-cousin can neither command anything of, nor forbid anything to his female cross-cousin. He can joke, tease, cajole, defy, beg or refuse – but so can she. For example, young men consider smoking their own prerogative and unfitting for girls, and a brother (including a close classificatory brother) is justified in hitting his sister if he discovers her smoking, but girls not only smoke in front of male cross-cousins, they demand cigarettes of them. Also, a girl is allowed to initiate a love affair, although given the double standard she has to be careful to avoid the epithet 'bitch'. Young men may coerce, intimidate or even force themselves upon much younger female cross-cousins, but girls of their own age are able not merely to refuse but to ridicule and humiliate them. This relation between young men and women as cross-cousins is inherent in the process of developing sexuality.

Little girls are shamed if they touch their genitals or allow them to be seen; toddlers of two or so will be smacked and older girls beaten. Boys, by contrast, may be seen naked without too much fuss being made about it.[14] Of a toddler who handles his penis someone may remark, '*Ia*, he takes hold of his *boci*!' (lit. uncircumcised penis) and others present may laugh, but the child is unlikely to be smacked. A boy of five or six may sit cross-legged, his genitals showing through a hole in his shorts, even after others have laughed and drawn his notice to the deficiency. After all, what other way can he sit that is *vakatagane* – manly?

The concern with covering female genitals even in early childhood is, I think, attributable to Christian conversion and colonization; in early and pre-colonial Fiji both sexes went naked until the time – often after puberty – when they were ritually clothed for the first time in barkcloth. But Christian puritanism seems to have suited Fijian predilections and the stricter attention to female nakedness to be oddly concordant with the proper mode of sitting *vakamarama*, in a ladylike way, with the knees together and the legs tucked back under the thighs, and with the earlier practice of tattooing girls' thighs, buttocks and vulva, a painful operation performed before puberty and said to make their vaginas *mamaca vinaka* – 'nice and dry'.[15] Men still say that the most desirable state in a woman is when her vagina is 'hot and dry', *katakata ka mamaca*, which suggests that for young women sex is perhaps at best frustrating if not in fact painful.

Judging by what I was told by both girls and young men, a boy's first sexual intercourse occurs around age 17, a girl's around age 15. However, one young man told me that when he was 18 he went with a girl of 11; when I asked him did he not think the girl too young, he said 'No, she knew her own mind'.[16] Thus, a girl's first sexual experience may occur when she is very young and may, despite the views of my informant, be forced upon her.

One day when I was walking outside the village I was joined by some little girls, aged between 10 and 12. They kept repeating the words 'nine minutes' in English and giggling like mad, but were reluctant to tell me why this was so funny. At last the youngest – an irrepressible child – revealed that another girl (aged 11) had been surprised by a boy of 14 when she was washing clothes in the stream and forced to have sex with him. The little girls knew all about it from another child who had watched from behind a tree. They placed the blame squarely on the boy, saying that the girl was afraid and that the boy was known to be 'wise in everything bad' (*vuku e na veika ca*); he was always putting his hands up the girls' skirts – even if they were only eight years old. They all joined hilariously in a circumstantial description of the event, making expressive gestures with their hands – a hole with the left hand through which they poked the index finger of the right. They used bizarre words – not Fijian – for the act itself, 'toponi' and 'prish prosh'; nine minutes was the length of time which the boy was overheard to announce as properly spent in the act.

That these acts by males are understood by both sexes to be essentially violent is clear in the foregoing and in the following information, given me by a young man in his early twenties. He had, he said, been slightly injured on his genitals by a girl of about 16 who struck at him with a kitchen knife as he lay sleeping. He was amused by the incident, said of it that the girl 'was joking with me' (*sa veiwali vei au*). Astonished by this story, I asked him why the girl did this – he was asleep and she just came and struck him with the kitchen knife? Yes, he said, 'because we are cross-cousins' (*ka ni keirau e veitavaleni*). When she was younger, he said, he used to touch her genitals even when other people were present. 'She used to be frightened of me then. Now she is not frightened, she jokes with me too, she begins to know that she is grown up.'[17]

Male pride in sexuality and an ability to rationalize violence as an inherent part of it is countered by girls' seeming indifference to sex itself. Where young men are represented as always prey to unsatisfied desire, young women are represented as calm, inhibited, uninterested; at best they passively accept the young man but remain essentially unaroused themselves. Being concerned to redress this imbalance and arouse female desire, young men (especially those who have been in prison) may resort to a form of sub-incision whereby small glass marbles are inserted under the skin of the penis. This practice is said to be a standard one among European gangsters who are known thereby to arouse their women to the very height of desire.

A young man may be concerned to arouse a girl's desire, but he is also concerned that she should desire only himself and no other. So her love is not allowed to be explicitly sexual, for if she desired men as men desire women, she would be a 'bitch'. Young women may *feel* desire, but it cannot be overtly recognized – even by the girls themselves. In their talks about young men, their schemes for attracting them or for illicit meetings, the notion that they may have sex together or that this is what the girl might want is not, I think, commonly acknowledged. Only one girl, with whom I discussed her love affair with a married man, seemed to feel at ease about sex and to like it, an impression I also had from young matrons of some years standing who talked fondly (or jokingly) of husbands who warmed the bed at night. Sexual desire in young women is only indirectly acknowledged by, for instance, tales of Daucina – 'The Lamp-bearer', one of the old Fijian gods – who spies on young women who bathe alone at night and visits them in their sleep.[18] He takes the form of a handsome stranger or a male cross-cousin; his power makes him irresistibly attractive and the girl can do nothing, only follow where he beckons, there to be taken as his wife. One girl of 19 was regularly visited thus in her sleep and at dusk she had seen Daucina in the form of her boyfriend from another village, crossing the village green; she called her mother's attention to the young man, but when her mother looked up there was no one to be seen and they knew, both of them, that it had been Daucina.

The presumed innocence of girls is such that they may tease and torment a man with their attentions in a public gathering and in doing so, promise nothing. Many times I saw young women in their late teens and early twenties gang up on an unmarried man to whom they were all cross-cousin and fête him with their attentions – they garlanded him with flowers, tucked frangipanis behind his ear, served him bowls of *yaqona*, addressed provoking remarks to him, giggled prettily in his direction and so on. If he was not thus forced to flee the gathering, the young man could only hang his head, overcome by shyness in the face of the onslaught. Consciousness of their power and their ideal inviolability is reflected in young women's body postures when they ask a man to dance. One properly adopts a low, stooping posture when passing among people who are seated and apologizes, *tulou tulou* as one does so. A girl who penetrates a group of men to 'touch' one of them in invitation to dance, adopts this polite, self-effacing posture; however, having touched him and turned again towards the lower part of the room, she walks upright with swinging hips and a proud smile. The very fact that in respectable gatherings in house or village hall a girl flirts and initiates dances is a mark of her ideal chastity and innocence. So, when male visitors are in the village, girls are expected to fête them in this way; it is hospitable and brings praise on the village. Lovers are said to be 'ashamed to look at each other in the light', so publicly flirtatious behaviour should be the best sign of innocence; that it is not necessarily so is because 'joking' is also understood to be a prelude to greater intimacy.

That girls are supposed to be innocently unconscious of the full effect of their behaviour on men is confirmed by the very circumspection that is expected of married women, and especially of young married women. Married women are assumed both to know what men are and what they risk by behaviour which, before marriage, would have been taken for granted. So young married women do not dance; nor do they flirt, joke, smile or laugh too much in front of men other than their husbands and especially not in the company of their cross-cousins. Villagers take it for granted that married men are jealous and newly-married men the most jealous of all. Jealousy is a recognized motive for a beating; even where the suspicion itself is known to be irrational, the jealousy it arouses is often thought to be the woman's fault. What struck me was that the beatings young married men inflicted on their wives were bound to occur – however impeccably correct the wife's behaviour.[19] One man of 19 beat his wife when she said she was going fishing; some men were also going fishing that day and she might have intended to talk and joke with them. This young couple was only a few months married and the beating prompted the wife to run back to her natal village, for already her husband had hit her so often that she was afraid. She was fetched back by her parents-in-law who went and begged her to return, promising that their son would never beat her again and had undertaken truly to change his ways. But some months later her husband himself had to go to fetch her back from another village nearby; she had run away to avoid his beating her because, in a public gathering, she had politely pledged a bowl of *yaqona* to a male cross-cousin.

Another newly-married man beat his wife even for gossiping with the girls because, who knows, she might have been using one of them as a go-between with another man. Two of the girls told me that after his marriage he had instructed his wife as to her behaviour – at the time they were both 21. He said, 'You must not stay up late at night, you must go to sleep early in the evening, don't go about visiting, just stay alone at home ... you are not to dance' and so on.[20] The girls said of this that it was bad, eh? (*sa ca e?*) and then, derisively *i tovo ci*! ('fart-like behaviour'). On the other hand it seemed likely that they would expect similar behaviour from men. As far as I could tell, couples split up only if the woman's kin as well as the woman herself considered the beatings too frequent and too severe – as happened with one of the two girls just mentioned and the father of her child with whom she had lived in Suva; he beat her, she told me, at least twice a week and always on Thursdays and when I asked her why said, '*Esi*! I don't know – he was drunk. He got paid on Thursdays. All I knew was that when Thursday came round I would be punched.'[21]

Young men in the first year or more of marriage seemed unable to control their extreme jealousy and anger and from what older women had to say about the early days of their marriages, this was a prevalent pattern. All the women, young and old, with whom I discussed male violence declared it abhorrent and unnecessary. Many old women had fearful stories to tell of dreadful beatings incurred in former days, where for example, a previously pacific and gentle husband on being told that his wife was dancing beat her so badly that she miscarried and, in one case, never again became pregnant. At the same time, most women *expected* men to be violent and found it hard to believe that I had never been so much as slapped; both sexes considered jealousy to be the most salient cause of violence and took it for granted that 'men are jealous' (*e dau vuvu ko ira na tagane*); one took exception only to too much. Girls however, objected strongly to jealousy in male cross-cousins with whom they were merely *veitau* ('friends'); several times I heard girls speak with contempt of one of their number who acted towards her boyfriend as if they were already married – i.e. she had stopped smoking, given up dancing, was shy (*madua*) in the young man's presence and no fun anymore. It was considered presumptuous in a mere cross-cousin to expect this of a girl though in a regular sexual liaison this pattern might well emerge; such behaviour was often said by girls to be a good reason for not getting married.

The jealousy, the beatings and the anger are all part of the process of turning a cross-cousin into a wife. Whether men admit this I do not know, though the Fijian anthropologist Nayacakalou remarked that men he knew sometimes argued that one should not marry a *known* cross-cousin because she would be 'difficult to control'.[22] The hierarchy across households that emerges in kava-drinking ritual is reckoned in terms of male household heads, and to be a 'head' one has first and foremost to be seen to be above one's wife. This husbandly superiority is constituted in the wedding exchanges and in every household meal. The wife's labour in the provision, cooking and serving of food is devalued by comparison with her husband's whose own contribution is the 'true food' (*kakana dina*) he labours for on his ancestral land. A wife eats by favour of her husband and his ancestors and this is acknowledged in her seating position *i ra*, 'below', at meals and in her attendance on her husband; she eats after him and her food is often of lesser quality than his. Indeed, she is herself 'his thing to eat'.

The significance of this idiom goes beyond any mere equation between sex and eating, for it was still true in pre- and early colonial Fiji of the mid to late 1800s that one ate one's enemies as an act of vengeful sacrifice;[23] these might be the same people with whom one intermarried. But women were not supposed to eat human flesh.[24] I do not know of any expression that describes legitimate female desire, though it is recognized that married women may properly have sexual feelings. But a married woman's desire should be naturally circumscribed, only for her husband; at least it was suggested to me by older women that a man might want variety, but that a woman can easily curb her desires. I knew of liaisons and of series of liaisons between young men and girls and of adultery between girls and married men, but I never heard of any case of adultery by a married woman. This was unsurprising; a married woman discovered in adultery would have been at risk of severe injury.[25]

A woman is said to become undesirable at some point in her thirties; she is 'old' and past her best. That she may still be desired by young men and regularly making love with her husband is not popularly recognized. So women in their mid-thirties to forties begin to enjoy a new freedom; their youngest children are at school, and they may now 'go about', visit sisters and parents elsewhere, go to weddings and so on – without their husbands. They may also joke with their male cross-cousins in a way that would have meant a beating ten, or even five years, before. By now their relation to their husbands is one of *veilomani*, mutual compassionate and familial love; so when a woman over 40 or so becomes pregnant after a long interval (say when her youngest child is about six) this is 'disgusting' and her husband is ridiculed behind his back. Sex is proper to marriage, but there comes a time when – especially in the view of rather younger people – it ceases to seem appropriate; for younger persons sex between long-married couples can only be either ludicrous or disgusting, unfitting for those who through their grown-up children (themselves perhaps parents) are now undeniably close kin. In the old days, a man did not properly consume the flesh of any of his close kin for fear his teeth would fall out; by the same token, a man is not supposed to want to 'eat' a woman whom he has himself helped to make a middle-aged wife. A woman thus gains a degree of autonomy only at the point where she ceases to be represented as an object of desire.

This is apparent in the joking behaviour of elderly women (those who are presumably past menopause) which may be aggressively sexual; they may 'stand up' alone without shame or even force a younger man into dancing – with much thrusting of hips and flashing of eyes. This behaviour does not bring into question the desires of the women themselves for they are not represented as having any, rather it displays an amused contempt for the desires of men. Old women fold their hands in the gesture which, in a traditional *meke* or sitting dance, signifies a spear thrust and thus signify in lewd mime the desires of men towards women. It is they who, at weddings, shame the bride with their remarks and comment loudly on the probable sexual prowess of the groom.

One might compare their behaviour with that of old men, who rarely attain this level of joking with young women and when, on occasion, they are so reckless as to try, earn only the mocking laughter and ill-concealed ridicule of the onlookers. Rather old men solace themselves with stories of witchcraft in the style of the Solomon Islanders (*draunikau vakaSolomoni*) who are said still to know the magic that 'carries away women'. I heard such conversation several times, always in the company of old men. On the occasion I recall here each one had his own story about some ugly old man, skin blackened by the sun, who could get any woman he wanted by use of *draunikau* (magic). One had only to rub one's hands with magically treated oil and then shake hands with the woman or give her something, a box of matches even, it didn't matter what. One had only to touch her and she would turn and follow one as in a dream. It could, I was told, happen to me too. 'Truly, mother of Manuel, it carries women away. You wouldn't know what you were doing. You would just follow. It's such a pitiful thing. It makes the women wretched.'[26] The men described girls who were young and fair, and what a waste it was when they followed men who were old and ugly. *Sa maumau dina*! Truly a pity! they said and shook their heads. One told a story of a remarkably ugly old man whose magic was so strong that he controlled a whole village in this way, the men just passively accepting it. Every morning he called out all the people and chose a woman to massage him and another to make love with him, or he entered a couple's house and took the place of the rightful husband in his own bed while the husband went off to sleep in the kitchen. These stories were greeted with exclamations of True! True! (*Sa dina! Sa dina!*) from the different listeners and *Sa!* – an expression of horrified assent.

It is not, I feel, overly fanciful on my part to find in these stories a desire transformed at last into a wistful projection of remembered violence that here signifies its own final defeat.

I have tried to show how men and women are represented as situated differently with respect to sexual love, which implicitly poses a threat to hierarchical relations between kin. Unmarried girls may provoke desire in young men even while they are themselves represented as ideally unmoved; unmarried young men and women may joke and tease each other with equal emphasis, but it is usually up to young men to realize the sexual potential of the situation. Female desire remains unspoken. A young man is explicit about his sexual feelings, but it seems that a young woman's desire should await arousal by her husband. After marriage a man's longing for a woman ceases to be represented as sexual love and becomes the legitimate wish to eat what is his. A married woman is assumed to feel desire, but for this very reason she must cease to joke with her male cross-cousins, for the sexuality that was before her marriage only implicit in that relationship is now revealed – but only for the time being – as its motive force. A woman's desire must be only for her husband and rendered subordinate to his – an end that is achieved perhaps in violence, for it is in the earliest years of marriage that a man is most likely to beat his wife. A woman with several children – the eldest already in primary school – is rarely so treated. If her husband comes home drunk she may even be heard loudly berating him for his behaviour – unfitting in the father of her children. Once her oldest children are past puberty and the woman herself in her mid to late thirties, she achieves a certain autonomy. No longer popularly represented as an object of desire and never properly acknowledged as subject to desire, she can again be safely allowed to joke with cross-cousins. The man is understood still to be prey to the sexual desire that has been the sign of his dominance since his youth, so in his mid-thirties and despite an apparently contented domestic life, he may still attempt to seduce young women who laugh at the advances of such 'old men' behind their backs. The older he gets, the more thoroughly is a man undone by desire, for the women who are most desirable in popular belief are those virginal girls whom he cannot have. And in old age, only a magical power could allow him once more to assert his sexuality. Old women, by virtue of their ideal detachment from desire, are able at once to make explicit the covert power that is a young woman's ability to arouse desire without apparently being subject to it, and the covert weakness that makes the man helpless in the face of his need. It is usually at weddings that old women represent this paradox in their own persons by dancing in mime a man's sexual desires and thus rendering him absurd.

Cross-cousins are kin to one another, kin who are potential spouses. For this very reason, if sexual love motivates a man to marry, it threatens the hierarchical relations between the ideal husband and wife with the competitive equality of cross-cousins. Marriage contains sexuality by virtue of the fact that even if sexuality initiates it, this is not represented as its *raison d'être*, which is rather the forging of kinship ties and the reproduction of kinship through the children of the marriage. Nevertheless, people do hold that sexual love is important in marriage, but in terms of married life as it is experienced, marriage as process transforms sexual love between equals (*veidomoni*) into the hierarchy of compassionate love between husband and wife (*veilomani*); when once a woman begins to become thoroughly a wife she can no longer be a source of threat to a man's authority. Then only may 'true love' (*veilomani dina*) begin, for the violence of the man's early desire is itself contained and rendered subordinate to compassion. If, in the first year or two of marriage, violence appears to be a consequence of sexual love, this is because a man's sexuality is at once his strength and his undoing while a woman's sexuality is an unspoken and potential source of power.

I am drawn to speculate on the beginnings of the developmental cycle of love in the manifold relations of childhood, whose interactions at once enter into and are the outcome of love. In the course of their growing up children learn that simple acceptance is the proper response of the junior party to any attention from a senior – whether it be in the form of the giving of food, affectionate gestures, an admonitory lecture, harsh words or ridicule or a disciplinary beating – for love is inscribed in all these acts. All these behaviours are defining attributes of kinship, and particularly of the close and always hierarchical relations within the household, and are encompassed by *veilomani*, mutual compassionate love.

However, not all kinship relations are hierarchical; one has one's peers, but by definition, they are not members of one's own household. Avoidance behaviours do not come into effect before puberty, so a child's peers are not only his cross-cousins, but all others of the same age, irrespective of the kin relation in which they stand to one another. Open, outgoing and lively behaviour is expected among one's peers and it is in this context that one can – and should – assert oneself, joke, play and even fight. Peer relations are fostered early in childhood; many times I saw two mothers, each encouraging the young child in her arms to punch out at the other, both children grinning and crowing with glee until one of them took too hard a blow and began to cry; then he or she was kissed and laughed over by the mother – the children being around eight months or older. These are the very gestures of friendship and love in which the mock punch, the playful knock with the knuckles are common indicators of intimacy and affection, both within and across sex, at least until one is in one's thirties or so. The love knock is not symbolic of a harsh blow; rather it is the opposite end of a continuum of meaning in whose terms love may be framed. So it makes little sense here to distinguish between a violence that is real and one that is symbolic for in any person's experience, each inevitably implies the other.

Each baby, child, schoolchild, young person, adult and old person plays out her or his own relations with peers and seniors, and observes the relations between others. This experience enters into each one's continuing cognitive construction of the meanings that generate her or his linguistic and other behaviour. And this behaviour itself becomes a constitutive of the meanings that that same person and others construct. This process informs the transformation of meaning over time – be it within a person's mind or the sweep of history – in respect of gender, of kinship, of hierarchy, of competitive equality, of marriage. Marriage generates kinship and so it contains within its own developmental cycle all the forms and expressions of love; here *veidomoni*, sexual love between equals, and *veilomani*, compassionate love that helps constitute hierarchy, are but two moments each of which contains the possibility of the other. In marriage as in other domains one shifts back and forth between relations of competitive equality and hierarchical relations; the alternations produce desire for *both* kinds of love.[27] In the married man's story that began this chapter, it was *veidomoni* – his own helpless (and unadmitted) sexual passion – that lay behind the beating he gave his wife; sexual love is by definition between equals because it is only allowed between cross-cousins, but it is also the locus of the constitutive violence that produces hierarchy. By contrast, *veilomani* is by definition hierarchical, but is also the site of the possibility of equal relations *within* marriage – for it is this term that my friend used to denote the 'true love' which began in his and his wife's covert recognition in laughter of what had become at other moments a passionate sexual love. That hierarchical 'compassionate love' comes *apparently* to dominate 'sexual love' between equals is a function of the fact that the developmental experience of love cannot be abstracted from politico-economic processes whereby the subordination of a woman to her husband within the household generates the patriarchal imagery of Fijian hierarchy. It is a wife's subordination that makes any man a chief in his own house. By the same token, in the image of the collectivity as the household writ large, a chief becomes the father of his people and his wife is simply not mentioned.[28]

Here I point out in passing that this analysis could be extended into the domain of transcendent power, where the Christian god may be represented as having both sexual and compassionate love for his human flock. The imagery is that of marriage, for as one preacher is reported to have said: 'God wants to put a wedding ring on your finger' – an action that would make wives of the congregation.[29] This imagery is a transformation of that which, in the past, informed chiefship and sacrificial offerings to the ancestors and which today is at once constituted and expressed in kava drinking.

In coming to a conclusion, what strikes me most forcibly is that while I have analysed elsewhere the playing out of the constituent processes of Fijian hierarchy in other guises and with respect to other domains of investigation, it now seems to me that love constitutes the most powerful explanation for the specific nature of that hierarchy. It is perhaps needless to say that it is also the domain that I least understand.

NOTES

1 Here I am indebted to Maria Phylactou for an enlightening discussion.
2 See Toren (1990) for an account of how these hierarchical relations are constituted in ritual.
3 See Toren (1990: 29–64, 168–247) for an analysis of the nature of this relationship in respect of children's understanding of gender and hierarchy, and Toren (1988) for an analysis of the way women's relation to men as either sisters or wives was constituted in respect of ritual. The hierarchical relation between husbands and wives is clear in the ethnographic literature especially in the nature of avoidance between them. Thus Waterhouse (1866: 309) says 'it is not in accordance with etiquette for the betrothed wife to mention the name of her husband. She will either speak of him as "the chief" or will use the personal pronoun "he".' Geddes (1948: 189–92) says women use the honorific term *Ratu* to their husbands, but that there is no reciprocal term for wives; he also remarks that a wife should be cautious in interrupting her husband and notes the dual standard of sexual morality.
4 Williams (1858, 1982: 182) refers to the *dredre kaci*, the 'call by laughing' as bringing a severe beating upon a married woman.
5 Cf. Brewster (1922: 197); Lester (1940: 283); Quain (1948: 339). Geddes (1948: 192) says that the virginity of chiefly women was especially guarded.
6 MacNaught (1982: 106) tells how the *taralala* 'spread like an epidemic' through the Fiji of 1925, to the horror of both chiefs and missionaries.
7 This violates the hierarchical spatial relations whereby a chief should always be above others; thus the internal space of house, church, and village hall has an area called 'above' where chiefs sit and an area called 'below' that is the place of women and/or young men. For an extended analysis of the way hierarchy is constituted in spatial relations see Toren (1990).
8 *E rawa ni daru lako vata? Isa! Lako vata ki vei*?
9 For an account of Fijian kinship terminology, see Nayacakalou (1955).

10 See Toren (1989) and Toren (in press) for detailed analyses of the ideal contrast between the European and the Fijian ways.

11 *Au sa kana tavioka wale ga e na veisiga, nikua e sega ni kana vinaka vei au.*

12 *Sa rui menemenea na yalewa o koya; e sega ni vakatagane.*

13 Thomson (1908, 1968: 24) gives *dogai* as 'what is called "broken heart" by Europeans'. I also thought the symptoms similarly suggestive and asked the young man who first told me about it whether *dogai* was the same as being broken-hearted – an expression that is used in popular songs (*kavoro na utoqu*, 'my heart is broken'). But I was told this was not the case. It seems likely therefore that Thomson was relying on his own reading of the symptoms. Cf. Brewster (1922: 198) who refers to *dogai* in Nadarivatu, north Colo, as an ancestral punishment for illicit love affairs before marriage, especially with reference to 'youths'.

14 Cf. Quain (1948: 317–18) who says that neither boys nor girls in Nakoroka, Vanua Levu, have to bother about concealing their genitals from view until puberty.

15 See Thomson (1908: 219). For other references on tattooing of girls see, for example, Williams (1858, 1982: 160); Seeman (1862: 113); Brewster (1922: 184–7); Quain (1948: 315). Cf. Hocart (1929: 149–50) on the confinement of Lauan girls of chiefly birth at puberty. Gell (1993) contains a fascinating comparative analysis of tattooing practices in Fiji, Samoa and Tonga. In Fiji boys were not tattooed; they were circumcised, as they are still today, see, e.g. Williams (1858: 166); Waterhouse (1866: 341); Quain (1948: 134); Sahlins (1962: 187).

16 *Sega. Sa tu vei koya na lewa i loma vakaikoya.* Lit. 'No, it was up to her [to make] the decision in her own mind'. Note that because sex before marriage is illegitimate, there seems to be no explicit notion of an 'age of consent', but I think it almost certain that adult men and women would consider sex between a young man and a girl so young to be an act of rape.

17 *E na gauna e liu, e a rerevaki au ko koya; nikua e sega, e sa veiwali tale ga vei au. E via kila o koya ni sa tubu levu.*

18 Quain (1948: 320, 321) notes that sexual experience in dreams is considered to be intercourse with devils and the souls of the dead; see also Herr (1981) who argues that, for Fijian women, 'sexual feelings are inextricably tied . . . with notions of being consumed and devoured and also of death'.

19 Cf. Amratlal *et al.* (1975) where a young woman is told by her father that 'her new boss was her husband and that she must listen to him' (p.44). Also: 'it was normal and accepted that a husband sometimes beat his wife' (p.47); 'women's position especially in the home has not changed that much . . . women accept that men should lead' (p.59).

20 *E dodonu mo kakua ni yadra vakalevu, mo moce vakayakavi, mo kakua ni veilakoyaki ka tiko vakadua e vale . . . kakua ni danisi.*

21 *Esi! E sega ni macala – sa mateni o koya, siga Lotulevu sa taura nai sau ni cakacaka. Au a kila ga ena yaco mai na siga Lotulevu au sa qai lauvacu.*

22 See Nayacakalou (1955: 48).

23 See Williams (1858, 1982: 210) and Henderson (1931: 57), who remarks that Tanoa, chief of Bau, had as his kava toast *sese matairua* [or perhaps this should be *saisai matairua*?], 'a spear with two points', apparently a metaphor for the breast of a virgin which Henderson says was a favoured delicacy. It seems possible that Henderson confused the sexual usage of 'eat' with the literal one.

Williams (op. cit. 211) says that, with respect to the epicurean properties of human flesh, it was the upper limbs, heart, liver, etc. that were praised. However, Tanoa's toast is interesting in respect of its sexual connotations, for here the virgin becomes at once that which slays and that which is 'eaten'. Cf. Sahlins 1983: 76, 1985: 89.

24 See Williams (1858, 1982: 211); cf. Clunie (1977: 40) who says that while human flesh was generally *tabu* to women, they did sometimes eat of it.

25 Hocart (1929: 158) records that adultery and divorce were common in Lau – apparently on the part of wives as well as husbands and Thompson (1940: 58) says that 'the discovery of adultery on the part of one's spouse usually causes only temporary friction'. It seems possible that Wesleyanism has wrought a change here – though I find it difficult to believe that in the past wives were allowed such licence; Williams (1858, 1982: 182) makes it clear that Bauan women were not, while Seeman (1862: 192) says that those discovered in adultery were put to death.

26 *E dina o tina i Manueli. Sa kauta tani na yalewa. O na sega ni kila na ka o cakava. O na muri koya ga. Sa dua na ka vakaloloma! E sa vakalolomataki ira na marama.*

27 I am indebted for this point to Marilyn Strathern.

28 See Toren (1990: 238–44). For an analysis of how Fijian chiefship can be understood as predicated on the antithetical and equally important values of competitive equality and hierarchy, see Toren (1994).

29 See Peck (1982: 348).

BIBLIOGRAPHY

Amratlal, J. *et al.* (1975) *Women's Role in Fiji*, Suva South Pacific Social Sciences Association, in association with the Pacific Women's Conference.

Brewster, A.R. (1922) *The Hill Tribes of Fiji*, London: Seeley, Service and Co. Ltd.

Clunie, Fergus (1977) *Fijian Weapons and Warfare*, Bulletin of the Fiji Museum, Suva.

Geddes, W.R. (1948) *An Analysis of Cultural Change in Fiji*, PhD Thesis, London School of Economics & Political Science.

Gell, A. (1993) *Wrapping in Images. Tattooing in Polynesia*, Oxford: Clarendon Press.

Henderson, G.C. (1931) *Fiji and the Fijians (1835–56)*, Sydney: Angus & Robertson.

Herr, B. (1981) 'The Expressive Character of Fijian Dream and Nightmare Experiences', *Ethos* 9(4): 331–52.

Hocart, A.M. (1929) *Lau Islands, Fiji*, Bulletin 62, Honolulu: Bernice P. Bishop Museum.

Lester, R.H. (1940) 'Betrothal and Marriage Customs of Mbau, Fiji', *Oceania*, X: 273–85.

MacNaught, T.J. (1982) *The Fijian Colonial Experience: a study of the neo-traditional order under British colonial rule prior to W.W.II*, Canberra: Australian National University.

Nayacakalou, R.R. (1955) 'The Fijian System of Kinship and Marriage', *Journal of the Polynesian Society*, 64: 44–56.

Peck, P.J. (1982) *Missionary Analogues. The Descriptive Analysis of a Development Aid Program in Fiji*, PhD Thesis, University of British Columbia.

Quain, B. (1948) *Fijian Village*, Chicago: University of Chicago Press.

Sahlins, M. (1962) *Moala: culture and nature on a Fijian island*, Ann Arbor: University of Michigan Press.

Sahlins, M. (1983) 'Raw Women, Cooked Men and Other "Great Things" of the Fiji Islands', in Brown, P. and Tuzin, D. (eds) *The Ethnography of Cannibalism*, Special Publication, Society for Psychological Anthropology.

Sahlins, M. (1985) *Islands of History*, Chicago: University of Chicago Press.

Seeman, Berthold (1862) *Viti: An Account of a Government Mission to the Vitian or Fijian Islands*, Cambridge: Macmillan & Co.

Thompson, L.M. (1940) *Southern Lau, Fiji: An Ethnography*, Honolulu: Bernice P. Bishop Museum Bulletin 162.

Thomson, B. (1908, 1968) *The Fijians. A Study of the Decay of Custom*, London: Dawsons of Pall Mall.

Toren, Christina (1988) 'Making the Present, Revealing the Past: the mutability and continuity of tradition as process', *Man* (N.S.) 23, 696–717.

Toren, Christina (1989) 'Drinking Cash: the purification of money in ceremonial exchange in Fiji' in Parry, J. and Bloch, M. (eds) *Money and the Morality of Exchange*, Cambridge: Cambridge University Press.

Toren, Christina (1990) *Making Sense of Hierarchy. Cognition as social process in Fiji*, London: Athlone Press.

Toren, Christina (1994) '"All Things Go in Pairs or the Sharks Will Bite": the antithetical nature of Fijian chiefship', *Oceania 64*.

Toren, Christina (in press) 'The Drinker as Chief or Rebel: *yaqona* and alcohol in Fiji' in McDonald, M. *Gender and Drink*, Oxford, Berg.

Waterhouse, Joseph (1866, 1978) *The King and the People of Fiji*, New York, AMS. (Reprint of the 1866 edition published by the Wesleyan Conference Office.)

Williams, Thomas (1858, 1982) (Rowe, G. S., ed.) *Fiji and the Fijians*, Suva: Fiji Museum. (A reprint of the 1858 London edition.)

2 Condor and bull

The ambiguities of masculinity in Northern Potosí

Olivia Harris

ANTHROPOLOGY AND VIOLENCE

In the towns and cities of Bolivia, collective memories lurk in people's minds of the unpredictable violence of the Andean peasants when they take action against their oppressors. Everyone has anecdotes to tell – uprisings, the sieges of cities and towns, murders, cannibalism. Indians are stereo-typed in the structure of everyday conversation as *brutos, salvajes*, at the same time as they are referred to more sentimentally by terms of endear-ment: *indiecito, caserito, muy bueno*. They are feared but also patronized. By contrast, in the Indian communities that I know it is not so much the physical force used by the townspeople, the traders, and the landowners that is recounted as the acts of flagrant injustice, often protected by the law, by which they have been cheated and robbed time and again of their land, their livestock, and produce.

These images of the Indians play their part in shaping the enduring racism in the Andean countries, where for all the supposed constitutional rights of citizens, most areas of life and culture are, in practice, founded on difference, the primary difference being between those who are Indians and those who are not, and then a multiplicity of differences depending on a person's precise location in the scale of class, culture, colour, and ethnicity, and which constantly deflects onto the Indians the blame for the country's problems. These stereotypes have, in turn, been sanctified too often by writers and researchers.[1]

The way in which violence functions so successfully as a sign of savagery is undoubtedly overdetermined. For the Judaeo-Christian tradi-tion with its Utopian message of universal peace, violence is transgression. So is it for the Enlightenment heritage which attaches such a high value to reason and self-control. The nation state too, as a political and legal form, has little official tolerance for acts of physical violence perpetrated by its citizens.

Given its ambivalent status in western thinking, violence is also a problem for anthropology. The classic period of social anthropology, with its Durkheimian paradigms and the artificial colonial peace within which it developed, tended either to ignore violence or to rationalize it in sociological terms (for example, Evans-Pritchard on the Nuer). In much anthropological writing, committed as it is to questioning through rational argument the bases of racist stereotyping, violence is either analysed as functional, or it is not mentioned. Such strategies have doubtless contributed to the view of anthropologists as irredeemably romantic and idealistic, and are ultimately self-defeating in that they also reproduce stereotypes, albeit of the 'noble savage' variety.[2] The issue remains, however, as to how far it is possible to give an account of aspects of life in an exotic 'other' community which are shocking, possibly abhorrent, for western sensibilities (such as the use of physical force or cannibalism) without strengthening a racist discourse which functions precisely by imputing to the other repressed aspects of the self? Or, on the other hand, by censoring such material, to perpetrate a view of the communities studied as outside the realm of the real.

Northern Potosí, a region of the central Bolivian highlands closely identified with its mining industry, is also known for the warlike behaviour of its *ayllu* inhabitants.[3] The famous hand-to-hand fighting in the *tinkus* that take place on many Catholic feast-days are a continuing irritant for the local representatives of the 'civilized' world – the subprefect, the police, priest and teachers – but they carry on, supported by the handsome profits of local traders, and by the quest of the more adventurous tourists for exotica to capture on film. The *ayllus* of this region were able to resist the wholesale alienation of their land to private owners at the end of the nineteenth century, not least because of their ability to coordinate large numbers of fighters and protect their lands by force (Platt 1982). But it is not only against non-Indian outsiders that each *ayllu* defends its land: there is also long-standing tension between neighbouring *ayllus* which breaks out into fighting from time to time.

The continued institutionalization of fighting in the form of the *tinku* must be seen in the historical perspective of colonial conquest and violence, of continuing threats to Indian property and livelihood, and a racist ideology which underwrites this.[4] Indian discourse takes up this violent imagery as a means of self-definition in a world of ethnic division. As Carlos Mamani Condori (1989) has indicated, the theme of violent action associated with the mythic feline serpent – *katari* in Aymara, *amaru* in Quechua – is an important part of Aymara mythology and historical consciousness. In some senses there is a greater ideological tolerance of the use of physical force than is typical of European cultures. It is not viewed as bad in and of itself which is undoubtedly one of the reasons why the non-Indian population is so alarmed by it (though how far the Indians are really more violent than non-Indians is obviously impossible to determine, since the non-Indian strata deny their own violence).

In view of these ambiguities it is relatively easier for anthropologists to explain violence in terms of pressures from outside than to investigate its parameters in everyday life. General discussions by anthropologists rarely address the issue of domestic violence (e.g. Riches 1986(b) *passim*). It is often less troubling to explain what, to the eyes of the dominant culture, is transgressive behaviour and values by an argument which traces the violence to an external source, for example colonial oppression. Indigenous violence may be interpreted as a form of self-defence (for example, Orlove n.d.), or symbolic protest (Riches 1986a), or connected to the common identification of humans with the wild and violent creatures of mythology. This identification is also found in Andean culture, and Allen (1983) suggests that it reveals the complexities of self-definition in an ethnically-divided world.

THE BATTLEFIELD OF LOVE?

Conquerors as well as conquered, the highland populations have their own memories and interpretations of the glories and the tragedies of war. But how is the mythologizing of physical force lived out in the texture of everyday life? At this more mundane level the meaning and legitimacy of the use of physical force is subject to constant negotiation. There is a widening disparity in what is considered acceptable, especially when the politics of gender come into play. This can be illustrated by a recent controversy over the incidence of domestic violence in Andean cultures.

Kristi Ann Stølen, on the basis of fieldwork in the mestizo community of 'Caipi' in the Ecuadorian highlands, published a book which reproduced detailed and harrowing accounts by women of the beatings and mal-treatment to which they were subjected by their husbands, within the context of a questioning and undogmatic feminism (1987; see also 1991). José Sanchez Parga responded in an essay provocatively entitled *¿Por qué golpearla?* ('Why beat the woman?'), in which he sought to reveal the inadequacy of a feminist reading of marital violence. His brief but wide-ranging argument includes probably every suggestion that has ever been advanced to account for wife-beating from a male perspective (1990).

Stølen's account, he suggests, reveals a 'female complicity' with her women informants. To counteract this he advances a variety of justifications for wife-beating: the pronounced dualism of Andean symbolic representations with a positive value placed on violence in the *tinku*; a family structure in which mothers are all-powerful in the home, excluding their husbands and creating excessive emotional bonds with their children; an emphasis on female chastity which men find sexually unappealing; femininity as a 'disturbing universe' full of 'occult powers'; the 'narcissistic wound' suffered by men because perfect complementarity can never be realized and women remain forever 'other'; men's physical aggression as either a response to women's verbal aggression or a substitute for their own verbal aggression which he claims is unacceptable in Andean culture; a compensation for the domination men suffer in the society at large; and a projection of the guilt they feel towards their wives because of their own infidelity. In the light of such a list Sanchez Parga's protest that he is not condoning wife-beating seems beside the point. Space does not permit a detailed discussion of his argument, but a few comments are relevant to the argument of this paper. First, some of the generalizations he makes about 'Andean culture', emphasizing the separation of male and female spheres, seem closer to the cultures of Southern Europe than to the native Andean communities with which I am familiar.[5] Second, while I am not unsympathetic with his concern to look at marital violence within a wider perspective of familial relations, psycho-dynamic processes, and ideas about femininity and masculinity, he undermines his own case by a 'male complicity' (identical to what he accuses Stølen of), which sees women as unambiguously responsible for the violence of their husbands, and by a hotch-potch of arguments many of which are based on introspection rather than on empirical observation. To attribute blame is a very inappropriate short-circuiting of the task of anthropology, which is to elucidate the context of such behaviour.

This exchange has aroused strong reactions in Ecuador. Apart from the incompatibility between the feminist and masculinist positions taken respectively by Stølen and Sanchez Parga, some people concerned about the oppression of the indigenous population feel that this emphasis on violence in a rural community can only strengthen racist stereotypes. Others point out that Stølen's material comes from a mestizo community, so that Sanchez Parga's generalizations about 'Andean' culture are misplaced. Many women are indignant at what they see as an evasion of the real issues in Sanchez Parga's justification of wife-beating in terms of indigenous structures of meaning, in particular the dualism which is a fundamental feature of Andean thought; while some anthropologists have disagreed more with his interpretation of this dualism.[6]

Dualism, found in virtually all spheres of social organization and symbolic representations, is a central concern for Andean anthropology. One of its most explicit expressions is the *tinku* battle, another is the gendering of elements which are represented in a relationship of complementary opposition. The issue arises as to how far the *tinku* – usually interpreted as balanced or symmetrical – can be identified with the complementary opposition of gender. Various authors have pointed out that there is a metaphorical equivalence between *tinku* as battle between balanced adversaries, and the 'amorous encounter' of a woman and a man (Bouysse-Cassagne 1987: 197; Molinié-Fioravanti 1988: 52; the phrase comes from Bertonio's Aymara dictionary of 1612). Allen makes a close association between *tinkuy* as violent fighting and as a 'love-affair' (1988: 206), and Platt indicates a number of analogies between the field of battle and the field of love, including the playful punches and tiffs between lovers which he equates with the fighting of the *tinku*, and the dances performed (1987: 97,111). Marriage rituals have been interpreted as a means by which the everyday inequalities between spouses are symbolically adjusted to achieve perfect symmetry (Platt 1986; Harris 1986), and a number of authors have analysed ways in which household organization and the sexual division of labour reflect the same principles at work in the economic sphere (Allen 1988: 78-87; Harris 1978; Isbell 1979; Silverblatt 1987: 20–39).

There is no doubt that physical aggression between lovers is not in the Andes viewed with such ambivalence as in western ideologies of romantic love (Allen 1988: 79; Millones and Pratt 1989: 41). However, there is a world of difference between 'lovers' tiffs' and wife-beating. Sanchez Parga recognizes that a direct analogy between the mutual blows of the *tinku* battle and the one-way violence from husband to wife cannot be drawn, and retreats to the vague statement that 'aggression rather than fomenting conflict signifies the reproduction of relationships between partners joined by strict complementary opposition' (1990: 27). This raises two questions: first whether all instances of dualism can be subsumed under the term 'complementary opposition' with its close association to gender complementarity[7] and second, whether the function of violence in the *tinku* is comparable to that between spouses. My conclusion is that in the concern to elucidate the workings of symbolic dualism, other important features of the ways that marriage, masculinity and femininity are represented have been ignored, and that looking at animal imagery and its associations with masculinity reveals a very different picture.

THE CONTEXTS OF VIOLENCE[8]

There are certain concepts and images at work among the *ayllus* of Northern Potosí which reveal a preoccupation with physical force in all its manifestations, and a recognition of its ambivalence in the reproduction of social life. I do not wish to argue that the semantic space occupied by the English-language term 'violence' is shared by any single stable concept in

Aymara or Quechua: quite the reverse, given its fundamentally transgressive associations. But I shall start from what would be classified as violent in English and what outsiders refer to as evidence of Indian 'savagery' in order to explore the vocabulary and imagery through which such behaviour is understood and conceptualized by the actors themselves.

In the Chayanta and Sakaka regions of Northern Potosí there are four contexts in which physical force is used and which, it should be emphasized, are in sharp contrast to the patterns of everyday life. People do not fight out of these contexts. Relationships between adult men are not acted out in daily life in a highly performative, agonistic style. Children are not encouraged to fight, nor is there any emphasis on physical punishment for children. It happens sometimes, but most parents say that hitting children is wrong: the way to teach them is to explain in words until they are old enough to understand. Nor do adults often recall violence towards them by their parents.

Starting from the socially most inclusive, these four contexts are:

1 feuds between *ayllus* over territorial borders which are known in the Aymara and Quechua of the region as *ch'axwa*[9];
2 the battles generally known as *tinku* which are highly institutionalized and closely associated with the ritual calendar;
3 the fights between individuals or groups which break out during fiestas as a result of interpersonal tensions;
4 the commonplace violence of men against their wives.

Let us consider each of these in turn.

1 *The ch'axwa*: Northern Potosí leapt into national consciousness in the 1960s when the Jukumani and Laymi *ayllus* of Bustillos province obtained firearms respectively from the government and the miners' union and their endemic border feud escalated into a bloody war in which hundreds died, and from which the reported cases of cannibalism caused a national scandal (Harris and Albó 1975; Godoy 1990). The feuds between neighbouring *ayllus* carry on to this day in spite of repeated attempts by the Bolivian state to suppress them. They escalate when fallow land on the *ayllu* border is brought under cultivation and one community takes the opportunity to extend into its neighbours' territory, reclaiming land which they consider to be rightfully their own. Slings and slingshot are the normal weaponry. As hostilities mount, raiding parties may attack hamlets and villages of the other side, burning houses, stealing and abducting livestock and raping unprotected women. *Ch'axwa* are not, however, an exclusively male affair. Women collect stones, prepare food, and join in discussing tactics. Captured warriors from the enemy side may be killed, and in

extreme cases their significant body parts (such as brain, heart, blood, tongue, testes) consumed raw on the battlefield. As far as I know women do not participate in this, nor are they consumed as victims.

Armed conflict on a wider scale is also *ch'axwa*, for example the action taken by Indians against the landowners after the 1952 revolution, the Chaco War of 1932–5 fought between Bolivia and Paraguay, or the Federal War of 1899 in which Indian troops, under their leader Zárate Willka, sought to defend their lands against increasing encroachment by outsiders.

2 *The tinku*: these encounters are fought between endogamous moieties at different levels of inclusiveness, in the squares of the old colonial pueblos during the main saints' fiestas. The men wear bull-hide helmets modelled on those of conquistadores, known as *muntira*, and also use wide woven belts and bull-hide breastplates to protect themselves. They fight with fists reinforced with woven belts, and often there is a stone, or a lump of lead, in the palm of the hand to give extra force to their blows.[10] Men go to the *tinku* as members of a sacred band of fighters who set out from their villages under the military discipline of a 'major' (*mayura*), playing the long bamboo panpipes known locally as *suqusu*.

Men are drunk when they fight, and they stamp their feet on the ground bellowing *soy toro carajo* ('I am a bull carajo' – the latter an onomato-poeically very satisfying swear word referring to the penis). They wait for an opponent to step forward swinging his arms and also bellowing like a bull. During the day the proceedings are overseen by townspeople who seem to enjoy being in the thick of the mêlée, though they affect to look down on the savage behaviour of the Indians which they control with a whip or stick. Sometimes things escalate beyond their control. Rarely a year passes in which there is not a death from the *tinku* somewhere in the region, which must eventually be equalized in time by a death on the other side. As Hartmann writes, quoting a man from the Cuenca region of Ecuador: 'one year the upper moiety sends the lower side running, another year the lower moiety sends the upper side running' (1978: 207).

The *tinku* is an important aspect of the ritual reproduction of the *ayllus*, and the duty of fighting falls particularly on the young men. Blood must flow on both sides as a sacrifice to the earth in order to produce a bountiful harvest (Alencastre and Dumézil 1953; Hartmann 1978). I remember an occasion when I was shocked to see the face of a friend mangled and bloody and hastened to sympathize with him, but he laughingly told me that he was pleased. To emerge unscathed is to miss the point of the ritual. For all the masculine imagery of bulls fighting, women participate too. Unmarried teenage girls accompany the men, one or two of them as *mit'ani* (flag bearers), who often support their male kin during the battle (e.g. by holding their musical instruments for them). Sometimes girls also fight, indeed, people say that girls should not marry until they have fought at least once. They do not aim to draw blood, rather to pull each other's hair and tear their clothes. Thus while men spill sacrificial blood in the *tinku*, women destroy each other's external covering of wool and hair, evoking the important role of cloth as a sacrificial object in Andean culture (Murra 1962).[11]

The distinction between *tinku* battles and feuds over land is not an exclusive one. Platt has argued that *tinku* and *ch'axwa* must be seen together as constituting a 'practical meditation on the relationship between hierarchy and equality' (1987: 98). The violence of the former has been 'smoothed down' and brought within the annual rhythm of religious feasting, in which balance between opposing parties is emphasized, while in the *ch'axwa* social controls are less tightly ritualized and each side aims to win (1986, 1987). Sallnow notes that *tinkus* in the Cusco region used to serve as a means of pursuing quarrels and disputes over land (1987: 136) and Abercrombie points out how vengeance for previous deaths or rout can be an important motivating force in drawing men to the *tinku* (1985: 259).[12]

3 *Fights during community feasts*: these also occur when people are well in their cups, and here too men claim to be bulls. But while *tinku* fights are the object of pride and boasting – a way for men to demonstrate their manliness and strength and for women also to demonstrate their vigour and vitality – the status of fighting with one's co-villagers, affines, and kin is more ambiguous. *Tinkus* are fought in liminal space that is a place of encounter between groups. This may be the town square, or a cemetery shared by several groups, or a wild place (*pampa*). By contrast, individual quarrels between co-villagers and kin are fought out at the centre of community space, where people are gathered for the prolonged drinking that is part of all ritual occasions. In contrast to local agrarian communities in so many parts of the world where conflict typically takes the form of psychic attack, in the Andes it is more likely to be expressed directly in physical blows. They save up quarrels for fiestas, quarrels arising from jealousy at a real or supposed adulterous relationship, from fines imposed in previous disputes, from the desire to take revenge. Above all, these are the occasions for a man to avenge the violence inflicted on his sister by her husband. Women also sometimes pick a fight with another woman, often jealous and angry because of an adulterous relationship, or an insult. Older women sometimes beat their daughters-in-law. The typical pattern is for the aggrieved party to shout 'Wait for the next fiesta and you will get what is coming to you'.

Nonetheless, while these fights are more explicitly motivated than the *tinku* usually is, they are controlled. Even when fighting escalates to include whole factions, people should only fight an appropriate opponent of the same sex and a similar age. Women and children mostly stay out of the conflict, trying to pacify the assailants, and dragging the sparring partners apart. One of the characteristics of a good wife is that she 'minds' and looks after her husband when he is drunk, pulling him out of fights.[13] There are occasions, however, when a woman is less inclined to stop the men, particularly where her brother is hitting her husband, and there are, of course, also clear criteria for what violence is unacceptable.[14] Godparents, kin, and village authorities remonstrate if they consider that one or both parties have gone beyond what is tolerable, and fines may be imposed.

4   *Wife-beating*: one of the reasons for violence between men in fiestas is the need for a man to avenge his sister. This is common for the simple fact that men beat their wives after drinking during a fiesta, some frequently, some only occasionally. A few women defend themselves with a stick, others escape to the house of a kinsperson, others take their revenge by refusing to cook. Women's complaints about their husbands' violence are frequently voiced in what can only be described as a highly conventional form. Many women during my early fieldwork envied my not being married, wiping a tear from their eyes as they talked. The lament of a woman from Cusco is repeated in essence throughout the Andes: 'From the day I got together with my husband, my life became just weeping and suffering' (Valderrama and Escalante 1977: 106), and is echoed in some of the stories recounted by Stølen. Harrison writes that one woman in Ecuador described the way her husband beat her as 'like you pound clothes on a rock in a river' (1989: 132). Women in Northern Potosí reiterate the refrain that it is hard and painful to be a woman. Many times in different communities they would look conspiratorially at me and say that when I left for England they would come with me to escape the pains of their life. Women do not justify their husbands' violence on the grounds that it is an expression of love, in the commonly reported cliché. Their view is that of the saying quoted by Sanchez Parga: 'of course he beats me, that's how husbands are' (*ha de pegar, marido es pues*) (1990: 38).

For most women the only direct retribution for the violence inflicted on them is when their brothers punish their husbands, by fighting them during a fiesta. We thus have a situation in which a man 'substitutes' for his sister. This acting out of the conflict over a woman begins at the marriage ceremony itself, when the bride's brother accuses his new affine of the way he will maltreat her in future. A wedding feast rarely ends without some kind of fight between the bridegroom and one of his new affines.

The generic status of wife-beating is hard to evaluate. Since men attack their sisters' husbands during the wedding feast itself, it is clear that this is a categorical, not a contingent matter. Some men are known to be far more violent than others, but all married men are thought of as wife-beaters.

Widows often say 'I don't want to remarry and get beaten again'. By contrast, the ways women defend themselves are specific to them and do not have the same stereotypical quality.

These four contexts in which physical force is used can be distinguished according to who attacks whom, and in what context. In some the opponents are balanced (2 and 3) while in others difference and dominance are apparent (1 and 4). Another distinction concerns the degree of collectivity in battles, and the privacy of wife-beating in contrast to other fights that are performed in public. Related to this is the question of the sacrificial quality of fighting. Allen, for example, distinguishes ritual battles from interpersonal 'drunken brawls' which have not been rendered sacred (1988: 212–13). And yet bloodshed or a death in other forms of fighting may well also be interpreted as a sacrifice to satisfy the 'hunger' of the mountains and earth. In general, the distinction between forms of fighting is not tightly drawn. We have already seen the close association between *ch'axwa* and *tinku*, where *tinku* may be the pursuance of *ch'axwa* by other means, or vice versa. All violence is unleashed in the liminal state of drunkenness, when everyday life is suspended and normal inhibitions are lowered. Those who are keen fighters in the *ch'axwa* are the same men who go enthusiastically to fight in the *tinku* when others of their age group have abandoned it, and also remorselessly pick fights with other men, and beat their wives. Some of this physical force is necessary for social reproduction, other manifestations are more a consequence of the way in which social relations are constructed rather than actively desired in themselves.

Linguistically *ch'axwa* is distinguished as a state of ongoing conflict between groups, also known as *kira* (from the Spanish *guerra* = war). In the Aymara of some regions the term *ch'axwa* refers to a pile of stones, or stony place (De Lucca 1983: 110), evoking an image of war fought at a distance with a hail of stones, away from domesticated space. Direct striking and beating, including hand-to-hand fighting is referred to by the root *nuwa* meaning to hit, strike, or beat. The local Aymara term for the *tinku* is *nuwasiña*. The use of the reflexive *-si-* emphasizes the mutuality of the *tinku* encounter; references to other forms of fighting and striking use the non-reflexive form which is directional (that is, 'X hit Y', rather than 'X and Y hit each other'). The way that people refer linguistically to these different expressions of violence is literal, emphasizing the form and direction of the attack and involving no apparent metaphor. The appropriate way to counter physical violence is by more violence. However, in contrast to this lack of metaphor in direct linguistic reference, the semantics of violent behaviour are rich with allusion and imagery.

OF BULLS AND MEN

Fighting is part of *ayllu* life, an inevitable and even necessary outcome of the ritual drinking which is so central to the expression of Andean religious worship. People speak of drinking and fighting as part of a single whole. When they talk about the Protestant evangelicals who have made some converts in the area they emphasize the fact that they do not drink or fight. 'But we do so we won't go to heaven.' It is the sacrificial fighting of the *tinku* that is most admired and valued, hence a man is not a man and a woman is not a woman until they have proved themselves in the *tinku*, pitting themselves against an equal opponent. Fighting between people of the same sex, age and strength is appropriate and respected. Men aspire to the state of bulls, and in fighting they become bulls. The 'poetics of manhood' (Herzfeld 1985) is organized around the importance of bulls, but it does not take the form of an intense mutual competition for prestige between men. Invariably as drinking progresses during any ritual, you can hear the men begin to bellow in their characteristic imitation of a bull, and they paw the ground as the bull does when it fights. For the *tinku* they wear the bull-hide helmet and breastplate, and by so doing they become bulls.

But while they fight as bulls, they also try to feminize their opponent, as a young bull may mount another. Izko recounts hearing a man shout at his fallen adversary *'no ves que te he montado'* ('see, I have mounted you!') (1986: 68). The standard insult to hurl at an opponent is *qincha* (malign whore) or *warmi* (woman). Zuidema has indicated how, according to many sixteenth-century sources, hierarchical relations between groups were gendered, and termed this the 'conquest hierarchy' (1964); Platt has similarly pointed to the gendering of the dual divisions of Andean society – the upper moiety being the warriors and the lower moiety playing the role of women (1987: 93–4; see also Harvey this volume).

The strength of bulls is greatly admired. In everyday life the animals are referred to as *waka*, while the term *turu* used in the context of ritual designates the wild strength that they embody.[15] This strength is also called *walura*, or *niñu*, the same terms that are used to refer to the ancestors, whose power ensures the continuing fertility of the land that they cultivate (Harris 1982). Much of the ritual calendar is organized around harnessing this spiritual force to help humans produce wealth and well-being out of a harsh and unpredictable environment. In the Chayanta and Sakaka regions, bulls are used extensively in ploughing, and their strength is vital for producing the crops. When I ask women what quality they look for in a man, the almost categorical reply is that he should be strong and vigorous, that he should take the team of bulls out for the first ploughing and break open the hard earth. Brute strength is the male contribution, and women reciprocate by taking out to them in the fields the best food they can cook.

Zuidema has suggested that in Andean thought agriculture is like warfare, in which human strength is pitted against the earth, and also against the power of water (1985). So agriculture is a means by which, in addition to the strength of the ancestors and bulls themselves, living men's bull-power is harnessed to attack the earth. One of the rites of passage by which boys become men is part of the sowing festival, and they are yoked in pairs to the plough and driven across the fields making real furrows, in which the sower girl who follows them places the seeds. As in the *tinku*, they wear bull-hide helmets and when set free from the heavy yoke, they career again across the fields, out of control, trying to mount the girls and other men. They drink *chicha* from bowls placed for them on the ground. In short, they behave just like strong young bulls. At another moment in the ritual cycle at the height of the dry season, all the bulls of the community are brought together to fight each other in a 'bull *tinku*' thus imitating the men who are in turn imitating them . . . .[16]

It is clear that in this region bulls have been thoroughly adopted into the symbolic universe, although they are not indigenous but imported from Europe in the sixteenth century. Quite apart from their significance in Mediterranean and Iberian mythology (Whitlock 1977), they correspond to key themes in Andean thought. In Northern Potosí, where they are yoked in pairs for ploughing, their duality is emphasized, and the *turu wasu* (bowls with a pair of yoked bulls on the base carved from a single piece of wood) are used at central moments in ritual performances to pour libations for fertility. This echoes the symmetric dualism of the *tinku*, though here fertility is induced not by the earth consuming the blood of the pair of fighters, but by the two matched bulls together 'fighting' against it. Their extraordinary and unpredictable strength is also celebrated, and it is this that is their most salient characteristic in other Andean regions where they are not used for ploughing. In Southern Perú they are explicitly identified with the *amaru*, the mythical feline serpent of the underworld which manifests itself in earthquakes, and in lakes, springs, and the confluence of rivers, and also in the power of the Indian peasants when they rise against their oppressors and enemies.[17]

MAN THE PREDATOR

To fight in the *tinku* is a rite of passage to adulthood, and a sacrificial offering to the earth. A man is obliged to pick a fight with his sister's husband, and in general to fight with equals is acceptable. To protect *ayllu* land against outside aggression is the duty of everyone who works that land. But mostly people do not approve when men beat their wives, nor do men boast of it openly (although it is often said that they coax their girlfriends into marriage in order to be able to beat them).[18] In practice, a man is usually very sheepish the following morning as his wife gives full vent to her indignation while she prepares the breakfast, or as he finds himself alone with a hangover, his wife having gone to 'visit' a kinsperson. He says 'I was drunk. I don't know what got into me'.

Why then do men beat their wives? They may justify themselves by claiming that she had had too many lovers before getting married, that she spent too much time with her family of origin, that she was flirting with another man, or had drunk too much. Such contingent explanations cannot account for the way wife-beating is generic within marriage, which makes it more susceptible to universalist accounts of male violence. However, universalist arguments tend to downplay the context within which such violence occurs. In Northern Potosí for example, there are various features which distinguish wife-beating from the typical pattern of bourgeois society. First, it is part of a context in which men's fighting qualities are important for the defence of communal land and thus for the future of the *ayllus*. Second, since all women suffer it (though to differing degrees), it does not have the psychological consequences familiar from western accounts, where women feel humiliated and isolated, unable to tell others what is happening, and in some sense responsible for it, and in which their self-esteem is seriously eroded. In Northern Potosí women talk about it openly and indignantly, and do not see it as their fault. Moreover, the fact that their brothers take revenge on their husbands is a public vindication of their sense of hurt.

What concepts are available within Andean culture for exploring the implications and ambiguities of this form of violence? Andean thought, as we have noted, operates in many contexts with the model of complementary duality exemplified in the metaphor of the married couple. However, there is another set of standardized descriptions of sexuality and marriage which reveal a very different emphasis. Young people are expected to have sexual experiences before marrying. In the typical story, repeated with variations by many people, the seduction scene takes place on the mountain-side where the young woman is herding her sheep or goats. She wears a little round mirror which glints in the sun, a sign of her unattached womanhood. The young man carries a flute or a *charango*, and wears a new hat decorated with feathers and with mirrors. He may say that he is going out herding, but people will smile knowingly at each other as he saunters past. The girl he desires always says 'no' and resists, though she may at the same time steal something of his clothing, for example, his hat or a decorative belt, so indicating her real feelings. The young man chases her and she runs away, but in the end she surrenders. (Another common scenario for sexual encounters is during fiestas.)

A vivid example of the ambiguity of this standardized seduction scene can be seen in *La Nación clandestina* by the Bolivian film-maker Jorge Sanjines. Many people who saw it at the London Film Festival in 1989 interpreted the scene as a rape, while recognizing that the woman had appeared previously to be encouraging the man. In some of the accounts I have heard from Laymi women the same ambiguity recurs. Was it rape, or was it seduction in which both parties were playing their appointed roles – the man to chase, the woman to resist?[19] In Andean cultural categories there are clearly defined concepts of rape which do not usually apply in such situations, and where the standard punishment for the man is a fine of llamas.[20]

When a young couple decides to live together the imagery of predation already present in the original seduction scene is repeated. They always run away together – usually with the girl's full connivance. Often she just abandons her flocks on the mountainside, and goes to her young man's home to hide, or the two run off to town for a few days without telling anybody. Although the girl is party to these events the process is nonetheless called 'stealing the woman' (*warmi suwaña*), and her family feigns great anger and resists the match even if they are in fact pleased with their new affine. Cohabitation, and the marriage rituals which may not be finalised for several years afterwards, are in this imagery a process of taming and 'socializing' the wild *tullqa* (wife-taker). After the marriage rituals are completed he enters into a series of obligations towards his wife-givers which he must discharge for the rest of his life.

The house is the appropriate place for sexual relations between spouses, while unmarried people encounter each other in wild places such as the mountainside, where the predatory man swoops down and captures his mate. I use this imagery intentionally, for the *tullqa* is likened to the condor, the vast Andean vulture which hovers over the mountainous landscape preying on the flocks and which is also the sacred embodiment of the mountains and the pre-social remote ancestors (*chullpas*). The common ritual name for a house is *condormamani thapa* (nest of the condor-falcon) which is related to a frequently recounted myth. The condor carried off a girl on his back to his mountain eyrie promising to feed her meat. ('Do you want meat? I will feed you meat' is a very common sexual joke here, as in so many parts of the world.) However, the meat is raw and the girl refuses to eat it. The condor flies off in search of better food for her, and meanwhile a parrot or a hummingbird appears who offers to carry her home. There her grandmother hides her in a large pot. The condor appears in pursuit and settles on the roof of the house where he scratches with his talon, trying to get at the girl he knows to be inside. Eventually he flies away, and the grandmother hurries to the pot to tell the girl that she is now safe. But when she looks inside she finds nothing but dry bones.

One of the messages this myth contains is that for marriage to occur girls have to accept 'raw meat', in other words to enter into a relationship with a wild being and give up the civilized customs of their own home, if they are not to be reduced to dry bones. In short, it suggests that marriage is tied for women to the status of a victim of male predation. I use this imagery advisedly. The condor is primarily a carrion-eating scavenger because its talons are not strong enough to carry off live creatures. However, unlike vultures in other parts of the world, its beak and wings are uncommonly powerful and condors *do* in fact carry off small creatures, sometimes it is said even human babies (Andrews 1982). The Indians commonly talk of the condor attacking their flocks. They call it 'horrible' (*phiru*) because it steals the creatures they have raised, who are like their own family.

A further way in which the wife-taker takes on the identity of a condor is enacted in a ritual. In certain feasts sponsored by his wife's brother or father, he puts on the head and wings of the huge bird and dances round the plaza, carrying his affine on his back. (Here again, as with bull-hide helmets, we see a person taking on the identity of another creature through incorporating its physical skin on their head.) When I asked what it meant I was referred back to the myth. In the myth the condor carries his 'wife'; in ritual he carries his wife's brother. This is the same transformation as when a woman's brother substitutes for her to punish her husband for beating her, and is typical of Andean symbolism of symmetrical dualism.

Thus, however nominal the 'stealing' of the woman from another kin group, however active the participation of the woman herself, and however much her kin group themselves approve, it is treated as a permanent loss, an enduring outrage. Part of the outrage is the loss of her labour, and the robbery of a child of the household, and part of it is the violence her husband will inflict on her. As compensation, the wife-taker remains in a permanent position of ritual subservience to his affines. When he carries his wife's brother on his back he is re-enacting the myth, but with a difference. From being the indomitable bird of prey who carries off his bride, he has become more like a beast of burden. Another of the common obligations of the wife-taker (whether sister's or daughter's husband) expresses a similar ambiguity. At key moments of ritual drinking it is the host's wife-taker who must serve *chicha* and rum to those present, and it is thus he who is responsible for inducting them into the desired altered state of consciousness which will give them access to the sphere of the ancestors, the mountains and all the powers that belong there, ensuring fertility and growth. In this context, the wife-taker serves the rest, but also leads them in the ritual.

To a degree, the wife-taker is tamed, his wild powers harnessed for the needs of social reproduction. But unlike bulls, condors as creatures remain firmly outside civilized space, and men are at their most condor-like when they are outside the domestic sphere on the mountains. It is there that girls are first seduced and abducted by their future husbands. It is also there that men assemble when they go to war. Historical accounts of uprisings frequently describe the Indian troops gathered menacingly on the mountain tops (Platt 1982). In war too, men become condor-like. During the *ch'axwa*, groups of men raid enemy villages, stealing their flocks, sometimes raping the women. Clearer still: they actually mimic the carnivorous predators in consuming the flesh of their enemies. Unlike marriage in which the condor–husband 'eats' metaphorically the raw flesh of his wife, in *ch'axwa* the condor–warriors eat literally the raw flesh of other men. This calls to mind the images detailed by the Andean writer Waman Puma when he describes the warriors of the pre-Inca period, evoking their many qualities of resistance, speed, cunning, and also predatory strength:

> It is said that in battle they became lions and jaguars and foxes and vultures and hawks and mountain cats . . . . Those who won in battle took the most renowned names of war leaders which were puma, falcon [i.e. Waman Puma's two names!], hawk, condor, red dawn sky, parrot, gold, silver, and so it is to this day.
>
> (1615 [1980]: 65)

Condori and Mamani (falcon) are indeed two of the commonest patronyms throughout the altiplano today.

I have never heard an explicit connection made between the condor identity of the wife-taker and the fact that men beat their wives, but there is circumstantial evidence to suggest it: the marriage ritual where the wife's brother focuses his complaints on the way his new affine will beat his sister; the house – the nest of the condor-falcon – as the place where a married couple have sex, and also the place where a man beats his wife. The wife-taker is explicitly identified in myth and ritual as the condor who offers the girl he has abducted raw meat (i.e. sex). But the metaphor of eating meat for sex is reciprocal, so that the condor/wife-taker who has sex with his wife is also 'eating her meat', just as the condor eats the meat of the lambs which women usually own, and with which they are, in some contexts, identified.

In the Aymara vocabulary of fighting and war analysed by Tristan Platt, the action of 'pounding' the enemy is a metaphor of conquest. This in turn is linked to the practice of food preparation, in particular pounding and grinding with stones, in which the concept of 'sweetness' applies both to food and to 'softening' somebody with blows as part of an eventual reconciliation (1987). The model of gender is certainly applied to the very unequal relationship between victor and vanquished in war and, indeed, to the striving for advantage in *tinku* confrontations. Are we to assume that metaphors from war reciprocally structure the behaviour of a man towards his wife in the matter of pounding her to a pulp? Given how generalized this imagery is across cultures, it is as well to recall that in the violence of marriage only one of the 'contestants' on the battlefield is physically active.

THE PARADOX OF VIOLENCE

Bulls are paradoxical creatures. They are dangerous and can, and occasionally do, kill people. They are a chthonic power representing the earth and the underworld not as a benign nurturing being but as violent and unpredictable. At the same time they are vegetarian and they are, to some degree, domesticated, and may be castrated if they are too uncontrollable. The carnivorous condor is not tamed, and yet it too is polyvalent. Its strength is not admired or emulated in everyday life. It is an enemy which hovers menacingly over the flocks and steals the lambs. In social life, the condor as wife-taker can be 'tamed', but his ritual obligations serve as a permanent reminder that at the heart of every household – the 'nest of the condor-falcon' – is the condor who has stolen his wife away from the security of her own kin-group, and whose sisters and daughters will in turn be stolen by another predator-outsider.[21]

Humans are condors not only when they steal girls, but also when they steal livestock from their enemies and when they prey on their flesh and blood. But condors are not only predators who steal the household flocks: they are also their ritual owners through their close identification with the mountains. The livestock they steal are theirs by right, seen by humans as a form of sacrifice. One of the commonest terms by which condors are invoked in ritual – *mallku* – is also the ritual term for the mountains, and for leaders of the *ayllu*. This association seems to derive especially from the identification of each *ayllu* with its land, and with the mountain guardians embodied in the condors that live on their craggy sides. It may also connect up to the war function of the *ayllu*, since all adult men must join together to defend their land, and become like condors in battle. We thus return to the paradoxical nature of the condor – on the one hand feared and disliked as a predator, on the other worshipped as the ancestor, guardian and source of fertility. Rasnake, in an illuminating description of Carnival in Yura (Southern Potosí), illustrates how the *mallku* as sacred embodiment of the whole *ayllu* is made manifest as a ritual staff which is thought to consume the blood of the sacrificial victim just as a condor does, and which is then imitated by the men who eat its raw heart (1987: 669).[22]

There are a number of obvious symbolic oppositions associated with the pairing of the condor and bull:

> mountain : underworld
> carnivore : vegetarian
> pastoralism : agriculture[23]

But it would be distorting to interpret the metaphors of bull and condor just as a contrasting pair, as quasi-mathematical functions. All men are bulls. They become condors as an additional, rather than an alternative, attribute. It would be particularly misleading to force too rigid a contrast in the context of fighting. Rather than two modes of fighting (for example *ch'axwa* versus *tinku*) at most they represent two aspects – brute strength and predation – which may be found in any fighting context. The qualities of raptorial birds are not systematically opposed to those of the predators of the earth and the underworld and, as Waman Puma illustrates, they are all admired in battle. When men gather on the mountain-tops to prepare for battle, they identify with the mountains and their embodiment in the condor; while the raging feline serpent from the underworld captures the spirit of rebellion, as witnessed by the fact that two of the main leaders of the great insurrection of 1777–82 – Tupac Amaru and Tupac Katari – took its name. Even the balanced equality of bulls fighting in the *tinku* slips into a sexual idiom in which men seek to feminize their opponent,[24] while a gender relationship which is manifestly unbalanced, in which a man beats his wife, is adjusted by cultural means into one that follows the Andean canon of symmetry, when the woman is replaced and avenged by her brother. It would, therefore, be more appropriate to see bull and condor as manifestations of powers and potentialities which overlap and merge in some contexts.

Urton (1985) and Isbell (1985) have pointed to the importance of animal metaphors in South American cultures for exploring the human life-cycle and particularly the transition from youth to maturity. The metaphors of bull and condor give meaning not so much to transitions in the life cycle but to the ambivalence of masculinity in Andean culture, balanced uneasily between the strength of the bull who ploughs, who sheds sacrificial blood in the *tinku* and whose vitality makes possible the reproduction of the household economy and the *ayllu*, and, on the other hand, the carnivorous condor, whose more threatening powers are feared but also admired and worshipped. An ambivalence which requires that men be strong, and that like bulls they not only plough but also fight, and yet which recognizes that fighting easily spills over into something more terrible and more destructive, which is at the same time found at the heart of domestic life.

A functionalist account of the role of physical force in the life of the *ayllus* would thus be one-sided, whether it asserts that domestic violence is a means by which men's domination over women is secured, or whether it is one that argues that Indian violence in general is a necessary response to colonial violence. I would want to emphasize that masculinity is contradictory and unstable even within its violent manifestations, as the two images of bull and condor reveal. Above all, violence cannot be equated with agency. Sometimes an individual man may acquire such a reputation as a violent fighter that others view him with repugnance. Some men dislike the complex of drinking and fighting and avoid both except in cases of explicit obligation, for example sponsoring a community ritual, or defending *ayllu* land. (These are the people most drawn to Protestant conversion.) But provided he complies with these obligations, an individual's reluctance to fight and drink has no material consequences. Even in marriage, women's actual behaviour seems to be only very partially a response to the threat of violence.

There are at least two very different ways of understanding Andean marriage within the terms of its own discourse: one in which the model of balance of the couple finds expression in their joint contributions to the household economy, and the other, evoked in the imagery of the condor, in which marriage is a permanently re-enacted scene of violent abduction. In these models we can see in a different context the same cultural play on the themes of equality and inequality, of symmetry and hierarchy which Platt has analysed at the collective level of *tinku* and *ch'axwa* (1987). The image of the condor is premised on the radical difference between women and men which is grounded in sexual difference, and which translates into terms of domination and victimization.

VIOLENCE AS OTHER

Of the different expressions of physical force I have described some are valued, some viewed with ambivalence. However, they share in common that they are performed in a state of 'otherness'. The consumption of alcohol is crucial to this state, not so much because of its chemical effects revealing 'the beast in every man' as because of its importance for establishing contact with the sacred by producing an altered state of consciousness, in establishing publicly and experientially the otherness of ritual performance.[25] It is when they have separated themselves through collective drinking from everyday life and when normal inhibitions are lowered that men embody and enact the sacred powers on which the life of the community depends, which are given form in the bull and condor. As an outsider I have called it violence, but it is a matter for continual negotiation what of this behaviour is considered legitimate and what is 'too much', as is clear from the number of formal complaints lodged with the *ayllu* authorities (including complaints from women about their husbands' violence) and which they have to adjudicate.

Violence is troubling and ambivalent. I suspect that it is a very common cultural strategy to represent it as 'other', to split it off from everyday life. It is in this sense that violence can be said to be 'symbolic' at the same time that it is very 'real' for the victim. There are many ways in which this other is represented and managed, in which this splitting can operate. In Anglo-Saxon culture, much of everyday violence and aggressivity is classified as a 'breakdown' of normality, or as accidents (viz. the role of traffic accidents which even when they involve lawbreaking are not classified in the statistics as 'violent crime'). In other instances, it is represented as an intrusion from outside – viz. the recurrent imputation of soccer violence to outside agitators or hooligans.[26]

In native Andean culture the logic takes a different form. Violence is explicitly treated as other, but as a necessary alternative state rather than a breakdown of normality. It is restricted to the moments of liminality in the context of religious performance when adults – women as well as men – enter into direct contact with the powers of the earth, the mountains and the ancestors, and it is preceded by the ritual suspension of normal activity, so that it is bracketed from everyday life. (The same is true of *ch'axwa* warfare.) A high value is placed on *losing control* in Andean cultures, which in this way differ from the conception of civilization rooted in western culture. It is men who act out this state in all its ambiguity. And yet there are no clear guidelines as to *how much* violence is good, and when it becomes too much. When a man beats his wife he may apologize afterwards, and if he is too brutal he meets with general disapproval and may be fined or sanctioned. Each time fighting erupts during a community feast people – women, children and men – are caught between a mixture of fascination, recognition and sometimes sympathetic indentification with one of the assailants, and at the same time a desire to limit the harm done. The *tinku* may sometimes lead to a death which most people will treat as a successful blood sacrifice to the earth, but of course for the kin directly affected it is a major calamity, the loss of a bull from the household.

Men's duty to act out the ambiguous part of these other asocial powers is not directly identifiable with agency, and in this sense too we can see it as a 'ritual'. Violence in Northern Potosí in general is neither excluded nor denied, neither used as a source of legitimacy nor expelled onto a putative periphery, but is located in an 'other' world in which it is harnessed to social reproduction, but at the same time recognized in all its ambivalence.

Male violence is symbolically elaborated in a way that women's is not. It is striking that men's identification with animals is far more pronounced than that of women, a feature which Urton suggests may be universal (1985: 9; see also Crocker 1985: 38). Turner in the same volume of essays on animal myths and metaphors in S. America, argues that it is the 'alienated aspects of the human (social) being . . . (which are) mediated by symbols of an ostensibly asocial, or "natural" character' 1985: 105). The violence expressed through bull and condor in Northern Potosí today fits Turner's argument well, although it is 'alienated' not so much in the Marxist as in the psychodynamic sense, in that it is attributed to a source outside the self.

It is clear that even physical violence is by no means a male monopoly. But whether in the *tinku* or in the community, women fight other women, although they may retaliate against their husbands in various ways (I remember one occasion when my *comadre* tied her drunk husband's hands behind his back with the aid of her sister and was still laughing when I went round to visit the next morning). It is not uncommon for women to justify other men beating their wives on the grounds of the woman's behaviour, but there is little they can do which directly reciprocates their own husbands' violence (such as verbal aggression, *contra* Sanchez Parga, or witchcraft). In this respect there is no balance between husband and wife, and it can only be achieved by the intervention of a third term, the wife's brother. Femininity, like masculinity, is contradictory in the symbolic representations of Northern Potosí. Women as well as men must have strength and vigour, and in some respects the relationship with their husbands is balanced. But, in other ways, as wives they see themselves as eternal victims, fated to be the objects of violence because they got married. Their predominant part in the practice of violence is to protest, to protest against their violent husbands, and to try to separate those fighting in fiestas.

Women weep for the sadness of leaving their homes and families, for the pain of endless pregnancies, for the hard work that fills most of their days. The physical hurt they suffer at the hands of their husbands becomes a synecdoche for all the sorrows of their lives. 'Men have no right to weep. We are the ones who suffer at their hands,' one woman told me as we watched the distress of a young man recently deserted by his new wife. But men do weep too for other reasons, and then when the drinking, the dancing, the fighting and beating are over, both women and men go back to work.

ACKNOWLEDGEMENTS

Different parts of this paper have been presented to a number of audiences: at the original conference in Oxford, then to Departmental seminars at the

Universities of Cambridge, London (SOAS), Oxford and Kent, and also in Quito at FLACSO (Facultad Latinoamericana de Ciencias Sociales) and at the Erasmus Seminar on 'Current Issues and Perspectives in the Study of Gender' at the University of Leiden. I am very grateful to many people for helpful criticisms and imaginative suggestions on these different occasions.

NOTES

1 See for example Vargas Llosa, writing of an ethnic group of Ayacucho, Peru: 'For the Iquichanos . . . violence is the atmosphere they live in from the time they are born until the time they die' (1983: 50–1), or the long list of negative assessments of Aymara character summarized in Bolton (1973).

2 Anthropological studies of witchcraft are a good example of this. Since the central issue has usually been the intellectualist one of rationality (how can people believe what is manifestly untrue?) there has been a serious understating and underestimation of the violence, death, or dispossession that could result from witchcraft accusations.

3 By *ayllu* I refer to the territory-based, largely endogamous groups of several thousand people. The northwestern part of the region where I have done research is Aymara-speaking, now shifting to Quechua. The *ayllu* inhabitants live mainly from agriculture and livestock rearing, at altitudes of 4,000–2,500m.

4 A point which Orlove (1989) emphasizes in his analysis of Andean ritual battles. But this region was also famous for its warriors who were 'the Inca's soldiers' before the imposition of Spanish rule (Platt *et al.* 1994).

5 Especially his remarks concerning Andean family structure, the sexual division of labour, and men as a 'cultural and domesticating force' (1990: 43).

6 I am grateful to a number of people in Quito for conversations on this issue, and particularly Xavier Izko.

7 I have discussed this at length elsewhere (1986). Platt's analysis of the *tinku* rests on making a comparable distinction between balanced symmetry and complementary antagonism (1987: 91).

8 This paper is based on the fieldwork I have carried out in different areas of the Laymi *ayllu* (Bustillos and Charcas provinces) at various times over the past twenty years, and also in the Sakaka region, Alonso de Ibañez province.

9 In the officially agreed Aymara orthography, 'x' is used for aspiration, like the English 'h' but stronger and further back in the mouth.

10 In this it contrasts to the *tinkus* found in other parts of the Andes – Southern Peru and highland Ecuador – which are fought with slingshot (Alencastre and Dumézil 1953; Hartmann 1978). In Northern Potosí slingshot is today used only rarely, when the battle heats up.

11 This contrast between men and women leads Arnold (1988) to suggest that the blood shed in the *tinku* is a magical imitation of women's menstrual blood which is thought to have supreme fertilizing powers.

12 As Harvey notes (this volume), in Southern Peru even in the context of 'ritual battles', prisoners may be taken and sometimes slaughtered. Sallnow's distinction between forms of *tinku* is useful in emphasizing variations in the rules of performance (1987: 141–4).

13 It seems to be common in many parts of the world for fights to take place in

public space, with the men acting as though they were unrestrainable, but in practice pulled apart by women and children (Fox 1989, chs 6–7).

14 For example, it is shocking for a man to hit men who stand in a parental or ritual kin relationship, while fighting between brothers does not carry the same degree of disapproval.

15 Both words come from Spanish. Cows are referred to as *qachu waka* – (female bulls), on the same principle as llamas. Bulls are rarely castrated unless they are becoming very dangerous.

16 July 31, on the occasion I witnessed it. Bullfights between bulls and men, which are held in many pueblos of Southern Peru and Bolivia, are very different from those of Spain in that the bulls are not killed, since they are not raised for beef, but kept as essential draught animals. Harvey (1991b) suggests that part of the symbolic importance of these bullfights is that they temporarily domesticate the powers of the landscape by bringing them into the centre of the village.

17 For example, Anrup (1990: 221) quotes the nineteenth-century traveller Raimondi: 'the Indians believe in an imaginary creature which they call Amaro which comes down the ravines when rivers are in spate . . . some people say they have seen it descending . . . in the form of an enraged bull'. Hocquenghem notes the identification between the amaru and water and thence with the ancestors (1987: 208). Of native Andean animals, llamas perhaps constitute a natural analogy for the human *tinku*. Abercrombie states that in the region of K'ulta the leading male llamas (*llantiru*) are the epitome of maleness, and are said to go to the *tinku* (1985: 153) and Penny Dransart (p.c.) confirms that male llamas fight.

18 Marriage operates in 'stages', which correspond to the amount of property vested in the new couple both individually and together, and are reinforced by the birth of children. As marriage rituals and property transactions are completed, it becomes almost impossible for a couple to separate.

19 This reveals the troubling ambiguities between desire, fantasy, seduction, and rape which are so hard to disentangle. When I gave a version of this paper to a multi-cultural audience at the University of Leiden most of the women present were disturbed at this description, but one in particular found it entrancing and said that it corresponded closely to the ideals of her Mediterranean culture of origin. This anecdote indicates the cultural variation in what is deemed acceptable and appropriate.

20 We can see here an apparent metaphoric equation of a woman's sexuality and the household flocks. Significantly, the compensation set for a man's death, in one instance I recorded, was a bull. Ward Stavig suggests that rape in colonial Cuzco was not a category used for adult single women (1988: 9), but this is not the case for Northern Potosí today.

21 The metaphoric range of the condor is far greater than that of the falcon in the Andes today. Bertonio's list of metaphorical associations for the falcon in early colonial Aymara includes that of a province and a lord with many vassals (1612, 1984: II: 213). The relative absence of the falcon in contemporary symbolism may reflect the disappearance of such large-scale organization while the condor, which represents a more local group, remains important.

22 According to Rasnake, in Yura people believe the condor is immortal, living off the blood of sacrifices. In reality, condors are known to live for at least 50 years. Mountains in the Andes are sometimes anthropomorphized as virile and cannibalistic warriors (Bouysse-Cassagne 1986: 205; Casaverde Rojas *et al.* cited in Sallnow 1987: 138), and as sexually voracious (Gose 1986: 203).

23 In the contrast between bull and condor we can see something of the split in Andean economy and history between agriculture and pastoralism noted by Pierre Duviols (1973). Mention should also be made of the contest between condor and bull enacted in some regions of Southern Peru (Arguedas 1941; Harvey 1991b).

24 Indeed, Izko notes that one of the games played by courting couples, known as *waka wakaku*, involves the woman enacting the role of cow who is pursued and 'captured' by the man/bull (1986: 157), so one way a man 'feminizes' his opponent in *tinku* fighting is reiterated in amorous encounters.

25 Saignes 1989; Harvey 1991a. Coca leaf which is also essential for ritual performance is used on a daily basis unlike alcohol and does not alter consciousness. While *ch'axwa* are not rituals in the same sense, they are, I understand, preceded by consumption of coca and alcohol.

26 The very term hooligan – of Irish derivation – implies this (Segal 1990: 110). The same discursive process seems to operate in Andean countries where the violence of the Indians serves to externalize the violence present at all levels of society.

BIBLIOGRAPHY

Abercrombie, T. (1985) *The Politics of Sacrifice. An Aymara cosmology in action*, PhD Thesis, Department of Anthropology, University of Chicago.

Alencastre, A. and Dumézil, G. (1953) 'Fêtes et usages des indiens de Langui' *Journal de la Société des Américanistes* 42: 1–118.

Allen, C. (1983) 'Of Bear-men and He-men: bear metaphors and male self-perception in a Peruvian community' *Latin American Indian Literatures* 7(1): 38–51.

Allen, C. (1988) *The Hold Life Has. Coca and cultural identity in an Andean community*, Washington: Smithsonian Institution.

Andrews, M. (1982) *Flight of the Condor*, London: Collins/BBC.

Anrup, R. (1990) *El taita y el toro*, University of Stockholm: Institute of Latin American Studies.

Arguedas, J. M. (1941) *Yawar Fiesta*, Lima: Librería Mejía Baca (1958).

Arnold, D. (1988) 'Matrilineal Practice in a Patrilineal Setting: rituals and metaphors of kinship in an Andean ayllu', PhD Thesis, University College London.

Bertonio, L. (1612, 1984) *Vocabulario de la lengua aymara*, La Paz: CERES, IFEA, MUSEF.

Bolton, R. (1973) 'Aggression and Hypoglycaemia among the Qolla', *Ethnology* 12: 227–57.

Bouysse-Cassagne, T. (1986) 'Urco and Uma: Aymara concepts of space', in Murra, J. V., Wachtel, N. and Revel, J. (eds).

Bouysse-Cassagne, T. (1987) *La identidad aymara. Aproximación histórica siglos XV, XVI*, La Paz: HISBOL.

Crocker, C. (1985) 'My brother the parrot' in Urton, G. (ed.).

De Lucca, M. (1983) *Diccionario Aymara-Castellano*, La Paz: CALA.

Duviols, P. (1973) 'Huari y llacuaz: agricultores y pastores. Un dualismo prehispánico de oposición y complementaridad', *Revista del Museo Nacional* (Lima) 39: 153–93.

Evans-Pritchard, E. E. (1940) *The Nuer*, Oxford: Clarendon Press.

Fox, R. (1989) *The Search for Society*, Rutgers: Rutgers University Press.

Godoy, R. (1990) *Mining and Agriculture in Highland Bolivia*, Tucson: University of Arizona.

Gose, P. (1986) 'Work, Class and Culture in Huaquirca, a Village in the Southern Peruvian Andes', PhD Thesis, London School of Economics.

Harris, O. (1978) 'Complementarity and Conflict. An Andean view of women and men', in La Fontaine, J. (ed.) *Sex and Age as Principles of Social Differentiation*, London: Academic Press.

Harris, O. (1982) 'The Dead and the Devils among the Bolivian Laymi' in Bloch, M. and Parry, J. (eds) *Death and the Regeneration of Life*, Cambridge: Cambridge University Press.

Harris, O. (1986) 'From Asymmetry to Triangle. Symbolic transformations in Northern Potosí' in Murra, J. V., Wachtel, N. and Revel, J. (eds).

Harris, O. and Albó, X. (1975) *Monteras y guardatojos. Campesinos y mineros en el norte de Potosí*, La Paz: CIPCA.

Harrison, R. (1989) *Signs, Songs and Memory in the Andes*, Austin: Texas University Press.

Hartmann, R. (1978) 'Más noticias sobre el "juego del pucara"' *Amerikanistiche Studien* pp.202–18, Collectanea Instituti Anthropos 20, Bonn.

Harvey, P. (1991a) 'Drunken Speech and the Construction of Meaning', *Language in Society* 20: 1–36.

Harvey, P. (1991b) 'Playing for Identity and Tradition – Southern Andean Bullfights', unpublished manuscript.

Herzfeld, M. (1985) *The Poetics of Manhood. Contest and identity in a Cretan mountain village*, Princeton: Princeton University Press.

Hocquenghem, A. M. (1987) *Iconografía mochica*, Lima: Pontificia Universidad Católica del Perú.

Isbell, B. J. (1979) 'La otra mitad esencial: un estudio de complementaridad sexual andina', *Estudios Andinos* 12: 37–56.

Isbell, B. J. (1985) 'The Metaphoric Process: "From culture to nature and back again"', in Urton, G. (ed.).

Izko, X. (1986) *Tiempo de vida y muerte*, La Paz: CONAPO/CIID.

Mamani Condori, C. (1989) 'History and Prehistory in Bolivia. What about the Indians?' in Layton, R. (ed.) *Conflict in the Archaeology of Living Traditions*, London: Unwin Hyman.

Millones, L. and Pratt, M. (1989) *Amor brujo. Imagen y cultura del amor en los Andes*, Lima: Instituto de Estudios Peruanos.

Molinié-Fioravanti, A. (1988) 'Sanglantes et fertiles frontières. A propos des batailles rituelles andines', *Journal de la Société des Américanistes* LXXIV: 49–70.

Murra, J. V. (1962) 'Cloth and its Function in the Inca State', *American Anthropologist* 64: 710–28.

Murra, J. V., Wachtel, N. and Revel, J. (eds) (1986) *Anthropological History of Andean Polities*, Cambridge: Cambridge University Press.

Orlove, B. (n.d.) 'Sticks and Stones: ritual battles and play in the Southern Andes', Unpublished manuscript.

Platt, T. (1982) *Estado boliviano y ayllu andino. Tierra y tributo en el Norte de Potosí*, Lima: Instituto de Estudios Peruanos.

Platt, T. (1986) 'Mirrors and Maize. The concept of *yanantin* among the Macha of Bolivia', in Murra, J. V., Wachtel, N. and Revel, J. (eds).

Platt, T. (1987) 'Entre *ch'axwa* y *muxsa*. Para una historia del pensamiento político aymara', in *Tres reflexiones sobre el pensamiento andino*, La Paz: HISBOL.

Platt, T., Bouysse-Cassagne, T., Harris, O. and Saignes, T. (1994) *Qaraqara/ Charka. Transformaciones históricas en el siglo XVI*, La Paz: HISBOL.

Rasnake, R. (1987) 'Carnival in Yura', *American Ethnologist* 14: 662–80.

Riches, D. (1986a) 'The Phenomenon of Violence', in Riches, D. (ed.) (1986b).

Riches, D. (ed.) (1986b) *The Anthropology of Violence*, Oxford: Blackwell.

Saignes, T. (1989) 'Borracheras andinas', *Revista andina* 7: 83–127.

Sallnow, M. (1987) *Pilgrims of the Andes*, Washington, DC: Smithsonian Institution Press.

Sanchez Parga, J. (1990) *¿Por qué golpearla?*, Quito: Centro Andino de Acción Popular.

Segal, L. (1990) *Slow Motion. Changing masculinities, changing men*, London: Virago Press.

Silverblatt, I. (1987) *Moon, Sun and Witches. Gender ideologies and class in Inca and colonial Peru*, Princeton: Princeton University Press.

Stavig, W. (1988) 'Love, Sex and Sexual Violence in Indian Communities of Rural Cuzco', Unpublished manuscript.

Stølen, K. A. (1987) *A media voz. Relaciones de genero en la sierra ecuatoriana*, Quito: CEPLAES.

Stølen, K. A. (1991) 'Gender, Sexuality and Violence in Ecuador', in Stølen, K. A. (ed.), *Gender, Culture and Power in Developing Countries*, Oslo: Centre for Development and the Environment, 80–105.

Turner, T. (1985) 'Animal Symbolism, Totemism and the Structure of Myth', in Urton, G. (ed.).

Urton, G. (ed.) (1985) *Animal Myths and Metaphors in South America*, Salt Lake City: University of Utah Press.

Valderrama, R. and Escalante, C. (1977) *Gregorio Condori Mamani: autobiografía*, Cusco: Centro Bartolomé de las Casas.

Vargas Llosa, M. (1983) 'Inquest in the Andes', *New York Times Magazine*, 31 July.

Waman Puma de Ayala (1615, 1980) *Nueva corónica y buen gobierno*, Murra, J. V. and Adorno, R. (eds), Mexico: Siglo XXI.

Whitlock, R. (1977) *Bulls through the Ages*, Guildford: Lutterworth Press.

Zuidema, R. T. (1964) *The Ceque System of Cuzco: the Social Organization of the Empire of the Inca*, Leiden: E. J. Brill.

Zuidema, R. T. (1985) 'The Lion in the City. Royal symbols of transition in Cuzco', in Urton, G. (ed.).

3 Domestic violence in the Peruvian Andes[1]

Penelope Harvey

The sexual violence which occurs in the towns and villages of the Southern Peruvian Andes is highly visible yet strangely inaccessible. Many Andean ethnographers have written about the confrontational courting style of young lovers who hurl insults and stones at each other and of the marriage ceremonies in which brides are forcibly dragged from their homes by the husband's kin.[2] However, most descriptions of Andean gender relations emphasize the complementarity of the relationship between husband and wife, which constitutes the focal point of each household or unit of production. Both men and women engage in productive work, own property, earn cash, take decisions about investments or other household ventures, and while men are more visible in political and religious office they require the active consent and participation of their wives to fulfil these public duties.[3] Andean women are strong forceful members of their communities.

The aspect of these relationships which is given considerably less attention in the ethnographic literature is the degree of violence which these women are prepared to tolerate from their husbands.[4]

The fieldwork on which this chapter is based was carried out in Peru in the Southern Andean village of Ocongate, Cusco.[5] During my stay in the village I had many conversations with women about their marital relationships. I was struck by the fact that their toleration of actions, which I found horrifying, was not based in a sense of shame or passivity; they talked with pride about how they fought back and were perfectly willing to complain to others about their treatment. The difference between their attitude and mine was that they appeared to accept this confrontational aspect of their relationships as one of the unpleasant consequences of falling in love and forming a stable partnership. Furthermore, despite the fact that I often witnessed them retaliating and giving as good as they got in domestic fights, when talking about such confrontation they did not present their husbands as directly responsible for the violence, even in very extreme cases. Any discussion of domestic violence in the Peruvian Andes should, therefore, consider the possibility that a person's gender is not taken as the cause of violent actions.

For example, Teresa, a woman of about 60, told me of how her second husband had nearly murdered her. She said that at that time he used to beat her regularly because he was seeing another woman and this always makes men particularly vicious towards their wives, especially when their lovers are not really under their control. In this case his lover was also the lover of one of the local police, and Teresa suffered the consequences. On this particular occasion they were the sponsors for a village festival. Her husband was very drunk and had come looking for her where she was dancing with the guests. He pulled her into the house by her hair and threw her to the floor and was beating her to death. She says that somebody must have called for help. A group of people came to her aid and as they struggled to pull him away from her he broke his shoulder. The man died while she was trying to cure him. Her mother-in-law accused her of murder and Teresa was imprisoned for a week during which time they did an autopsy on her husband which showed that some combination of alcohol and restricted circulation had caused his death. The death was thus put down to his struggle with her helpers and not to her attempts to care for him, and she was released.

This confrontation had particularly extreme consequences yet the basic dynamics of alcohol-induced violence, the exacerbation of the wife's position by her husband's kin and the displacement of male responsibility onto other problematic circumstances are as evident in other less dramatic accounts that women gave of their relationships.

Marta had been beaten many times by her husband Juan when he was drunk and she attributed the frequency of his drinking bouts and the violent behaviour towards her to witchcraft and to his close relationship with his half-sister, Flora. She believed that Flora's ex-lover was punishing Juan for enabling Flora to end the relationship. Marta told how she had recently been punched in the face by Juan for interfering in a quarrel that he was having with Flora. Flora was accusing him of irresponsibility for allowing their father to get drunk, despite the fact that Juan knew he was likely to go home and beat his wife (Flora's mother/Juan's stepmother). Marta had tried to defend Juan saying that the old man had been drinking long before and Juan gave her a black eye for her trouble.

Accounts such as these present very particular problems for anthropological analysis. Many contemporary ethnographers are aware of the negative stereotypes that so easily attach to the peoples they study. Anthropologists project otherness through the mere selection of their research topics and to focus on wife-beating implies a disassociation from the violence and drunkenness and creates a separation between observer and observed that can all too easily be used to strengthen racist attitudes.

One response to this problem has been to simply not write about these aspects of people's lives. Andean ethnographies are filled with references to drinking but seldom mention drunkenness.[6] Thus, paradoxically, the participatory aspects of fieldwork which enable researchers to witness these confrontations can also lead them to turn a blind eye out of loyalty to those with whom they have formed close attachments. It is certainly the case that men who beat their wives when drunk are usually generous, caring friends and spouses when sober. However, the prevalence of violence between sexual partners is such that the denial of this aspect of gender relations irreparably inhibits any more general consideration of the topic.

The other standard response is to disassociate drunken violence from indigenous culture and attribute it to the negative influences of western mestizo lifestyle. However, this implicit division of local practices into the authentically indigenous and the imported western or mestizo has equally detrimental effects both rendering most contemporary Andean social practice inauthentic, and essentializing a notion of authentic indigenous culture in opposition to, and separate from, recognizably western practices. For the past five hundred years Andean peoples have engaged with outsiders – Europeans, North Americans, each other! There is no justification for limiting Andean cultural authenticity to the pre-Hispanic.

What is interesting about both these responses is that despite the fact that one attempts to emphasize the distance between observer and observed while the other seeks to minimize it, both treat the relationship between wife-beating and drunkenness as familiar and recognizable. Cross-cultural comparison is thus rendered unproblematic on an epistemological level despite the difficulties it produces on the political level.

Riches has suggested that for a cross-cultural study of violence the 'situational level of experience' must be separated from 'the representational level of knowledge'. He claims that the former is relatively unproblematic for anthropology in that it seems likely that 'the notion of contestably rendering physical hurt (i.e. violence) has cross-cultural validity' (1991: 295). I would argue that we cannot simply disaggregate facts from their representation and this chapter, therefore, seeks rather to articulate the links between situational experience and representational knowledge, by drawing attention to the notion of contestation as the defining yet variable aspect of the situational experience of violence. Individual women contest their treatment and thus render it violent. Nevertheless, both men and women acknowledge a husband's right to hit his wife. This attitude produces a situation in which women can experience 'violence' while accepting, at the level of representational knowledge, that such acts could be legitimate and thus 'non-violent'.

The first part of this chapter looks at the relationship between situational experience and representational knowledge in this respect and contrasts the contextualizing effects of consanguineal (kinship) and affinal relationships. It is argued that the antagonistic aspect of the relationship between spouses is not motivated by gender difference but has more to do with the nature of affinity. This point is reinforced in the second section of the chapter which looks at how the idioms of kinship and affinity are applied to the conflictual social relations enacted in ritual battles and in interactions with the supernatural. Finally, I return to the specificity of the concrete instances of violent confrontation between spouses to look at why wives are particularly likely to be beaten when men are drunk, and why their experience of 'violence', their contestation of physical hurt, is not recognized in the ways that they and others commonly describe these experiences.

OCONGATE: FROM KINSHIP TO AFFINITY

Childhood

Children are taught from a very young age, both explicitly and by example, that they should respect their parents and their older siblings, who should in turn protect and care for them. Harmonious kinship relations depend upon a recognition of this hierarchy and the assumption of the responsibilities that your particular position entails. Those who do not learn this respect do not become social human beings. When they die they become *condenados* (wandering spirits condemned to eternal exile from the general social universe of the dead) and, more particularly, from the Christian afterlife. Very small children are rarely punished or chastised but once they are deemed able to understand, a stage which coincides with linguistic proficiency and is reached at approximately four or five years of age, they can expect frequent and often severe beatings from their parents or from older siblings.[7] As one man remarked to me concerning his sister: 'Sometimes I hit her, I have the right because I'm older' (*A veces le meto la mano, siendo mayor tengo derecho*).

On another occasion a woman told me about a recent incident when she had been drinking with some of the helpers from her family bakery. At one point they thought they heard her older brother arrive, and she laughingly recounted how they were considering mass suicide in preference to being caught.

As might be expected such use of force within kinship, or rather for kinship, is generally accepted as legitimate by adults. The beatings are an expression of a relationship of hierarchical respect and, as such, they are not questioned or contested, either in cases of other households or, on the rare occasions when respectful relations were enforced, among adult kin. Furthermore, acceptance can be seen in adult accounts of their own child-hood experiences. People sometimes cried at how hard their life had been and at how much they had had to suffer, but they never directly criticized their parents or older siblings for beating them, although they might complain of undue severity. Thus a woman cried that her father had beaten her until she bled because she had not looked after the animals properly but she emphasized that he did look after his family: 'Our father hit us hard but he fed us well'. Parents feed their children, they give them strength and teach them endurance, thereby enabling them to grow up and lead adult lives. Their actions produce relationships of respect, which are manifest in the uncontested beatings.

To challenge the legitimacy of the rendering of physical hurt by a parent would constitute a dispute about the legitimacy, and thus the closeness, of the kinship relationship itself. People distinguish between legitimate kin and other social relations with the term *pariente legítimo*. *Parientes legítimos* are close consanguineal kin, traced through one's own parents or siblings but not through second marriages of a parent nor through one's own or a sibling's spouse. Respect is the only appropriate behaviour within the hierarchy of legitimate kin. The only other people who are rigidly included in this respect hierarchy are godparents and co-parents (*compadres*). The relationship between godparents and godchildren is seen as a sacred parental relationship and demands extreme respect and formality. The co-parent relationship is more akin to a sibling relationship with the ritual parents in the role of the older sibling. These notions of hierarchy and respect are powerful norms in the community and coincide with the teachings of the Church and the school. Children are quite explicitly taught that acceptable social behaviour requires such respect.

However, as might be expected, relations within the hierarchy are negotiable to an extent, especially when the legitimacy of the behaviour of one kin member is challenged in defence of another. Exceptionally harsh or frequent punishment might be contested, a man might even beat his father in retaliation for the beating that the father had given his mother, but such contestation is risky and emotionally harrowing for all involved.

Adolescence and forming couples

Children are thus brought up in an atmosphere of imposed hierarchy where respect is demonstrated by their parents' ability to beat them. Lack of physical strength and the intractibility of kinship hierarchy make confrontation difficult for children. They often respond by leaving home. One way of achieving this break is to move beyond kinship relations and form a sexual partnership, eventually setting up a separate household. Such breaks are themselves embedded in idioms of violent separation. Parents expect children to go through a phase of 'adolescence' (*adolescencia*) during their teenage years. Adolescence is manifest as an uncontrollable obsession with the other sex. The process of separation from kin is thus objectified as something that happens to you, something which you are not ultimately responsible for. Female adolescence particularly is treated as an illness. Schoolgirls were concerned to know how adolescence was handled in Britain, and parents told me that it was as well for a girl to have adolescence in her youth otherwise she might get it as an old woman when an obsession with men would be totally inappropriate.

Adolescence is the driving force behind male pursuit of young women. Male accounts of adolescence stress the risk of life and limb as they evade irate parents, distract vicious dogs, climb walls and perilously hang from rafters. In this construct of virile, active masculinity it is men who take the initiative in creating the links with their desired young women – sending love letters, singing or playing music, lending things such as cassettes and most intimately giving items of clothing.

The strongest positive strategy for women faced with adolescence is to adopt an attitude of obsessive disdain. Teenage girls tend to be obsessed with men in general but are extremely dismissive of any particular young man. They talk incessantly about the young men of the village and enumerate the reasons why they could not possibly imagine forming a relationship with any of them. They are adamant that they never reciprocate male feelings of desire. Their relationships with men are relationships of active resistance. They enjoy teasing men, tempting them, but not giving in to their advances. The freedom of these non-hierarchical social relations is seen as symptomatic of the life of the single woman, the time when women can do whatever they like. Older women complain that young girls today give in to men too easily and get pregnant as if they were animals. One old woman told me that in her day young women would not let the men anywhere near them; furthermore, the men did not stand a chance with them as they knew that the women would break every bone in their bodies or worse! They suggest that, in their day, adolescence as an erotic and confrontational idiom of separation was less rapidly resolved into the subsequent relationship between spouses.

One aspect of the onset of adolescence is that young men and women begin to drink alcohol. While they refuse to drink with higher-ranking kin, and would never get drunk in their presence, amongst themselves and away from adult control the consumption of alcohol plays an important role in the initiation of sexual relations. As I have discussed in earlier studies of Andean drinking practices, drinking is widely associated with the achievement of potency, creation of community, and the establishment of links with the world of indigenous supernatural power.[8] Adolescent drinking takes place outside the social space of kinship hierarchy and the adult world of the established couple, and it is in this conceptually wild, out-of-community space that sexual relations are usually initiated; the *puna* grasslands above the village by day, the nearer cultivated land at night. In keeping with their idiom of disdain young women never admit to having willingly had sexual relations with men. They always say that they were tricked into it – 'he deceived me' (*me engañó*). Active resistance is expected and is often understood by the men as an expression of desire. It is interesting to note that adolescent sexual relations are said to occur with greatest frequency during Carnival, the most important festival of the rainy season, when the Andean world is believed to be in direct contact with the wild powers of the dead.[9] The most propitious season for marriage, on the other hand, is during August, at the height of the dry season. Adolescent sexual relations are thus associated with wild, non-social, non-hierarchical space in which respect has no place, in contrast to the formal affinal relationship constituted in the establishment of a separate hearth or household. The formation of this new social unit, which marks the move to adult status, reorients the relationship between these sexual partners back towards the kinship hierarchy. The formation of new households usually coincides with the birth of children through which the sexual partners now begin to relate as kin.

Despite the image of the single man or woman as living a carefree life and enjoying the privilege of being able to escape the demands of kinship hierarchy, kin react strongly to the knowledge that adolescents are forming sexual liaisons. Nearly everyone I talked to had some tale about how they themselves or their lover, usually both, suffered beatings at the hands of their respective kin while they were courting. The formation of intimate relationships outside kinship facilitates a move away from the immediate kin group, but it is a move that has to be fought for.

As I have noted above, it is very difficult, given the social importance of respect, for young people to stand up to their kin and their response is thus usually to elope. They run away from home and return only when the woman is pregnant. The woman's pregnancy constitutes the couple's new status and the families will usually accept the new relationship although not without a period of remonstration in which parents continue to assert their authority.

The marriage ritual itself often emphasizes the necessity of this struggle as an integral component of courtship. Marriages are traditionally celebrated in a spirit of competition. The celebrations take place over several days, first at the bride's house and then at the groom's. Each household tries to outdo the other in the serving of food and drink and the provision of music for dancing. In many areas of the Andes, although not in Ocongate itself, the groom's family has to capture the bride.

> Albo compares the wooing of the girl's kinsmen by those of the youth to the storming of a fortress. The parents of the prospective groom must kneel before the parents of the bride to plead for her hand on their son's behalf. As the groom's party escorts the bride away from her home, her kinsmen make a mock sally against them, and her father must be prevented by force from following her. The final reconciliation is enacted only at the house raising and demands the participation of the community as a whole. At the conclusions of this ceremony a dance is held in which people pair off without regard to sex or kinship affiliations. The dancers first threaten one another, then whip one another, and at last display complete amity.
>
> (Lambert 1977: 10)

As couples begin to establish their relationships, and marriage rarely occurs until couples have lived together for several years, physical confrontation becomes more frequent between the 'spouses'. In fact, at this later stage of consolidating relationships, such confrontation is jokingly referred to as an expression of sexual desire – the famous 'Andean love' (*amor andino*). I never heard a woman use this idiom to describe a beating that she had received. However, men often depict female attacks on them as motivated by desire, an extension of female adolescent behaviour, and outsiders to the relationship may also take up this interpretative option.

The use of physical force is thus simultaneously an idiom of integration and separation. Parents hold their children and wrest them away from potential spouses while affines achieve a unity and interactional intensity in the same terms with the difference that the relationship is no longer one-way. This complementarity is demonstrated most forcefully in the relationship between spouses who both feed and beat each other.

Marriage and jealousy

Marriage ideally marks the formation of a kin-based unit through the birth and rearing of children. Women particularly seek legal legitimation of their sexual unions in the hopes of thus securing material and emotional support for bringing up their children. This support is found in the mundane social relations of the village and in the institutional backing of the family as a social unit by both Church and state agencies. Images of motherhood are strong, positive and pervasive and present women as those who are most able to form close bonds with their children and take responsibility for them and the immediate environment in which they are raised. A woman shows her love for a man by having his children and bringing them up. It is motherhood that confers adult status and motherhood that places women firmly in a world of sexual differentiation and complementary agency.

As mothers, women are responsible for the running of the home, and to be worthy of respect a woman must show herself to be hard-working in this regard. Men are not expected to display aptitude or interest in the day-to-day maintenance tasks such as serving food or cooking. This ability in women is thus seen as something worthy of respect and the man who *can* perform these tasks will let it be known with pride, often as evidence of his autonomy – a valued male characteristic. A lively clever woman will represent the interests of her household behind the scenes in informal networks and in the subtle manipulation of the man over whom she has some influence. An ideal woman is quick-witted (*viva*), hard-working (*trabajadora*), tender (*cariñosa*), and attractive (*simpática*) – a quality which combines physical and moral attributes. There is no ideal of passive receptive femininity. A bad woman is one who is not effective because she is lazy (*floja*), stupid (*sonsa*), or uses her abilities for anti-social purposes (*mala*).

The dominant image of masculinity in this community is associated with physical strength and an autonomous spirit. Heterosexual virility is an aspect of this strength. Women insult men by suggesting that they are no longer sexually active, an insult which hinges on the perceived failure to display effective male agency. The association between maleness, sexual virility and indomitable autonomy leads to a general acceptance of the inevitability of sexual infidelity. However, to be worthy of respect a man must show both effective engagement in the public life of the community and also authority in his role as head of the household, where he operates as the guardian of order and discipline.

The birth of children brings a husband and wife into a pseudo-kinship relationship. Spouses most usually employ kin terms to address each other and point out that these terms are particularly affectionate. However, it is interesting to note that the terms used are generally cross-generational, and thus carry the implications not only of trust and respect but also of hierarchy. They most commonly refer to each other as mother/father (*mama/papa*) or as son/daughter (*hijo/hija*). A husband can feel he has the right to hit his wife, and in principle, it is a right which the woman herself may recognize. This recognition is implied by the way in which women respond to mis-treatment by other men, as, for example, in the following comment: 'Am I your wife, what right have you to treat me like this?' (*Acaso soy tu mujer para qué me trates así?*). Thus women are aware that when they form a stable partnership with a man they enter into a relationship which is based on the kinship ideal of mutual respect, trust and love, but which is ultimately hierarchical, the man having the highest authority in the household. However, given that husband and wife are not in fact *parientes legítimos* the legitimacy of the use of physical force between spouses is, in fact, very commonly contested.

One of the most common motives for marital violence is male sexual jealousy (*celos*). This sexual jealousy is aroused in men by female sexual infidelity, real or imagined. Women are often beaten for their past sexual experiences and may also be punished for the deeds of other women. A woman once told me that she had been severely beaten by her husband and, when I pushed her to tell me why, she said that the wife always suffers, that he had beaten her for all the faults of his other lovers, even calling them by name as he did so. This woman's body thus became the register of her spouse's previous relationships, relationships in which he was unable to objectify his control in this way.

Both men and women are thought to be desiring subjects, even into old age. Old men particularly are prey to sexual desire and can still feel jealous of their wives, although this attitude tends to be laughed at by younger people. Married women are assumed to experience sexual desire and their husbands should ideally control that desire through satisfying the woman's needs. Indeed, men frequently joke about the strain that women put them under in this respect, constantly demanding their sexual services.

The most distinctive aspect of male attitudes towards sexuality is their exaggerated concern with female infidelity. Indeed, female infidelity appears to be far more threatening to men than male infidelity is to women. I suggested above that male infidelity is a commonly accepted aspect of normal masculinity. There are plenty of stories of female jealousy in which women are accused of practising witchcraft against men, or lying in wait in order to inflict severe physical injury, but such behaviour is always presented as abnormal and as such illigitimate. Beatings are not about revenge or punishment but about establishing and expressing particular kinds of appropriate relationships. It is not appropriate for women to exact revenge even though their physical attacks on men are nearly always in response to a man's proven liaison with another woman, often even involving the desertion of the established family. The acceptable and, indeed, common way for a woman to deal with such cases is through the courts where they have recourse to the institutionalized representation of the family as an inviolable unit and can thus make a strong case against a man.[10] Men defend themselves in terms of other discursive modes, usually the let out of drink or the masculine 'need' for sexual autonomy. A man would rarely use the courts against a woman as he would thus further damage his injured masculinity by calling in a higher male authority. An appeal to the judge would also require the narration of the event in terms that would force him to acknowledge a breakdown in the order of the household which he should control.

. Since domestic authority ultimately rests with the man, and since residence is most frequently virilocal, a man can carry on sexual relationships with other women without disrupting the kinship hierarchy of his domestic unit, especially when his affairs are conducted away from the village, and away from his wife's kin. A woman's sexual infidelity, on the other hand, automatically challenges the man's position in the domestic hierarchy as it places him in a disputed relationship not only with his wife's kin, an unavoidable aspect of affinity, but also with his wife's male lover.

My suggestion is that the particular image of masculinity as hierarchically dominant and controlling is, in fact, threatened in the Andes as much by the fact of a wife's affinity as by her infidelity. A husband and wife ideally live in a pseudo-kin relationship yet their relationship is complicated by the fact that it is complementary. They feed and enable each other, they do not live together in the one-way hierarchical relationship of kinship. Affinity is threatening to the ideally kin-based family unit because, although it is a relationship of mutual dependence, it is not a relationship of undisputed hierarchy. As will be clearly illustrated below with reference to the nature of supernatural power and the practice of ritual battles, Andean complementarity is essentially a hierarchical notion. The bringing together of distinctive elements to form the complementary whole is confrontational however because the hierarchy is not the prescribed, respectful, trusting hierarchy of kinship but the achieved hierarchy of conquest.

The regenerative power that the complementary whole embodies is predicated on this joining of difference. Affinity is necessary because there can be no regeneration through kinship alone. Incestuous sexual relationships are ultimately sterile, those involved are not social beings, their offspring will die. Hierarchy within marriage must thus contain, but not negate, difference.

Marriage is thus predicated on difference, a difference that is attested to by the sexual nature of the relationship and a difference that is necessary to the reproduction of the domestic unit. However, the domestic unit is simultaneously predicated on the reproduction of the kinship hierarchy to which the in-marrying spouse must be assimilated. An in-marrying wife thus finds herself in a very difficult position. She is expected to respect the authoritarian unnegotiable hierarchy of her husband's kin group yet she is never fully assimilated as kin. A man may hit his wife for not obeying him or even for not behaving appropriately towards his parents or siblings, in other words, for failing to treat his kin as if they were hers.

As might be expected, a husband has far less control over his wife in the rare cases of uxorilocal marriage. In such marriages women remain in strong hierarchical relationships to parents and siblings and a man can never hope to fully transfer her allegiance to himself and to his kin. In all marital relationships there is a conscious struggle on the part of the husband to get the wife away from the influence and protection of her own kin. Women tend to resist as long as they can and early marital disputes often occur over these split loyalties.

The argument that sexual jealousy is about affinity, rather than gender, is strengthened when we look at how women deal with their spouses' jealous accusations. All the strategies they adopt entail the stressing of their pseudo-kinship relationship and the playing down of affinal difference. One common tactic is for the woman to engineer to stop sleeping with the man. Children are often used as the excuse. Women move into separate beds to nurse young children. Less frequent sexual relations paradoxically seem to diminish a husband's jealousy, presumably because celibacy diminishes the mutual interaction which challenges the kinship hierarchy. Another strategy is to play down the importance of a husband's use of force, to treat it as the legitimate imposition of respect by kin rather than as the disputed 'conquest' of affinity.

One woman reported to me in a quite relaxed fashion, in the context of a longer interview in which she had wept as she recalled the treatment she had suffered at the hands of her father, that she had a very happy marriage despite the fact that she and her spouse were always fighting. She said, laughing, 'Sometimes he hits me because I am crazy, sometimes he's been on the verge of going for me with an axe'. By not contesting her treatment she depicts her relationship to her spouse as closer than that which she had with her father.

Finally, a woman will tend to look to her husband's kin rather than to her own for support if she wants the situation to be resolved rather than escalated. Typically, she will turn to an aunt or uncle who have the hierarchical rank to admonish the spouse. Co-parents and godparents are also appealed to in this respect. Men too will use this tactic when in dispute with their wives. If a woman turns to her own kin however, the problem is likely to escalate as her kin have no accepted authority over her husband. Nevertheless, however skilfully a woman follows these strategies she can never establish herself as adult kin because her husband's *parientes legítimos* will never fully accept her as such. In other words, there are parties to the negotiation of her status which she can never control. Women are very aware of this when they cry about being all alone having married out of their own kin groups into groups that never fully accept them. When a woman has married in from another community her position is even more vulnerable. This vulnerability continues however well a woman gets on with her affines. Affinal relationships between brothers and sisters-in-law and parents-in-law with daughters/sons-in-law are often quarrelsome and difficult. Arguments often arise over responsibilities. One party accuses the other of irresponsibility and they in turn are accused of being interfering and unnecessarily critical. There is no established or mutually acceptable hierarchy.

Children and in-marrying spouses, nearly always women, are thus both closely connected to the undomesticated world that exists outside of the established hierarchy of kinship. Their domestication to this hierarchy occurs through the teaching of respect. Children are transformed into fully social beings, *parientes legítimos*, wives, on the other hand, occupy a more ambiguous position. They should ideally act as *parientes legítimos*, but they themselves can never command the respect which is due to kin as their husband's kin can always invoke their affinal status. Thus, unlike Toren's Fijian example (this volume) where wives become kin through the process of marriage, in the Andes the process of marriage does not create a relationship of kinship between spouses. The kinship that is created is between parents and children. It is in this sense that I understand women's reasoning that they remain in violent partnerships for the sake of their children. For if a woman leaves her husband she deprives her children of the pivotal kinship relationship with the father, from whom the child learns respect and from whom the child receives a legitimate place in the hierarchy of local kin.

IDIOMS OF VIOLENCE AND AFFINITY

Ritual battles and the supernatural

I now want to turn briefly to the wider South Andean ethnography on ritual battles and on the relationship between humans and supernatural powers, to illustrate those ways in which the rendering of physical hurt is not contested but is seen as beneficial and even enjoyed as fun. I also wish to draw attention to the explicit reference to the affinal relationships between the parties to these legitimate 'violent' interactions.

Ritual battles occur throughout the Andean region from Ecuador through Peru and Bolivia.[11] The fights are ritualized in the sense that they are recurrent events that take place on traditionally established dates, in specific places, and between specific social groups. The two fights with the largest number of participants, up to 1,000 with many more spectators, are named after the mountain ranges that dominate the *puna* battlefields – Chiaraje and Toqto. Two well-defined groups fight with slings and stones often inflicting considerable, even fatal injuries. In the case of Toqto these groups are two provinces of the Cusco Department and in the Chiaraje case two sectors of a single province. In these particular battles it is only the men who fight, while the women watch, encourage the men with songs and shouting, and provide them with stones. They also serve food and drink during the interval.

In many places the fights, while still employing weapons that inflict wounds and in some cases death, consist of a series of individual encounters rather than a general battle fought by larger groups. Representatives of the opposing groups take it in turns to receive or to try to avoid the blow from their opponent. Again participants are largely male and number about fifty.

The fights entail particular notions of winning according to injuries inflicted or territory encroached on, but it is important to stress that the outcomes are essentially unpredictable and are usually disputed. In the Chiaraje and Toqto fights it has been suggested that, territorial consider-ations apart, the winning side is the one that takes the most prisoners, weapons and clothing from their opponents. Captives are ridiculed and made to dance, often in women's clothing. Many sources state that the women of the losing group are taken by the winners as marriage partners. Other reports say that women are taken as captives but later released, having been stripped of their clothes but not sexually violated. To give clothes in the Andes is very closely associated with the giving of sexual favours.

There are other ritual fights in which people are not literally killed, and if wounded then not seriously so, as the weapons are objects such as fruits or cornstalks. There are also fights that take the form of dramatic perform-ances in which the actors stick to an established sequencing of events, often leading to the symbolic 'death' of one of the groups. It is fights of this nature that I witnessed in Ocongate.

After the pilgrimage to the shrine of the Señor de Qoyllorrit'i which occurs at the feast of Corpus Christi the two ritually most important dance groups confront each other in the village square.[12] The Ch'unchu dancers represent native Amazonian peoples, the Qollas represent *puna* pastoralists and traders. In this fight, in which the dancers chase each other around the square swiping at each other's legs with their whips, the Qollas are eventu-ally defeated by the Ch'unchus. On one occasion the Qollas dressed up in women's skirts and spent most of the fight simulating sexual intercourse with each other and making lewd suggestions to the crowd both through their body language and the sexual obscenities they yelled in Quechua. They were finally 'killed' by the long wooden sticks that the Ch'unchus carry and which had been used to represent the phallus during the extended buffoonery that comprised the greater part of the fight. This feminization of the defeated group is consistent with practices reported in connection with many of the other fights to which I have referred.

The connection between gender and conquest or submission is obviously being drawn in the ritual battles described above when male captives of the losing group are dressed as women or taken as sexual partners. However, it is important to note that it is women's sexuality, not their association with motherhood and home-making, that is stressed in these cases. This emphasis on the sexual availability of the feminized group places them clearly in an affinal relationship to the victors. The ritual battles thus involve two opposing yet complementary groups, interdependent in the wider order of social relations yet not ordered into the social hierarchies that ensure stable continuing relations. As Platt remarks concerning the Bolivian Macha:

> ritual warfare (enacts), in the language of inter-moietal rivalry, the balanced relation between complementary forces that is necessary to organic reproduction.

(Platt 1987: 164)

The immediate outcome of these fights ranks the two opposing sides and the emergent hierarchy is gendered. However, the emphasis on the sexuality of these gendered groups reminds us that we are not dealing with the ordered hierarchies of kinship but with the unstable relationships between affines.

People fight in ritual battles for fun. They are occasions for festive drinking, singing, and dancing. In many fights the emergent hierarchies are immediately contested and disputed. The confrontations are always enacted through these idioms of desire. Far from establishing order the ritual battles appear to acknowledge, and even eroticize, the disorder that lies at the heart of productive relations. It is worth noting in this respect that ritual battles are often referred to as amorous encounters. Thus we can see a direct parallel between what has been described as 'the battle for regeneration' at the level of community with that of the violent domestic relationships entailed in *amor andino*.[13] I believe that violence between affines is expected on one level. It is both erotic and funny, enjoyable. Perhaps people laugh about domestic confrontation and *amor andino* because it appears to be about the establishment of ordered domestic hierarchy, while in fact it merely emphasizes the irreconcilable differences on which human productivity precariously depends.

Human relationships with local supernatural powers also emphasize confrontation and difference, although unlike the encounters of the ritual battles, these interactions appear to invoke both kinship and affinal modes of relatedness. These powers, particularly the mountain spirits and the earth spirits, ensure the fertility of crops and animals, and the successful continuity of human social relations. The relationship between humans and the spirit world is rigidly hierarchical yet it is highly problematic, unpredictable and potentially destructive.

As has been shown for many otherwise distinctive areas of the Andes, the relationship between human beings and the supernatural powers of the Andean landscape is essentially one of mutul consumption.[14] To briefly summarize the argument, mountain spirits spend their vital fluids during the growing season in the form of rain which enables humans to grow crops, to eat and to reproduce their community. However, these spirits need feeding in return. Mountain spirits and humans exist in a relationship whereby they feed on each other and thus have to restore each other's vital force if the regenerative cycle is to continue. In return for the rain, humans offer their vital substance to the spirits in sacrificial offerings. Just as the mountain spirits can waste away and lose their power if they are not fed and attended to, similarly human beings exist in a very dangerous relationship to these powers because the ultimate sácrifice is human vital substance itself rather than a metonymic substitute. Feeding and wasting are two sides of the same coin.

This relationship is also discussed in these terms in Ocongate. Humans and the spirit world exist in a hierarchical relationship whereby the hunger of the spirits is both unpredictable and, at times, voracious. Human men and women depend on the power of the spirit world yet they can never rely on the beneficence of these spirits. These powers that can bring life and fertility can also cause death and sterility. If angered, or if their needs are not minutely attended to, they will avenge themselves on human beings. Furthermore, humans are collectively responsible for the maintenance of good relations with these spirits and individuals can thus never ensure a harmonious relationship with the spirit world.

Gose's study of sacrificial offerings to the supernatural powers in the Southern Andes revealed a strong affinal metaphor in local discussion of how the human and the supernatural worlds are related.[15] Although human sacrifices are rarely, if ever, offered today, historically the ultimate offering that could be made to the mountain spirit was a young virginal woman from the community. Gose's analysis suggests that such women stood as metonyms for the human community which then entered into an affinal relationship to the mountain spirits as a wife to her husband.

Harris (1982: 65) also describes this relationship between the supernatural and notions of affinity in her discussion of the concept *niñu* in the Norte de Potosí, Bolivia. *Niñu* are in one sense the children of the Sun and Moon with a close association to the Christian God and the Virgin Mary.

Niñu however has also a multiplicity of other meanings that undermine this clear identification with the moral force of celestial deities. It can, for example, be used to refer variously to severe fevers, the carrion condor, the mountain spirits, bulls, and wife-taking affines . . . . wife-takers, identified in myth and ritual with the condor, are necessary for reproduction but also the source of discord and fragmentation. Many of the meanings of *niñu* are clearly sources of power which are not fully controlled . . . *niñu* also refers in some contexts to the mountain spirits.

(Harris 1982: 65)

The affinal relationship between humans and the supernatural is clearly articulated in the notion of mutual consumption which stresses the inter-dependence, the sense of difference and the inevitability of violent interaction. The supernatural powers of the landscape do not behave with trust and respect towards humans but are unpredictable and potentially destructive. Like affines they have to be wooed and placated. However, the rigid hierarchical relationship between humans and the supernatural powers also suggests that these relationships are not simply and unambiguously affinal. These powers are of the local landscape, they identify indigenous tradition and it is through their association with these powers that local people articulate their ethnic autonomy. Despite the use of affinal idioms the spirits of the landscape are also frequently referred to as ancestors. In this sense the idiom of mutual consumption becomes one of incorporation.

It is interesting to note at this point that human sexuality is also talked about in terms of feeding and wasting. Sex is commonly referred to as eating. When I returned to Ocongate weighing some thirty pounds less than when I had left, people joked with me that I was very thin and had obviously been eating a lot. The reference was to the supposition that I had been actively engaging in the wildly unrestrained 'free-love' that they imagine European sexual relations to entail.

The relationship between sex and eating depicts sex as both destructive and productive. The central idea seems to be that in a sexual relationship partners both feed on and are fed by each other. The parallels between spouses and the relationship that humans have with the mountain spirits is obvious. I would also suggest that in the ritual battles the sexual union with the losing group can, through the metaphor of eating, be taken as a reference to their assimilation. The winning group is thus regenerated through the assimilation of the losers taken as captives.

Attitudes towards incest reinforce this notion of destruction and pro-duction. To have sexual relations with kin in the terms of this metaphor would be to feed on yourself, on your own community, and the act is thus highly threatening. Those who commit incest are believed to become *condenados* (dangerous wandering spirits). Stories concerning *condenados* frequently refer to their voracious appetites, and to the dangers entailed in their ability to take on a human form and trick men and women into having sex with them. Sex with a *condenado* leads to almost instant death by wasting away. It will be noted that the relationship between sex and eating is not directly related to gender difference. It can be seen as a statement on the nature of affinity, but affinity as it effects both men and women.

Affinity thus appears to centre on notions of dangerous predatory difference which entails both disorder and desire, exacerbated in the relationship between spouses who feed each other. Kinship, on the other hand, entails order, hierarchy and authority. Kinship is the result of having been fed by others whom one does *not* feed. The hierarchy is one-way.

The rendering of physical hurt can acquire an uncontested legitimacy if it expresses either the erotic disorder of affinal relations or the hierarchical order of kinship relations, for in both these circumstances the outcome can be beneficial and productive. Where violence is intolerable is in those cases where it works against the order of kinship and respect.

Such interpretative possibilities are obviously highly relative and context dependent. In the final section of this chapter I thus wish to return to concrete interactions and consider the relationship between drunkenness and wife-beating and the question of why it is so difficult for women to voice an effective contestation of these acts.

VIOLENCE AND DRUNKENNESS

I have discussed elsewhere the central importance of drinking and drunkenness to ritual in Andean villages. People drink to 'enliven' themselves through the formation of closer links to the supernatural powers of the landscape and to each other. There are appropriate and inappropriate occasions for drunkenness, and within any drinking event there are moments when people are expected to drink in moderation and other moments at which excess is expected, indeed required. The sanctions for inappropriate drinking are not immediately visible – people tolerate drunkenness but an undisciplined drinker will gradually become isolated, disapproved of, disliked, even pitied.

Drinking is ostensibly about enhancing social relations but drunkenness very frequently leads to conflict and disruption. As people get drunk they feel more able to articulate the problematic aspects of their social relations and they feel empowered to vocalize complaints and to act on the focus of their dissatisfaction. Men and women become very sensitive to their position in the household hierarchy and it is with reference to the need to impose respect and draw attention to the order of the kinship hierarchy that much domestic violence occurs. Men hit their wives and children, women hit their children.

However, the primary motive for drunken violence is male sexual jealousy which cannot simply be explained in terms of the threat to a man's position in the kinship hierarchy as the woman's infidelity is often imagined or displaced as wives stand for lovers that the men have no authority over.

Drunkenness most frequently occurs in ritualized contexts in which drinkers affirm pride in an autonomous indigenous identity. However, the affirmation is tentative and qualified. When drunk, people constantly refer to the fact that their indigenous identity both is and is not their power. They make positive assertions about insider identity, and about their Inka past, but they also cry about their poverty, their loneliness, and their vulnerability. Drunkenness is a state in which people make explicit reference to the limitations of their indigenous, insider identity in their realization that this dimension of power is not only ultimately inaccessible but also is a power that can be and has been defeated. Linguistically, drunks achieve this qualification by using Spanish rather than Quechua to assert their indigenous authenticity. Male violence towards their wives might perhaps offer another such qualification. Men and women occupy an inferior feminized position in relation to the supernatural powers whose presence legitimates the drinking sessions. Drunk men sometimes refer quite explicitly to their own menstruation or pregnancy. When a man beats his wife out of sexual jealousy he is drawing his attention to their affinal relationship. The social disruption that his actions bring about is a recognizable aspect of affinal relations. By dominating the woman he feminizes her and asserts his own masculinity. His actions will not be condoned but they are recognized and understood. From the outside people might remark that he was imposing respect, or that he was simply drunk and acting somewhat inappropriately. If the woman complains to local judges in these circumstances they are likely to detain the man until he calms down, but sanctions are not severe and people will tend to joke about his actions rather than express any strong disapproval. Women are often blamed for provoking the man. Were a man to beat his mother, aunt or sister in these circumstances his actions would be totally unacceptable and people appear genuinely horrified when such confrontations occur.

Women find themselves in a very different position. In terms of the kinship hierarchy it is totally unacceptable for a woman to hit her husband and such behaviour will draw strong disapproval from the husband's kin. People do accept and enjoy women's retaliation within the affinal idiom but she is expected to constrain rather than aggress. There is no institutional or discursive support for a woman's domination and feminization of her husband. Such actions would ultimately shame a man and undermine the complementary nature of their partnership.

Furthermore, the final blow to female autonomy is that women are expected to be the guardians of drunken men. This role of guardian is not particularly the role of the wife but rather the role of a man's female kin. In so far as a woman becomes part of the community of kin then she has the moral obligation to look after her drunken husband despite the fact that regardless of her behaviour he might stress her affinity.

Thus, while both men and women when drunk subject those in subordinate positions to themselves to physical abuse, it is particularly wives who are vulnerable to the consequences of male assertions of affinity through reference to sexual jealousy. It makes no sense for women to beat men as an assertion of their superiority in an affinal idiom because there is no discursive space in which it makes sense for men to occupy a position of feminized defeat. This position can only be occupied by women. Women do attack men in ways which they present as being purely instrumental and which are directly designed to bring an end to a particular and real extra-marital relationship in which the man is engaged. Women who do so are thought to be crazy, and there is no cultural norm that allows them to avoid the implications of their actions. Women do not attack men for fictitious relationships nor do they treat men as metonyms for past relationships.

CONCLUSIONS

Anthropological analyses of domestic violence entail the dilemma of how to reconcile politics and epistemology. The analytical distinction between situational experience and representational knowledge enables the relativization of the various ways in which violent acts are contextualized and interpreted without the implication that the physical act of rendering hurt has not really taken place. By concentrating on the social relationships that these acts both express and produce I have tried to look at the relative ability of people to legitimate or contest and thus define the parameters of violence.

This chapter has offered some possibilities by looking at the particular relationship of kinship and affinity that constitutes the domestic space in which wife-beating occurs. Relationships of kinship embody order, hierarchy and respect. Men are valued for showing strength, authority and autonomy, women for diligence, motherhood and nurturing. These qualities complement each other. As members of a married couple young people become fully social and productive persons. These notions of masculinity and femininity, of order and discipline are naturalized and enshrined in the institutional practices of state and church and in the daily interaction of village life. Affinal relations express difference and work against the ordered hierarchical complementarity of kinship. Affinity is necessary for productive sociality yet it implies disorder, confrontation, instability. Affinal relations are not contained by principles of ordered hierarchy. They cannot be assimilated to this idiom of kinship or they would cease to embody the difference essential to reproduction or to inspire the erotic desire of *amor andino*.

In their relationship to the supernatural powers of the landscape people recognize that they are engaged with forces which cannot be controlled and which threaten the very fabric of their social life. In their inferior position the assertion of kinship relations to these powers offers the possibility of a mutual respect and trust. Within the domestic unit affinity threatens the autonomy and control of the household head. The in-marrying spouse, usually the wife, is constituted as the necessary but dangerous outsider. Yet this image does not offer a positive femininity for women. This is because the idiom of affinity offers no positive feminine subject position – femininity is strongly associated with conquest and domination. Given the strength of these metaphors and the way in which they resonate with institutionalized norms of church and state which disempower women in terms of patri-archical values, it is very hard for women to effectively challenge the legitimacy of a beating; they protest yet their protests are defused by their reintegration into the very systems of meaning that allow such behaviours to occur – i.e. the patriarchical and paternalistic structures of the legal system, and the symbolic expressions of kinship and affinal relationships.

Wives thus occupy an uneasy position as affines yet potential kin – just as humans occupy a similar vulnerability in relation to the supernatural powers of the landscape. As a woman gains more adult children her position improves as she becomes more firmly established within her own kinship hierarchy. In this chapter I have thus attempted to develop an explanatory framework which could handle the apparent intractability of Andean gender hierarchy without falling back on naturalizing or essen-tialist explanations which offer no possibility of change and no analysis of how social power is constituted. I wanted a politically aware explanation that recognized the importance of differential access to social power with-out attributing necessary determinant force to any particular set of social relations. I hope to have shown that while we might recognize certain elements in the particular conjunction of violence and sexuality in the Andes, fuller contextualization renders familiar actions unfamiliar without positing a total separation between our experiential worlds. The refusal to allow this separation also makes it possible to consider western respon-sibility for certain local practices without the implication that these local practices are thereby rendered inauthentic.

NOTES

1 The first draft of this paper was presented to the conference on sex and violence held at the Cherwell Centre, Oxford with the collaboration of the Centre for Cross-Cultural Research on Women and I have subsequently presented versions to the Congress of the Latin American Studies Association in Miami – 1989, to the seminar at CLASCO (Commission for Latin American Social Science) Quito – 1990, and to the IEP (Institute of Peruvian Studies) Lima – 1990. I am grateful to the participants of these seminars for their comments and support. Special thanks are also given to C. Blondet, P. Gow, C. McCallum, M. Phylactou, D. Poole, S. Radcliffe, M. Strathern and C. Toren who have taken the time to read drafts and discuss the topic at length with me.

2 See, for example, Allen (1988); Bolton and Mayer (eds) (1977); Harris (1978); Harrison (1989).

3 Allen (1988); Bolton and Mayer (1977); Harris (1978, 1980); Harrison (1989); Isbell (1978); Platt (1986); Silverblatt (1987); Skar (1981).

4 The following authors do note the 'violence' but do not go into Andean people's understandings of such interaction. Bourque and Warren (1981); Harris (1978, 1980); Stølen (1987).

5 This chapter is based on three periods of fieldwork in the village of Ocongate. The first, 1983–5, was funded by the ESRC, the second, 1987, was funded by the British Academy, and the third, 1988, was funded by the Nuffield Foundation. The Institute of Latin American Studies at the University of Liverpool also supported the two latter research trips.

6 Examples of Andean ethnographies which refer to drinking practices are Allen (1988); Bastien (1978); Carter (1977); Gose (1986); Harris (1978); Harvey (1987, 1991, 1993); Isbell (1978); Sallnow (1987); Wagner (1978). For a bibliographic review see Heath (1987).

7 Harris has noted that 'The different stages of the formative years are defined by the child's relation to language; a baby becomes a boy or girl when it can speak' (1980: 72). However, it is important to point out that the Laymi of Northern Potosí, Bolivia, do not deem it appropriate for parents to beat their children. Beating in this context would be associated with punishment, and punishment is inappropriate because children have imperfect command of language and thus imperfect understanding of what they have done.

8 See Harvey (1987, 1991, and 1994).

9 See Harris (1982).

10 The courts in Ocongate are very personal institutions. The judge is a local resident, chosen by the provincial authorities. His office is a room in his house and he is the sole arbiter of the cases brought before him. He has the power to impose fines or short periods of imprisonment at the local police post. Any serious cases are referred to the provincial authorities. Domestic violence is not thought of as serious in this way and the local judge is expected to be able to mediate these domestic concerns.

11 Alencastre and Dumézil (1953); Barrionuevo (1971); Contreras (1955); Gorbak, Lischetti and Muñoz (1962); Harris (1978, 1980); Hartmann (1971–2); Platt (1987).

12 See Sallnow (1987).

13 Platt (1987).

14 Gose (1986); Harris (1982); Nash (1979).

15 Gose (1986).

BIBLIOGRAPHY

Allen, Catherine (1988) *The Hold Life Has: coca and cultural identity in an Andean community*, Washington DC: Smithsonian Institution Press.

Alencastre, A. and Dumézil, G. (1953) 'Fêtes et usages des indiens de Langui', *Journal de la Société des Americanistes* XLII.

Barrionuevo, A. (1971) 'Chiaraje', in *Allpanchis*, Cusco: Instituto de Pastoral Andino.

Bastien, Joseph (1978) *Mountain of the Condor: metaphor and ritual in an Andean ayllu*, New York: West Publishing Company.

Bolton, Ralph and Mayer, Enrique (1977) *Andean Kinship and Marriage*, Washington DC: American Anthropological Association.

Bourque, Susan and Warren, Kay (1981) *Women of the Andes: patriarchy and social change in two Peruvian towns*, Ann Arbor: University of Michigan Press.

Carter, William (1977) 'Trial Marriage in the Andes', in Bolton, R. and Mayer, E. (eds) *Andean Kinship and Marriage*, Washington DC: American Anthropological Association.

Contreras, G. (1955) 'Las guerrillas indígenas de Chiyaraqe y Toqto', *Archivos Peruanos de Folklore* 1.

Gorbak, C., Lischetti, M. and Muñoz, C. (1962) 'Batallas rituales de Chiaraje y de Toqto de la provincia de Kanas', unpublished manuscript.

Gose, Peter (1986) 'Sacrifice and the Commodity Form in the Andes', *Man* 21(2): 296–310.

Harris, Olivia (1978) 'Complementarity and Conflict: an Andean view of women and men', in La Fontaine, J. S. (ed.) *Sex and Age as Principles of Social Differentiation*, New York: Academic Press, 21–40.

Harris, Olivia (1980) 'The Power of Signs: gender, culture and the wild in the Bolivian Andes', in MacCormack, C. and Strathern, M. (eds), *Nature, Culture and Gender*, Cambridge: Cambridge University Press, 70–95.

Harris, Olivia (1982) 'The Dead and the Devils among the Bolivian Laymi', in Bloch, M. and Parry, J. (eds), *Death and the Regeneration of Life*, Cambridge: Cambridge University Press, pp. 45–73.

Harrison, Regina (1989) *Signs, Songs, and Memory in the Andes: translating Quechua language and culture*, Austin: University of Texas Press.

Hartmann, R. (1971–2) 'Otros datos sobre las llamadas "batallas rituales"', *Folklore Americano* XIX–XX(17): Lima.

Harvey, Penelope (1987) 'Language and the Power of History: the discourse of bilinguals in Ocongate, Southern Peru', PhD dissertation, London School of Economics.

Harvey, Penelope (1991) 'Drunken Speech and the Construction of Meaning: bilingual competence in the Southern Peruvian Andes', *Language in Society* 20: 1–36.

Harvey, Penelope (1994) 'Gender, Community and Confrontation: power relations in drunkenness in Ocongate', in McDonald, M. (ed.) *Gender, Drink and Drugs*, Oxford: Berg.

Heath, Dwight (1987) 'A Decade of Development in the Anthropological Study of Alcohol Use, 1970–1980', in Douglas, M. (ed.) *Constructive Drinking: perspectives on drink from anthropology*, Cambridge: Cambridge University Press, pp. 16–69.

Isbell, Billie-Jean (1978) *To Defend Ourselves: ecology and ritual in an Andean village,* Latin American Monographs 47, Austin: Institute of Latin American Studies, University of Texas.

Lambert, B. (1977) 'Bilaterality in the Andes', in Bolton, R. and Mayer, E. (eds), *Andean Kinship and Marriage,* Washington DC: American Anthropological Association.

Nash, June (1979) *We Eat the Mines and the Mines Eat Us: dependency and exploitation in Bolivian tin mines,* New York: Columbia University Press.

Platt, Tristan (1986) 'Mirrors and Maize: the concept of *yanantin* among the Macha of Bolivia', in Murra, J., Wachtel, N. and Revel, J. (eds), *Anthropological History of Andean Polities,* Cambridge: Cambridge University Press, pp. 228–59.

Platt, Tristan (1987) 'The Andean Soldiers of Christ: confraternity organization, the mass of the sun and regenerative warfare in rural Potosí (18th–20th centuries)', *Journal de la Société des Americanistes,* LXXIII, 139–92.

Riches, David (1991) 'Aggression, War, Violence: space/time and paradigm', *Man* 26(2): 281–97.

Sallnow, Michael (1987) *Pilgrims of the Andes: regional cults in Cusco,* Washington DC: Smithsonian Institution Press.

Silverblatt, Irene (1987) *Moon, Sun and Witches: gender ideologies and class in Inca and colonial Peru,* Princeton: Princeton University Press.

Skar, Sarah (1981) 'Andean Women and the Concept of Space/Time' in Ardener, S. (ed.) *Women and Space: ground rules and social maps,* London: Croom Helm.

Stølen, Kristi Anne (1987) *A Media Voz: relaciones de genero en la sierra ecuatoriana,* Quito: CEPLAES.

Wagner, Catherine Allen (1978) 'Coca, Chicha and Trago: private and communal rituals in a Quechua community', PhD Dissertation, University of Illinois, Urbana-Champaign.

4   Ritual and the origin of sexuality in the Alto Xingu

Cecilia McCallum

In the literature on the peoples of lowland South America, it is hard to find a clear account of matters of gender. It is sometimes assumed that relations between men and women in lowland South America are basically antagonistic and predicated on actual or threatened violence by men against women. Proponents of this view characterize the small-scale societies there as 'patriarchal', based upon male control of women. The charter for this control – or alternatively its psychological expression – is said to be 'myths of matriarchy' – stories of a time of female 'rule' that was overturned by men – and the ultimate male sanction against women is said to be the threat of ritual gang rape.

This chapter disputes the validity of such an approach, focusing on one Amazonian social complex – the Alto Xingu area of central Brazil. Through an analysis of the Xingu material on myth, ritual and kinship it seeks a more exact understanding of gender and power than a simplistic notion of patriarchy or male control would allow. It looks in particular at two ritual complexes, the male sacred flute rituals and the female rituals of the Monstrous Women. It is careful to distance itself from the assumption that male sexuality is in some sense a locus of power, a view derived from the specific nature of gender constructs in the west,[1] and not pertinent to the ethnography discussed here.

I began with a simple question in mind – Is it possible to give an explanation to ritual gang rape other than that it is a way for men to control women? – but I soon uncovered a host of other problems. In the Alto Xingu, there is strong moral emphasis on respect for others, on self-control, and on pacificity. This is highly elaborated and well documented in the literature.[2] Such an emphasis does not tie in easily with an assumption that people seek control over others. Alongside explicit insistence on the theme of respect and pacificity a look at the actual tenor of day-to-day life reveals further difficulties with the thesis of male control. Here, it is often noted that Xinguano people form close emotional attachments to each other, to friends, kin, spouses, and lovers – affective bonds of a lifetime's duration. Whilst there is internal variation (Arawakan speakers are generally politer than Carib speakers, for example), male–female relations in day-to-day life are not primarily hostile at all. But what if one were to attempt a structural analysis of social organization, focusing perhaps on the division of labour, the ownership of the means of production and distribution, or the organiz-ation of first marriages? Again the analyst loses his or her footing. To argue that 'men control women' boils down to subjective opinions on the part of the anthropologist, appeals to experience of life in the village and evalua-tive statements that can be disputed on the grounds that they are impossible to prove or disprove.

In the face of such problems some anthropologists, such as Bamberger and Gregor, have turned to the analysis of myth and ritual to sustain their position that male control is a central facet of social organization. The position they seek to justify requires a particular – and extremely prob-lematic – theorization of myth and ritual. Myth is viewed through a double lens as, on the one hand a charter for an ideal type of social relations and, on the other, as a manifestation of unconscious psychological conflicts implicit in the realization of such relations. Thus myth is said to tell the story of how men came to dominate women – providing a legitimation of such control. At the same time it is said to reflect male anxiety over the castrating vagina. This theoretical approach *assumes* that ritual and myth are indigenous forms of representation – so that myths become blueprints for 'performances' representing, and thus recreating, ideal type social relations. There are no grounds for *a priori* equating ritual with repre-sentation or political theatre in Alto Xingu and such an assumption about the ethnography leads to all kinds of difficulties.[3]

A strong theme in the literature on the region is the great emphasis placed upon the real power of ritual. Such power is connected to, and indeed crucially channelled through, the bodies of both performers and 'spectators'. In the Alto Xingu vision, motion, scent, sound, and touch are thought to act upon the body and enact transformations in it. These changes are essential to the daily process of life. Ritual is 'doing' – direct action – not fiction imposed upon reality, but an aspect of reality itself. The power of ritual comes through changes made in people's bodies, whether on a collective or individual basis. It is a power that is made and built up over time (usually years) through many different individual actions by both performers and their backers, and is bound up with kinship, politics and economic organization. To begin to see the complexity of the beast makes one realize, then, that ritual 'gang rape' is no simple phenomenon, and no simple explanation will do.

In what follows, I will not deal with rape or gang rape as an experience.

I have neither the data nor the inclination to do so. I can say that both secular rape and ritual gang rape occur, though the incidence of the latter has declined considerably in the past 20 years. A normal target for such attacks would have been, it seems, women of low status who were orphans and had no male kin to defend them, and women from other villages than that of the attackers. This is consistent with the data on sexual violence from elsewhere in lowland South America.[4] It is possible that ritual gang rape is a relatively recent phenomenon produced by the particular historical and epidemiological events of this century.[5] I should stress that anthropologists who work in the Alto Xingu report that both men and women there find the subject distressing. The idea of sanctioned sexual violence conflicts with the normal tenor of male–female relations and the Xinguanos' strong preference for calm, peaceful and respectful social interaction.

MYTH

In 1974 Joan Bamberger published a paper entitled 'The Myth of Matriarchy: Why Men Rule in Primitive Society'. In it she analyses variations of myths of the 'Rule of Women' (sic) found in widely separate areas of lowland South America, arguing that they are social charters for male dominance. These stories tell how certain women in ancient times possessed powers (such as sorcery, spirit-masks, or musical instruments) whilst their men were 'held in subjection' or suffered in other ways, such as from sexual deprivation. The men 'rise up' and take the masks or musical instruments away from the women. This primordial theft leads to the construction of the first 'men's houses' and the inception of secret male cults. Henceforth women are 'forbidden' to see the trumpets, flutes, or masks upon pain of death and/or rape. The normal order of male–female relations is established. Such stories are also found in Alto Xingu. The following is such a one, a Mehinaku version summarized from Gregor (1985: 112). This is one of a series of myths about the Monstrous Women Spirits known as the Yamurikuma. It concerns the origin of the modern sacred flutes.

> In ancient times the men lived alone far away. They lived badly, naked, with no proper possessions, no weapons, no fire, no hammocks. They were forced to masturbate instead of have proper sex. The women on the other hand lived in a proper village with a female chief. They owned everything that is needed for a civilised life, such as houses, cotton, feather headdresses and the Kauka flutes which they had made. They wore male ornaments and body paint. They had a house for the Kauka flutes. The men saw the women playing the flutes there. They said 'this is bad, the women have stolen our lives' and they decided to take action.

They made bullroarers. They thought they could have sex with their wives very soon. Running into the village whirring the bullroarers they managed to catch all the women and rip off their male decorations. They lectured them, telling them that they should wear female ornaments alone and leave the flute-playing to the men. The women ran to hide in their houses. At night the men came in the dark and raped the women. In the morning the men went fishing. After that the women could not go into the flutes' house.

The Alto Xingu is in the *Parque Indígena do Xingú*, the most famous demarcated indigenous territory of Brazil, and has been a showpiece of successive national governments. The Mehinaku are one of the 10 groups making up the Alto Xingu social complex (which excludes Gê-speaking peoples like the Kayapó and the Suyá in the north of the Park). Each group in this complex is based in a single village with a population of a hundred or so and is represented by a distinct language belonging to one of four different language groups, including Arawakan (spoken by the Mehinaku, the Yawalapíti and the Waurá), Carib (spoken by the Kalapalo, the Kuikuru, and the Nahuquá-Matipu) and Tupi (spoken by the Kamaiura and the Aweti). Alongside the linguistic diversity, and some other differences, the people of these villages share an impressive cultural uniformity. This is manifested, for example, in the shape of the villages, which are circular. Large elliptical houses situated around the circumference surround a central plaza where ceremonies take place and a smaller house for the flutes and other ritual items is built. The Alto Xingu social complex appears to have been forged gradually by successive groups of migrants to the area. As a system, it functions admirably to create a peaceful social environment. There is constant trading and ceremonial interaction between the villages and intermarriage is common. With regard to social identity, Gregor writes that:

> villagers do not regard themselves as members of rigidly defined social units. Being a Mehinaku is a matter of degree and depends upon a multiplicity of factors, including the network of involvements with other groups. Hence a villager can reasonably explain that he is a lot Mehinaku, a little Waurá, and a tiny bit Kuikuru.
>
> (Gregor 1977: 318)

This anti-essentialist philosophy of being is a marker of Xinguano culture, as Basso (1973) shows with regard to kinship and Viveiros de Castro (1977) with regard to cosmology and personhood. The nature of things is a matter of degree not of absolute opposition; and, as I will show, things and persons must be actively made by the intervention of others. Being is transient and dependent upon the productive agency of others, just as stories change in the telling and are the creatures of the storytellers.

Basso (1985: 261–308) gives a Kalapalo Yamurikuma story about the origin of the Yamurikuma songs. In this story, the women who live alone rub their genitals with pepper and stinging things and grow penises. They ignore the men's desire to have sex with them and refuse the fish that the men try to give them. Instead these 'monstrous women' seduce and kidnap women from another community, leaving the men in the cold. In the end the men forcibly take male ornaments and possessions back from the women and have sex with them.

Bamberger suggests that in such myths there is an 'obvious relationship between viewing, touching and forbidden sex . . . . the association should perhaps be seen as part of a complex set of cultural laws establishing the proper set of behaviours expected between the sexes' (1974: 274). For her sexual hierarchy is a major theme of the myths. Thus, whoever possesses the tribal secrets sit in authority, able to dominate the other sex and 'enjoy a life of relative leisure'. She writes 'In no versions do women win the battle for power. Instead, they remain forever the subjects of male terrorism, hidden in their huts, fearing to look out on masked spirits and trumpeting ancestors' (ibid.: 274–5). This argument is persuasive by its simplicity. Men are the powerful ones, and the symbol of their authority is their ownership of the phallic trumpets. Women are afraid and confined to their 'huts' (a description not suitable for the large houses typical of the Xingu). Rape and sexual murder are the instruments of their oppression. The evidence available to us now goes against Bamberger's argument, it seems to me, yet it continues to persuade.

A recent formulation is to be found in Gregor's 1985 study of Mehinaku sexuality and social life, *Anxious Pleasures*. Gregor uses a neo-Freudian perspective on sexuality. His point is that among the Mehinaku 'there are striking similarities of sexual desires, fears and defensive reactions' (1985: 200) to western ones, despite the apparent exoticism. He says that Mehinaku society is close to a 'sexual Utopia' for men since they can have numerous affairs without becoming involved, or risking their reputations or community standing (sic; ibid.). The male 'sex drive' according to Gregor is not matched by the female. He suggests that a 'lower female libido' is probably innate and a universal. Hence men in Mehinaku society, just as in North American society, are chronically sexually frustrated (Gregor cites the 1981 *Hite Report on Male Sexuality* in support of this view). Mehinaku men are also sexually anxious, he suggests, drawing upon myth as supporting evidence. Men are afraid of women, he says, for menstrual blood and sex are thought to make men ill and stunt the growth of male adolescents. 'The psychological flip side of fear of women is antagonism towards them' (ibid.: 205). Masculine hostility is institutionalized in male discourse and in the 'men's house' (sic) 'with its bullroarers and sacred flutes'. The most shocking expression and instrument of institutionalized male hostility is gang rape. And Gregor draws a comparison between rape in American society and the threat of gang rape in Mehinaku. For him the major difference is that rape is 'legal' and sanctified (in ritual form) for the Mehinaku and not in the USA. He explains this 'excess' in terms of the extreme 'clubby' nature of Mehinaku masculinity and the related sharp sexual division of labour. Citing the Murphys' work on the Mundurucu as further evidence, Gregor concludes that 'the masculine ethos' finds its clearest expression in the 'tribal community' because the sexual division is enshrined in social and economic structure. His analysis falls in with Bamberger's view that men rule universally in 'primitive' society. It goes further, however, in its claim that male–female interaction is universally tortured and fearful.

Gregor treats myths as if they are dreams showing the subconscious fears and desires of Mehinaku men, vehicles exploring the basic hostility between men and women. He treats associated rituals in a similar vein. The central section of his book is an analysis of the Pequi fruit rituals which he sees as expressions of pure sexual antagonism and indeed he labels them 'Gender Wars'. Whilst he argues that men are the victors in this 'war' it seems more likely that the central concern of the rituals is not sexual hegemony at all, but rather the creative interaction between male and female. The Pequi rituals consist of a series of games pitting male wit, ingenuity, and strength against female, and vice versa. They are concerned with human sexuality, and in particular with fertility and productivity.[6] In contrast, the flute and Yamurikuma ritual cycles are concerned with the original creation of sexuality, not with sexuality *per se*.

THE RITUALS

The Kauka sacred flute ritual cycle and the Yamurikuma Monstrous Women ritual cycle both last many months and at times involve periods of intense activity by both men and women. The performers are all male in Kauka ceremonies and all female in Yamurikuma ceremonies. Public performances in both involve apparent 'gender reversal' – men appear to 'play' female spirits and women to 'play' male spirits. The so-called 'myth of matriarchy' is closely linked to them.

The Kauka sacred flutes are a 'representation' of the chief of the spirits (Gregor 1985: 99). They must be played regularly in order to appease the spirit and 'ensure the well-being of the community' (ibid.). This statement about the purpose of the flute rituals is important, if maddeningly vague.

Xinguano informants do not seem to elaborate on exactly how the flute spirits 'ensure the well-being of the community', except in a negative sense – if they are not played properly then the spirit becomes angry and takes vengeance. Nevertheless, it seems reasonable to surmise from the literature on breath and blowing in Amazonia that the flute playing itself acts upon the women and children listening from their houses, and the men in the flute house or on the plaza, in a direct sense. This same observation would be true of the beneficial effects of women's singing during Yamurikuma.[7]

The flutes themselves are kept in their own house in the centre of the village and, according to Gregor, women should not enter lest they see them. However, according to Basso, Kalapalo women may enter the house when the flutes are not there, and are stored instead in the rafters of a flute sponsor's house. The flutes are said to be 'menstruating' at these times (Basso, 1985: 304 on the Kalapalo; Viveiros de Castro (p.c.) in general).[8] They are taken to the sponsor's house during periods when they are not played. One such period would be during those stages of the Yamurikuma cycle when women take over the flute house. Gregor asserts that any woman would be gang-raped if she entered the flute house but he seems to be conflating entry into the house with sighting of the flutes. (Perhaps during his fieldwork the flute house was never without a set of flutes.) The flute house is primarily a male domain. The flutes are played there during the day, men sit there talking and making things, male shamans sit outside it at dusk smoking, and the flutes are brought out and played on the patio around it at night (Viveiros de Castro 1977). Nevertheless, it is referred to as the 'flutes' house' and not the 'men's house'. It is unclear how long the flutes are kept, or whether they are renewed when they rot, but Gregor says that at the time of his first fieldwork there were three sets of Kauka flutes in the men's house and each was a different manifestation of the spirit Kauka (1985: 326). Each set had a slightly different version of the ritual performed on its behalf. Gregor stresses that Mehinaku religion is open to individual innovation.

The Arawakan term 'Kauka' or rather *kawíka* deserves some discussion. Both the Yawalapíti and the Waurá use the term *kawíka* although only the latter are reported to name the flutes thus (Ireland p.c.). The Yawalapíti name the flutes *apapálu* but they say that the flute ceremony is the most *kawíka* of all ceremonies because the women cannot see it (Viveiros de Castro 1977: 196). In this usage, the term means 'dangerous' or 'fearful'. Viveiros de Castro shows that it encapsulates a central notion and value of Yawalapíti life best translated as 'respect'. To have *kawíka* is to be generous, calm, peaceful; to respect one's affines; to obey one's parents. It indicates a relation of distance between people or beings (ibid.: 197). It can be both negative (involving danger) or positive (bringing benefits to the parties involved). The flute spirit as *kawíka* is both extremely dangerous and potentially beneficial to the community.

One person's illness, caused by the spirit, heralds the flute-playing ritual. A shaman, whilst curing the victim (either a man or a woman), might 'see' that a spirit has shot arrows into his patient and stolen the soul. He proceeds to recover the soul and remove the arrows. If the shaman sees that Kauka is the culprit, then Kauka's victim becomes the sponsor of a ceremony that will socialize the spirit and control its future relationship with humans.[9] This man or woman becomes the flute sponsor for life (although according to Viveiros de Castro she or he can transfer ownership of this benefit to another (ibid.: 230). The term glossed 'sponsor' (*wekehe* in Mehinaku; *wïkïti* in Yawalapíti; *oto* in Kalapalo) denotes both a relation of ownership and of parenthood or asymmetrical kinship. This is a central relation in Xinguano social organization. In this context it means both owner and maker of the ceremony – and the ceremonies are referred to as the 'children' of the sponsor.[10] He or she will have to care for the ceremony just as a parent cares for a child. This person, with his or her spouse, will have to provide food for the participants in the ceremonies in the months and years to come. He or she appoints 'organizers' who sort out the logistic details of the rituals.

> When Kauka, the demon of the sacred flutes and the 'chief of the spirits' steals a soul, the patient selects several ritual organizers and purchases 3 flutes for them. Between himself (the sponsor) and the organizers, there is now a relationship which may endure the rest of their lives. Every few days the organizers and other villagers play the flutes while the spirit is 'fed' large buckets of manioc porridge provided by the sponsor and actually consumed by the entire village. The garden from which the manioc comes is cleared, weeded, and harvested by all the men working collectively, and they are 'paid' with gifts of fish by the sponsor. In the course of many months the sponsor and especially his wife will have invested a great deal of labour in preparing the manioc flour for porridge.

> (Gregor 1977: 324)

The Yawalapíti also refer to the food that the sponsor and spouse make in these kind of circumstances as 'the spirit's food'. The spirit is thus 'represented' by 'the community' – the people who are fed the spirit's food – and not just the flutes (or other object in the case of other spirits). The organizers eventually arrange a 'gift-giving' to which other Xinguano villagers are invited. Valuables, such as shell belts and necklaces, are given to the sponsor who keeps them as Kauka's property. He or she may not trade them but may wear them. Basso says that the major ceremonies of Kauka and Yamurikuma are *egitsu* (a Kalapalo term) – that is, other Xinguanos from other villages are invited to participate (though apart from the gift-giving this appears to happen only at the very end of the cycle). Most of the ceremonial activity involves the villagers alone. It takes place during the dry season when food is relatively abundant. Considerable preparatory economic activity and coordination are required so that sufficient amounts of food can be accumulated by the sponsors 'for the spirit'.

Yamurikuma is 'sponsored' in the same way as Kauka. The sponsor, spouse and close kin begin work when the pequi is ripe at the end of the dry season like other such *egitsu* rituals. (Pequi is a tree planted in groves which bears a fruit whose pulp is edible and can be stored for long periods underwater.) At this time (September to November) certain songs are sung by the women collectively in the plaza while the sponsor harvests pequi and stores it underwater ready for the next dry season and the main events of the ritual. After this there is a lull until April and the end of the rains. During this time the sponsor accumulates food – mainly manioc starch processed from a specially prepared garden. Later it will be given, accompanied with fish and pequi, to the women performers and to the visitors at the height of the festivities which take place during the dry season. The preparation for the spectacular events of the dry season – the *egitsu* – are an important aspect of the ritual cycle. The massive labour invested in the food preparation symbolically underpins all the events that follow. The meanings created resurface in the relation between the producing couple and the consuming community 'representing' the spirit that is honoured. The work of sponsorship and the consumption of the products of that work thus form a particular relationship between the original victim and the 'spirit' embodied in the other villagers. This cumulative process is paralleled by the work of the flute-players and singers in the ceremonies themselves.

Basso, in her analysis of the Kalapalo versions of Kauka and Yamurikuma, points out that both rituals involve musical statements about sexuality that are 'antagonistic if not actually violent in their expression' (1985: 261). But, she stresses, the performers do not embody male or female sexuality in opposition to the non-performers (who are always of the opposite sex). The sexual attributes of the opposite sex that are referred to during the performances are the most repellent and dangerous ones – the insatiable vaginal mouth and its menstrual blood; dangerous male semen and the 'angry' and voracious penis. Basso writes:

> In both Kagutu (i.e. 'Kauka') and Yamurikumalu, neither male sexuality nor female sexuality alone is inherently violent or merely aggressive, but in conjunction they become seriously threatening. As the myths

propose and the Kalapalo enact during their musical rituals, this combination is socially lethal, and it can be extremely dangerous – even fatal – to a member of the opposite sex.

(Basso 1985: 307)

The performers are in a state of ambiguous sexuality (like the Monstrous Women who grew penises from their labia) and not (as Gregor suggests) of heightened own-sex sexuality.

The ethnography supports this analysis amply. The Kalapalo liken the flutes to female sexual organs, and call their mouths 'vaginas' (Basso 1985: 304). They are said to menstruate when they are stored in their sponsor's house and male sponsors are supposed to refrain from fishing for the flute-players at this time just as men refrain from fishing for their wives when menstruating. Some of the flute music is originally composed by women as women's songs for Yamurikuma or in other contexts (ibid.: 305). Basso says that women are interested in the flute music, for they listen from inside their houses and discuss who composed them. They could often name the players. In Yamurikuma too some of the songs the women sing are said to have originally been composed by men. In both ritual cycles the style of performance, the costumes and the instruments carry sexual meanings that refer to the opposite sex.

During the women's ritual, if a man comes too close to the performers, he is in danger of attack. 'During the time of year that the Yamurikumalu ritual is held, women attack and beat up any man other than the sponsor who dares enter the plaza' (ibid.: 307). The women pound the man's body, pull his hair and smear him with a red body paint that only women use (*ondo*) and that according to some of her male informants is associated with menstrual blood. Gregor (1985: 109) had a similar story from the Mehinaku. They told him that in past times any intruding man except for the sponsor would have been gang-raped by the women. For the Kamayurá, on the other hand, Menezes Bastos says that female attacks on intruding men are treated as games and do not involve serious violence (p.c.).

Men can safely watch the women singers from a distance. Women, however, are in danger of being raped if they see the men playing the flutes. This only applies if the unfortunate woman is seen by several flute-players, for one man alone would be more than likely to pretend he had not seen her. Basso says that such rape is considered a compulsive effect of performance observed rather than a punishment by men of women who have violated a rule. The women are afraid of rape but not of the flutes – it is the combination of the sexual feelings of male flute-players and the sexuality of the flutes themselves that have such an effect on the performers. The rape, the Kalapalo 'suggested' to Basso, is a reaction caused by the combination of male sexuality (characterized as aggressive) and an intense form of female sexual feeling embodied in the instruments. The raped woman would probably become seriously ill as a result of the rotting semen of many men which could not agglutinate to form a child. In any case, some men suggested that she might be taken to a place in the forest where there was a hornet's nest and left to be stung to death. An alternative to rape, according to a Yawalapíti informant, would be to bury the woman.

Basso does not report any cases of actual rapes, but Gregor has a few accounts of a gang rape that took place about 1940, and he mentions a Waurá woman who was raped. A woman inadvertently saw the flutes and was tricked by a lover into going to the forest where the flutes were played 'whilst the spirit Kauka' raped her. The woman was not killed but taken home and cared for. She later delivered an 'oversized' baby that was killed because 'it had too many fathers' (1985: 102). (Ireland, p.c., comments that the Waurá told her that only the babies of unmarried women would have been killed.) Gregor's male informants explained to him that the rape had to be done because, if not, all the men would die. Gang rape for Mehinaku men is a precautionary measure to save themselves from the anger of Kauka. Yet even though they say this the men are reluctant to report a woman who sees the flutes. Only one man said he actually would tell on close female kin, and several men remarked that they would not tell on any woman unless other men also saw her. Gregor remarks that the men used 'distancing' devices to describe the events of a potential rape, always using the third person for example. What is more, it is always ascribed to the spirit and not to the men. The women also ascribe the rape to Kauka and are even ready to tell on other women who are said to have seen the flutes. The men ignore this 'gossip' according to Basso and Gregor. Importantly, by this evidence the woman must be seen by 'Kauka' as well as seeing 'it'. Kauka's desire must be aroused by vision which the walls of the house normally impede.

I will not discuss the occurrence of gang rape or female ritual violence against men further here. When such things do happen there can be no simple explanation of the events, nor underestimation of the horror of the experience for the victims. All kinds of factors, such as inter-community politics, appear to have been involved in such cases in the past.[11] What is clear from the above is that the sexuality of the performers is abnormal when they perform and that this manifests itself in a potential for excessive violence. This is dangerous and to be avoided. Whilst the flute-players are overcome with violent sexual desire by the sight of a woman, the singers seem to experience a compulsion to violence which is symbolically sexual rather than overt and is aroused by the proximity of a man rather than the sight of him.

It is not clear whether the flute-playing occurs only during certain seasons. The dangerous public activity of Yamurikuma, on the other hand, picks up with the start of the dry season. Pairs of women dressed in male costumes dance from house to house. They sing *kagutukuegï* songs ('other' or 'monstrous' *kagutu*/Kauka) whilst the sponsor brings fish, manioc soup, and pequi to the plaza where they are performing. The sponsor (or where this is a woman, her husband) will be helped in his fishing by most of the other men of the village when the time for the climactic events and the arrival of the visitors draws near. The women relax in the flute house after a collective singing session. As in a Kauka ritual cycle, the end is marked by the arrival of guests. The climactic day is a 'dramatic display of feminine strength and beauty' during which the women wrestle female champions from amongst the visitors. When the women have finished the men also wrestle. Finally, an adolescent girl might be brought out of her seclusion and her hair cut.

MAKING AND UNMAKING

The 'ritual cycles', as I have dubbed them, thus follow several distinct phases. We can distinguish these phases by focusing on many criteria, but perhaps the central movement is the developing relationship between the spirit and the human community. From the bodily crisis of one person, founded upon the untimely conjunction of human and spirit, it moves to a display of corporeal well-being of human beings in their prime, founded upon the separation of human and spirit. This movement is effected through the ritual creation of separate, gendered, human sexualities. It reflects and actively constructs the Xinguano philosophy of production and person-hood, which is founded upon concepts to do, on the one hand, with making, ownership, parenthood, and correct, restrained sexuality; and, on the other, with 'unmaking', with loss, death, aberrant sexuality, violence and destruction.

The ritual cycles begin with the 'unmaking' of a human body. An encounter in the forest or the gardens causes the individual to fall ill and brings about the intervention of a shaman. The spirit is visible to shaman and also to patient, in his or her dreams and delirium; but whilst the shaman is able to experience this vision safely, for the patient the vision signals death and the approaching disintegration of the body. During this first phase the patient and close kin must observe dietary restrictions in order to 'remake' the afflicted body. The cause of the illness – the flute spirit or the Monstrous Woman spirit (called 'Ñafegi' by the Kuikuru[12]) – is distanced by this means from the body, so that it may be thus reconstructed, restoring the patient to a state of health. So begins the next phase of the cycle. Here the work of the new, special relationship with the spirit begins. The victim has now become the 'owner' of the rituals deemed his or her 'children'.[13] It is his or her labour, together with that of spouse and kin, that over the following months constitutes and builds up the relation with the spirit.

In the first stage, the nature of the spirit is relatively unproblematic. It is an immortal and normally invisible being that haunts forest and gardens outside the village. Its traces are 'arrows' seen by the shaman in the body of the person whose soul it has taken. In the second stage the identity of the spirit – or of the humans who incarnate it – becomes more problematic. It is not separation but conjunction that the rituals and the feasts that follow achieve. Yet this conjunction is of more than one kind. It alternates between two forms: performance and feast. During the public performances the performers, their music and musical instruments combine as both spirit and human, both male and female, in a measured and formal process that benefits those who listen. The blowing or singing – the sacred noise achieved through the expulsion of breath from their bodies – rebounds upon the silence of the listeners to mutual benefit. No bodily communication, whether through touch, smell, oral or sexual consumption, takes place. Only the arousal of angry desire in the twisted, inhuman, semi-spirit bodies of the performers leads to such contact. The sight of women and the close proximity of men stimulate such untimely and vicious passions in the performers, who act out physically their emotions upon the unfortunate bodies of helpless human victims, effecting the unmaking of their bodies and, sometimes, the making of monstrous spirit children. Yet if all goes well such violent interaction is avoided, and the performers mediate between the world of the spirits on behalf of the humans peacefully and beneficially, by embodying and generalizing the spirits' breath and song.

During the feasts, the opposite is happening. The community, occupying the place of the spirit, eats the food made for it by the sponsor. Now the Xinguanos say that spirits eat peppers and tobacco smoke, not the fish, manioc and pequi prepared and distributed by the sponsors. The melodious breath of the spirit is a form of prestation. It helps the 'well-being' of the human community. We could see the sponsor's food as a reciprocal offering. So what does this return of human food to the spirit signify? What change does it cause in the spirit? By making the food of the spirit and feeding those that take its place – the performers and everyone else – the sponsor makes a new relationship with the spirit. He or she 'tames' it, makes it like his or her child, treats it like kin. The prestation of food makes the spirit more human and less spirit. It seems fitting that those who have merely listened – taken in the invisible power of the spirit – are those who eat – taking in the bodily substance made by one who is their distant kin or affine and who is now all human, not unmade by the spirit at all.

So during this second, and lengthiest phase of the ritual cycle, the relationship between humans and spirit alternates between one where sexual and oral conjunction should not take place, and one where oral consumption creates a substantive relationship between them. These forms appear to be crucially interdependent. In both, the spirit is present, the presence mediated through the bodies of either performers or consumers – but never both together, if all goes well. It is a presence, but a presence 'once-removed', so to speak, in contrast to the earlier phase of direct contact between spirit and human.

In the final phase, the intervillage ritual, the spirit itself is not present for the major festivities. The ceremony seems to mark the visible absence of the spirit from the village. The relationship with the spirit has now moved from an intensely personal one to a collective one, as the immediacy of its presence, manifested in visibility and pain, diminishes, and as the scale of its public ceremonial increases and moves from presence-once-removed to controlled absence.

On this final day, two events take place marking the highest achievement of Xinguano production – wrestling and (whenever possible) the release from seclusion of an adolescent girl. Champion wrestlers and young women in seclusion embody a supreme aesthetic and moral value in Xinguano eyes. They are the tangible accomplishment of their kin and co-villagers, perfect men and women, strong and beautiful of body, self-disciplined, skilled, and respectful of others. For Viveiros de Castro wrestlers embody the 'ideal type of Xinguano'. Skilled wrestlers, especially, are *kawíka* in the double sense of respecting, pacific, generous and, at the same time, to be respected in the fight. The wrestlers are worthy of respect; the girls, of longing and desire. Both are just embarking on their lives as married and producing adults. They are the culmination of years of 'making' on the part of their kin and, especially, their parents. In turn, they are ready to begin such work themselves.

Xinguanos say that wrestling is the opposite of war, as Viveiros de Castro (1977) makes clear. Thus, participants must be restrained and not resort to undue violence. Wrestling acts as a form of socialization in self-control. Not only is it the culmination of years of work on the part of parents, strengthening and training their son, but it is also a form of continued education. The skills learnt are essential to the social process. Viveiros de Castro writes: 'When villages visit each other, in ceremonies, wrestling is the first activity to take place, after which the distribution of food – an incorporation of the stranger in terms of substance. Physical corporal confrontation and afterwards "commensality": the system of hospitality works admirably to integrate a poly-linguistic society with a pacific ethos, like the Xinguano' (ibid.: 218). Finally, these mature men, powerful and beautiful, are the most sexually attractive of all Xinguano men. Their counterpart in this is the secluded girl.

The girl emerging from seclusion is marked off from other girls and women by her physical appearance. Her skin is very white and attractive from one or two years of confinement in the house. Her body is rounded and plump – 'strong' in Xinguano eyes – from the special diet and from her sexual adventures. Her hair grows down over her eyes to her chin forming a fringe which cuts off, so to speak, her vision of the world. As she comes out, and when her hair is cut, she presents the appearance of someone who is ready to engage in the productive activities of daily life – she is knowledgeable of female skills, physically strong, sexually experienced, and the epitome of female beauty.

Therefore, the final day of the ritual cycles consists, in large part, of the public presentation of people embodying male and female sexuality, bodily strength, and also (as we shall see) productive knowledge. This final ceremony is the end-product of months or years of labour; so too are the splendid young men and women in whom the Xinguanos take such pride. They are the product of many years of labour and self-deprivation by their parents. Making a child is a complex process involving many activities and not just sexual intercourse. In order to make their children, parents must endure periods of abstention – couvade, dieting during illness, sexual abstention at certain times – and also periods of intense activity – fabricating the foetus with repeated intercourse; fishing and processing manioc to feed the child, or secluded adolescent, and make it grow; teaching it gender-specific skills and knowledge, gathering medicines and emetics to 'change its body' and to transform it into a strong and productive person. On a broader scale, ritual, in the Xingu, always makes persons.

If one considers this work and privation of the parents as part of a process that constitutes and underpins social organization in all its complexity, the Kauka and Yamurikuma rituals can be understood as complementary both in form and in rationale. As we have seen, production, ownership and parenthood are closely linked. A basic principle of action seems to be 'who does, owns; who owns, shares identity with what is made'. Kinship, according to this principle, is *a priori* the product of repetitive action, a result of process and not simply a fact of shared essence. In this case the parents, linked by complementary difference, cooperate in the work of creating persons empowered with male or female agency – that is men and women who in the future will engage their acquired agency in complementary interaction with their own spouse. It is gendered agency – what parents do to their adolescents – that gives people the ability to produce and to reproduce in their own right. It is the interaction of such individual agencies which both allows for the production of persons in

Xingu (in the specific form here of husband-wife complementarity) and which constitutes sociality. By making their children, parents at once make kinship and make the possibility of future sociality on a village and, indeed, inter-village scale.

Kauka and Yamurikuma are concerned, in parallel fashion, with the construction of separate male and female agencies, but on a collective rather than an individual scale. But before I explore this claim in greater detail, it is necessary to look more closely at the construction of male and female agency in Xingu eyes.

The Xinguano view of social life is a person-centred one – a point Viveiros de Castro's study makes elegantly and convincingly.[14] Social organization centres on the construction of personhood and not the construction of 'corporate groups' or 'society'.[15] It constantly engages the people of the Xingu in social, economic and ceremonial processes centring on persons, such as the 'owner-sponsors' of Kauka and Yamurikuma. The construction of personhood is conceived of as a corporeal process, one that is founded, in my view, upon the distinction between male and female agency. Sexuality is an integral aspect of the Xinguano concept of male and female agency – so it is logical that the origin of sexuality is of such major significance in the most important of Xinguano ritual cycles.

Sexuality is a product of the intervention of outside agencies in a child's body – an intervention controlled and engineered by the parents in large part. They know that food and sexual substances 'penetrate' the body and either promote health or illness. A complex conceptual system distinguishes kinds of food, sexual substances, and medicines and links their consumption to specific bodily states.[16] The major oppositions in this system are between manioc and fish; fish and meat; blood and semen; emetics, pepper, tobacco and food and the crucial distinction is gender. Different combinations and restrictions help produce differing kinds of bodies and sexualities depending on the specific state of the person who consumes. Parents in some villages in the Alto Xingu allow secluded girls to secretly meet lovers, knowing that semen will help them to grow. Secluded boys, on the other hand, should abstain from sex altogether as losing semen makes them stunted. Boys and men who engage in too many sexual adventures become weak and uncertain wrestlers. Thus, when Gregor writes that men are in danger of becoming ill if 'their penises do not eat enough' one should be careful how to interpret this.

Sexuality is constrained within the framework of kinship. One should, according to the Mehinaku, only have sex with certain kin (ideally cross-cousins) – foreigners are thought to be disgusting. Sex is a pleasure for both men and women, a possible danger for both (under the wrong circumstances), a matter of sensuality and fun, and also a deadly serious business, for sex leads to pregnancy and a woman must be careful how many men she makes love to since too many fathers make her ill rather than pregnant with a proper child. Women who go with too many men will give birth, it is said, to deformed or monstrous children. A man who sees a woman giving birth or who comes into contact with menstrual blood or female sexual fluids is in danger of losing his male skill and strength. He loses his ability to wrestle. Indeed, losers have insults hurled at them such as 'sex-maniac' implying that they have rendered themselves weak by too much sexual contact with women. Such situations are not irremediable. Men sometimes observe women to whom they are very close give birth (Ireland p.c.). According to Viveiros de Castro's informants, such contact with women's blood by sight, smell, or any other method, means that the man's 'belly' fills up with blood, it becomes blocked so to speak, and only by dint of observing dietary and sexual restrictions can the man restore himself to health. The same author stresses that couvade in the Xingu is even more concerned with the health of the father than that of the newborn child. Women can intrude their bodies into men's by means of menstrual blood, then. One might note that such intrusion is similar in its effects on the male body to the effects of too much semen on the female.

Xinguanos have many sexual relationships besides with their spouses – both passing seductions and steady sexual partnerships with lovers. For Gregor this means that the Xingu is almost a male sexual Utopia. Men can take their pleasure, he suggests, 'without becoming involved' and women must be generous with their bodies, he stresses, for men are said to become ill when their passions remain unfulfilled. Yet the idea that men do not 'become involved' seems to me unreasonable. How could this be so in such a small community where the average village population is about one hundred? Whilst brief affairs with outsiders probably bring no long-lasting commitment, other affairs are a different matter. Ireland says:

> Marriages, on the whole, are exceptionally stable and enduring when compared to those in our society . . . . Husbands and wives treat each other with the respect that their mutual reliance on each other naturally engenders. Waurá husbands do not order their women around, and there is no such thing as casting off your wife because she has become old . . . . The Waurá call an extramarital lover for whom a deep attachment is felt one's 'other wife' or 'other husband'.

> (Ireland p.c.)

Whilst this may be the case, love affairs must always remain hidden. Franchetto says the following apropos of the Kuikuru:

> What can be said about the expression 'the vagina is expensive'? The

payment (*ihipïgï* in Kuikuru) in order to have access to a woman's sex is high. The 'vagina payment' (*igïgï ihipïgï*) is both the name given to the long years of work a son-in-law puts in for his parents-in-law during the first years of marriage and also any 'gift' given to a woman lover or one so desired. These goods enter generally and immediately into circulation in the ritualized exchanges of women (feminine *moitaká*). The women say they do this in order to prevent the husbands suspecting that such objects from lovers should be among the belongings of their wives. Women look after the love affairs of their daughters and sisters and administer to the rapid exchange of the goods obtained.

(Franchetto p.c.)

Steady relationships always include flows of prestations between the man and woman, whether they are lovers or spouses. The man gives fish to her and she cooked food to him. Men eventually take it upon themselves to help look after their lover's children even where these are fathered by another man originally (Gregor (1985): 37). These prestations are more than tokens of affection. To give food and to have the prestation accepted and consumed creates a specific kind of relation, essential to the construction of kinship. The food, consumed, makes the body of the recipient in terms of the logic of gender. Thus manioc, produced by women, converts into semen in the bodies of men; fish, produced by men, stimulates the over-production or the coagulation of blood. Men in couvade and menstruating women afflicted with excessive blood may not eat fish, because like blood it is 'strong smelling'. One might venture that if women's produce makes semen, then men's produce makes blood. This is clear evidence that male and female agency underlie the cyclical creation, destruction and reconstitution of persons in a complex and interdependent process involving work, sex, eating and abstention.

The intrusion of a spirit's darts into a human body acts in a way similar to sex or eating, affecting the body's state directly. But sex and eating are properly carried out reciprocally between humans, not humans and spirits, and although dangerous at times for the health of men and women are essential to the production of kinship and sociality. Illness and death, caused by spirit darts or the darts of human sorcerers, are the antithesis of such human activities. If the sick person dies, and his or her spirit travels to the land of the dead, he or she will find a world where there is no sex and there are no children. Dead children are transformed into mature young adults – like the wrestlers and adolescent girls of *egitsu* ceremonies – when they reach heaven. Indeed, the singing, dancing and wrestling of ritual, the visual display of perfect persons, are activities pleasing to the spirits, reminiscent of the heavenly pastimes of the dead. The activities of the living in daily life, working, having sex, eating, defecating, smelling, touching, are by contrast abhorrent to the spirits. It seems to me that the Kauka and Yamurikuma rituals are concerned, in particular, with defining the relationship between these two contrasting forms of activity, here on earth.

The relationship between the victim and the spirit can be transformed, as I have shown. From a phase when the spirit 'consumes' the human, comes one when the human makes 'the spirit' consume human food. While the 'spirit' consumes human food, and not spirit food (tobacco and pepper), it is forbidden contact with human flesh. Kauka and the Yamurikuma must not have sex with men and women. As long as the spirits keep away from the bodies of humans, people will be able to fully engage their male and female agencies in sex and work in the making of a properly human sociality.

The shaman removes the physical traces of the spirit by sucking them out. The patient henceforth is the mediator of the villagers' relations with the spirit. He or she can then have a lifelong pseudo-kinship with it that begins with the penetration of the body and continues even beyond death (although in some cases the 'owner' of a ritual can declare his or her obligations over saying that he or she will sponsor the complete ritual for the last time (Franchetto p.c.)). After death he or she might visit another person in his or her dreams and direct that person to become the next associate of the spirit (Basso 1985). He or she is the 'owner' of the spirit's ceremonies and responsible for the relations constructed between the spirit and the human community which represents it in public. The making of these relations at once effects a separation between spirits and humans – the spirits are fed so that they will eventually leave the humans alone; and they effect a separation between male and female agencies – of which sexuality is a crucial aspect. The productive power that the spirits embody at the height of the ritual is extremely dangerous and potentially violent. The productive power that the humans are left with at the end of the ritual is both safe and non-violent.

If a woman is raped by the flute spirit her capacities to produce are seriously endangered and the child that might result could be put to death. This is wrong and should be prevented at all costs, so the women must fear, respect, and avoid the spirit. Human and spirit must remain mutually invisible. Similarly, only male sponsors may enter the plaza during Yamurikuma because they have already established a safe relationship with the spirit through the work of feeding it. Their continuing domestication of the spirit acts to their own and everyone else's benefit. The spirit has been driven out of their body and back into the forest only to be later called back into the village and 'made kin'. The spirit is treated by the sponsor and his or her spouse like a child or like a relative with whom sex would be impossible. The relation of potential affinity (a sexual one) is avoided – and a safe relationship of kinship is constructed. In return the flute spirits through their magical breath and the Monstrous Women Spirits through their song impart fertility and strength to the villages before finally returning to their place in the other world. Human fertility, based upon the double separation of spirit and human and male and female, has been gained.

Nothing could be more fitting then, than the final events on the climactic day of the ritual, after the pubescent girl has left seclusion. Her fringe is cut and her vision restored to her. Now she is ready to join her prospective husband in the economic and sexual activities of marriage. It seems particularly appropriate that the beginning of her life as a proper woman should coincide with the end of a ritual constructing properly gendered agency and sexuality out of a state of ambiguity. After her presentation, the villagers take advantage of the presence of visitors to engage in sexual liaisons which under normal circumstances are difficult. Secret meetings with visiting lovers take place and new affairs are started. Thus a process which began with the personal affliction of an individual and led to the reconstruction of her or his personal and corporeal capacity, ends with the secret but generalized celebration of sexuality on a collective scale.

CONCLUSIONS

In interpreting sexual violence or any form of symbolic action we must be aware of the way that individual action and experience are bound by historically specific social and cultural contexts. Feminism has made anthropologists particularly sensitive to these issues.[17] Any analysis of myth and ritual can benefit from the deconstructive critique typical of feminist scholarship. Moreover, in such an ethnographic context as this it is vital to employ a clear view of symbolic form and action. As Gow (1989b) argues, we cannot assume that people in lowland South America employ the same theories of representation in graphics, ritual, or narration as our own. A theory of representation applied out of context invalidates an analysis of ritual, and what is more in such a case as this, where we are dealing with questions of gender and power, defeats the purpose of analysis. Cameron and Frazer, using a different methodology and focusing on the history of western thought, make this same point in Chapter 7. They argue that representation has a power and importance in western culture that should not be seen as universal. In the west sexual murder is the killing of a representative object of sexual desire and this representative object is a specifically western construct. To assume that this form of symbolic violence is universal is to ascribe debased forms of symbolism and representation to other cultures. Such debasement is likely to go hand-in-hand with the imposition of a western theory of human sexuality. Indeed, a failure to theorize representation and a failure to get to grips with gender and the cultural construction of sexuality are closely related ailments. Gang rape in the Alto Xingu – whether as an idea or as an event – is many things: what it is not is a manifestation of a supposed universal male desire to overpower and humiliate women.

Feminist scholars like Cameron and Frazer have discussed the nature of representation in the west extensively,[18] arguing that the realist portrayal of women as objects for male consumption – in painting, in literature, in the media, in pornography – constructs a specific view of power as gendered. This view rests upon a popular theory of the 'nature' of sexuality – in our culture, male sexuality is symbolic of dominance because of its supposed *nature* – and the supposed nature of female sexuality as its complementary natural opposite.[19] The set of ideas positing the essential and innate nature of male and female sexuality is constructed, articulated, and reaffirmed in western representation – in painting, literature, television, cinema, pornography – typically by creating a female object to be consumed and at once controlled by the male viewer. The cultural complex involving such representation is the product of a specific historical trajectory, the specific social, economic, political, and cultural processes that characterize western capitalism. Such processes – including as they do the conditions for male domination of women – do not characterize life in the Xingu.

ACKNOWLEDGEMENTS

This paper is based upon my reading of the literature on the Alto Xingu. I am extremely grateful to a number of anthropologists who have studied with the people there and who read and commented upon earlier versions of this paper for me. Émilienne Ireland was kind enough to send me extensive comments and suggestions, correcting the worst of my interpretive excesses. Eduardo Viveiros de Castro gave me inspiration and the confidence to finish, as well as excellent editorial advice. Bruna Franchetto's exact comments were invaluable. As well as helping to polish the paper, conversations with her about the people of Xingu helped keep my feet on the ground. Rafael José de Menezes Bastos was kind enough to listen to a version of the paper and give me lively and stimulating discussion. Carlos Fausto also kindly read and commented on it for me. The paper was first presented at the conference in Oxford and I am grateful to all those who discussed it. Thanks also to the Sussex anthropologists who listened to the next version. Finally, many thanks go to Peter Gow and Penelope Harvey, both of whose lively interest all the way along kept it rolling. All responsibility for any errors or misinterpretations is my own.

NOTES

1 The literature on gender constructs in the west is too extensive to discuss here but see, for example, Jackson (1987); Weeks (1981 and 1985); Segal (1987); Jordanova (1980).

2 The paper is based upon my reading of the ethnography of Basso (1973 and 1985); Gregor (1977 and 1985); Viveiros de Castro (1977). See also Villas Boas (1970). For an excellent discussion of the literature prior to 1977 see Viveiros de Castro (1977). In the same work Viveiros de Castro discusses notions of respect, fear and shame in the Xingu, as does Basso (1973). On gender in lowland South America see Overing (1986a, 1986b); Goldman (1963); Descola (1983 and 1986); Dole (1974); Gow (1987, 1989a, 1991); C. Hugh-Jones (1979); Siskind (1973); Lea (1987); McCallum (1989 and 1990); Brown (1986).

3 I do not discuss the literature on ritual here, but the paper does have implications for the theorization of ritual. In particular it disputes the idea that ritual is a 'performance' aimed at constructing 'society' through the representation of ideal values or rules.

4 Peter Rivière (p.c.) observed that the important criteria in such matters is lack of kin rather than gender. Orphans are the most underprivileged of persons in lowland South American societies. The few first-hand reports of sexual violence in the literature bear this out. Wagley (1977: 249–57) witnessed a Tapirapé gang rape. The woman was an orphan, an epileptic and unmarried. She had refused to work and was publicly denounced as 'without brothers' by her uncle. The rape followed immediately (ibid.: 254). Lizot (1985: 36) tells how Yanomami people he knew mistreat both men and women who have few kin and Biocca (1970) bears this out. Siskind (1973) and Arhem (1981) show how the uxorilocal Sharanahua and the virilocal Makuna, respectively, tend to mistreat in-marrying strangers.

5 This is pure speculation but it seems logical that the large number of orphans and the severe trauma produced by the epidemics might have led to an increase in violence.

6 Mehinaku informants told Gregor that the pequi games act as increase rituals (Gregor 1985).

7 I am thinking of a possible relationship to shamanic breath and blowing. This is a point that needs further ethnographic investigation. What effect do different kinds of speech and song have upon the bodies of the listeners? For example, see Seeger (1987: 78–81).

8 The Barasana also say that their sacred flutes menstruate (Hugh-Jones 1979).

9 Gregor says that the ceremony is 'designed to prevent the spirit returning' (1977: 323). But Viveiros de Castro (p.c.) emphasizes that the spirit should keep on returning in order to benefit the community.

10 Viveiros de Castro (1977: 216).

11 Ireland (p.c.).

12 Ñafegi (the Kuikuru name for the Monstrous Woman Spirit) is one of the most fearful *itséka* (spirits). She lives in the forest, appearing as a very beautiful

woman dressed in Yamurikuma ornaments to seduce men walking alone. It is fatal to have sex with her.

13 In the original (Viveiros de Castro 1977: 216) the ceremonies are said to be the 'daughters' (*filhas*) of the owners but this is a misprint and should read as *filhos* (children) (Viveiros de Castro p.c.).

14 See also Seeger, da Matta and Viveiros de Castro (1979) and the discussion in McCallum (1989).

15 I am making a theoretical point here about the use of terminology to describe social groupings. I do not mean to imply that personhood is opposed to the social. As Franchetto pointed out (p.c.) there is a vital link between the construction of the person and the fabrication of social groups like the village or the *otomo* (sibling group, kindred – out of *oto* (owner, parent) and *mo* (pluralizer)). The construction of social groups depends on the dialectic between us and them, kin and affines. The construction of gender is inextricably linked to this dialectic.

16 I base this section mainly on Viveiros de Castro (1977). See also Gregor (1985).

17 See Moore (1988); MacCormack and Strathern (1980); Strathern (1988).

18 In this volume. Their paper is part of a broader movement in the feminist critique of representation in relation to power and gender. See, for example, Kappeler (1986); Kuhn (1985); Williamson (1978); Cameron (1985); Segal (1987).

19 M. Jackson (1987); Weeks (1985).

BIBLIOGRAPHY

Arhem, Kaj (1981) *Makuna Social Organization: A study in descent, alliance and the formation of corporate groups in the North-west Amazon*, Uppsala: Academiae Upsaliensis.

Bamberger, J. (1974) 'The Myth of Matriarchy: Why men rule in primitive society', in Rosaldo, M. and Lamphere, L. (eds).

Basso, Ellen B. (1973) *The Kalapalo Indians of Central Brazil*, New York: Holt, Rhinehart & Winston.

Basso, Ellen B. (1985) *A Musical View of the Universe*, Philadelphia: University of Philadelphia Press.

Biocca, Ettore (1970) *Yanoama, the Narrative of a White Girl Kidnapped by Amazonian Indians*, New York: Dutton.

Brown, M. F. (1986) 'Power, Gender and the Social Meaning of Aguaruna Suicide', *Man* 21(2): 311–28.

Cameron, D. (1985) *Feminism and Linguistic Theory*, London: Macmillan.

Caplan, P. (ed.) (1987) *The Cultural Construction of Sexuality*, London: Routledge.

Descola, P. (1983) 'Le jardin de Colibri: Procès de travail et catégorisations sexuelles chez les Achuar de l'Équateur' *L'Homme* XXIII: 61–89.

Descola, P. (1986) *La nature domestique: symbolisme et praxis dans l'écologie des Achuar*, Paris: Editions de la Maison des Sciences de L'Homme, Fondation Singer-Polignac.

Dole, G. (1974) 'The Marriages of Pacho: A woman's life among the Amahuaca', in Mathiason, C. J. (ed.) *Many Sisters: women in cross-cultural perspective*, New York: Free Press.

Goldman, Irving (1963) *The Cubeo: Indians of the Northwest Amazon*, Urbana: University of Illinois.

Gow, Peter (1987) 'The Social Organization of the Native Communities of the Bajo Urubamba, Peru', Doctoral thesis, London University.

Gow, Peter (1989a) 'The Perverse Child: Desire in a native Amazonian subsistence economy', *Man* (N.S) 24: 299–314.

Gow, Peter (1989b) 'Visual Compulsion: Design and image in western Amazonian cultures', *Revindi* 2: 19–31.

Gow, Peter (1991) *Of Mixed Blood: Kinship and history in Peruvian Amazonia*, Oxford: Oxford University Press.

Gregor, Thomas (1977) *The Mehinaku: The drama of daily life in a Brazilian Indian village*, Chicago: Chicago University Press.

Gregor, Thomas (1985) *Anxious Pleasures: The sexual lives of an Amazonian people*, Chicago: Chicago University Press.

Hugh-Jones, Christine (1979) *From the Milk River: Spatial and temporal processes in Northwest Amazonia*, Cambridge: Cambridge University Press.

Hugh-Jones, Stephen (1979) *The Palm and the Pleiades: Initiation and cosmology in Northwest Amazonia*, Cambridge: Cambridge University Press.

Jackson, Jean E. (1985) 'Rituals of Gender and Domination in the Vaupés', Paper presented to the annual meeting of the American Anthropological Association, December 1985.

Jackson, M. (1987) '"Facts of Life" or the Eroticization of Women's Oppression?', in Caplan, P. (ed.) *The Cultural Construction of Sexuality*.

Jordanova, L. J. (1980) 'Natural Facts: A historical perspective on science and sexuality', in MacCormack, C. and Strathern, M. (eds) *Nature, Culture and Gender*, Cambridge: Cambridge University Press.

Kappeler, S. (1986) *The Pornography of Representation*, Cambridge: Polity Press.

Kuhn, A. (1985) *The Power of the Image: Essays on representation and sexuality*, London: Routledge & Kegan Paul.

Lea, Vanessa (1987) *Nomes e nekrets Kayapó: Uma concepção de riqueza* (3 vols), Doctoral thesis, Museu Nacional do Universidade Federal do Rio de Janeiro.

Lizot, J. (1985) *Tales of the Yanomami: Daily life in the Venezuelan forest*, Cambridge: Cambridge University Press.

McCallum, Cecilia (1989) 'Gender, Personhood and Social Organization among the Cashinahua of Western Amazonia', PhD thesis, London University.

McCallum, Cecilia (1990) 'Language, kinship and politics in Amazonia', *Man* (N.S.) 25: 412–33.

MacCormack, C. and Strathern, M. (eds) (1980) *Nature, Culture and Gender*, Cambridge: Cambridge University Press.

Moore, Henrietta (1988) *Feminism and Anthropology*, Cambridge: Polity Press.

Overing, Joanna (1986a) 'Images of Cannibalism, Death and Domination in a "Non-violent" Society', in Riches, D. (ed.) *The Anthropology of Violence*, Oxford: Basil Blackwell.

Overing, Joanna (1986b) 'Men Control Women? The "Catch-22" in the Analysis of Gender', *Journal of Moral and Social Studies* 2.

Rosaldo, M. and Lamphere, L. (eds) (1974) *Woman, Culture and Society*, Stanford: Stanford University Press.

Seeger, Anthony (1987) *Why Suyá Sing: A musical anthropology of an Amazonian people*, Cambridge: Cambridge University Press.

Seeger, Anthony, da Matta, Roberto, and Viveiros de Castro, E.B. (1979) 'A construção da pessoa nas sociedades indígenas Brasileiras', *Boletim do Museo Nacional* (N.S.) 32: 2–19.

Segal, Lynne (1987) *Is the Future Female?: Troubled thoughts on contemporary feminism*, London: Virago.

Siskind, Janet (1973) *To Hunt in the Morning*, Oxford: Oxford University Press.

Strathern, Marilyn (1988) *The Gender of the Gift: Problems with women and problems with society in Melanesia*, Stanford: University of California Press.

Villas-Boas, Orlando and Villas-Boas, Claudio (1970) *Xingú; os índios, seus mitos*, Rio de Janeiro: Zahar.

Wagley, Charles (1977) *Welcome of Tears*, Oxford: Oxford University Press.

Weeks, J. (1981) *Sex, Politics and Society*, London: Longman.

Weeks, J. (1985) *Sexuality and its Discontents: Meaning, myths and modern sexualities*, London: Routledge & Kegan Paul.

Williamson, J. (1978) *Decoding Advertisements: Ideology and Meaning in advertising*, London: Boyars.

Viveiros de Castro, Eduardo B. (1977) *Individuo e sociedade no alto Xingu: os Yawalapíti*, Rio de Janeiro: Master's thesis, UFRJ, Museo Nacional.

5 Man the hunter

Gender and violence in music and drinking contexts in Colombia

Peter Wade

INTRODUCTION

Explanations of male violence towards women can fall into the trap of constructing monolithic and universalistic concepts of masculinity: male dominance is effected through actual physical violence. While this is undoubtedly a probable consequence of such acts, this view over-simplifies the processes involved in the constitution of masculinity, and may even take at face value some of the representations of masculinity as 'naturally' aggressive. Instead, masculinity has to be seen as a range of possible positions which men constitute over time in relation to others and in relation to cultural representations of masculinity which may be varied and conflicting. The same clearly applies to femininity and indeed to subjectivity in general (cf. Moore, this volume; cf. also Pleck 1981). Violence is a possibility that derives from a context in which power differences, usually with a material basis in the sexual division of labour, are implicit and explicit in the cultural constructions of gender which give to certain representations of masculinity a dominant status.

In this chapter, I examine different masculinities and femininities in a specific Colombian context, analyse how these interact, develop and conflict, and look at the strategies, violent and non-violent, that people adopt as they try to constitute in their lives specific subjective positions as 'men' and 'women'.[1]

THE FAMILY IN THE ATLANTIC AND PACIFIC REGIONS OF COLOMBIA

The Pacific and Atlantic coastal regions of Colombia that concern me here have both been strongly influenced by black slave populations. The Pacific region is still 80–90 per cent black, very poor and underdeveloped; while the Atlantic region, usually known as *la Costa*, is much more of a tri-ethnic mixture and is also more urbanized and developed (see Wade 1993).

The family structures of both regions have a certain amount in common which distinguish them from the white/mestizo Andean interior of the country. The high frequency of *unión libre*, roughly speaking common-law marriage, is obvious. Changes of spouse during a lifetime are quite common and both men and women frequently have two or more consecutive partners. Norman Whitten (1974) identifies a pattern he calls 'serial polygyny' in which a man goes through a series of temporally overlapping unions. In such a pattern, women also obviously change partners, although the possibility of a temporal overlap is for them, not unexpectedly, much more restricted. A result of this is a host of half-sibling relations. A further corollary is the presence of a relatively high proportion of female-headed households, which in fact are often temporary stages in the dynamic of serial polygyny. There is also the development of the so-called matrifocal family in which a mother becomes, over time, the central point of identification and continuity for her children and sometimes her grandchildren, as men come and go in a more impermanent fashion (Dussán de Reichel 1958; Gutiérrez de Pineda 1975). Even if the male is permanent, he frequently has relations with other women and may maintain other households, so that again the focus of the family centres on the woman and her children.

Another feature of affinal arrangements in these regions is polygyny of a more usual kind in which a man maintains approximately equal relations with two or more women. This ranges from cases in which a man might have two common-law relationships of a relatively long-term nature with two women in separate households, to rather rare cases in which his *mujeres* (women) live under the same roof. Both forms are more common in the Pacific region where, as a recent investigator reports, women simply say, 'Here the custom is that men have the right to have more than one woman at the same time' (Maya 1987: 134). There are also many cases of men with a principal wife, legally married, sometimes known as the *mujer de asiento* (*asiento* has various meanings, including seat, settlement, and stability), and other women, often called *queridas* (lovers or mistresses). This, a more urban pattern, is more common in the Atlantic region.

These flexible changeable arrangements do co-exist with stable conjugal relationships, but they are characteristic of these regions and distinguish them from the Andean interior where Catholic marriage is much more frequent, female-headed households more rare, monogamy is the norm, and men are more permanently attached to a single domestic unit based on the marital tie. There is, of course, variety between and within these coastal areas. In the Pacific region, male mobility, serial polygyny, polygyny with equal status *mujeres*, and low rates of marriage are all more common than in the Atlantic region. In both areas, the greater respectability of marriage and conformity to patterns characteristic of the Andean interior mean that class structures and status affect family structures.

This is not the place to examine the explanations for these particular family structures. It is important to note, however, that for Colombia various commentators have laid particular emphasis on male mobility, both as a means of coping with dispersed and/or unstable resources and income-earning activities, and as a cultural norm (Whitten 1974, Gutiérrez de Pineda 1975, Friedemann 1974).

GENDER IMAGES AND RELATIONS

These family structures are reflected in some of the ideas people in these regions have about what 'men' and 'women' are like, ideas recognized by men and women alike. These are not simple, single images of gender, but rather a number of concepts in relation to which people intersubjectively constitute a sense of self as a 'man' or a 'woman', and which they can use to represent themselves as such, both to themselves and to others. I look briefly at some central concepts, drawing out basic oppositions and potential areas of conflict. As part of this, I will use the lyrics of a popular Costeño[2] musical genre called *vallenato* which expresses certain aspects of these concepts, specifically viewed from a male perspective, since these songs are written and performed entirely by men.

A central and powerful concept of masculinity, recognized by both men and women is that of man as nomadic, moving from one woman to the next, changing partners. This is probably rooted in real patterns of male mobility. Whitten (1974: 125) notes, for example, that a man's movements are generally connected to economic strategies, but also that part of the process of becoming a grown male in the Pacific region is to *andar y conocer* (move around and become acquainted), in which *conocer* includes sexual knowledge. An extension of this image is the man as *mujeriego* (woman-izer, philanderer), engaged in the sexual conquest of women even when based in a relatively stable conjugal union. A second and inseparable image of masculinity is that of the *hombre parrandero*, the fun-loving drinker and dancer who is always ready to party with his male friends and stay up all night, drinking rum, listening and dancing to music, telling jokes and stories. There is, however, a second rather different concept of masculinity: that of the good father who provides for his *mujer* and children. In the Chocó province of the Pacific region, the sign of a man's adulthood is being able to take a woman from her home and provide for her and the children he has by her (Maya 1987: 116). When a conjugal union breaks up, a man continues to have residual responsibility for the children who bear his surname (Whitten 1974: 119), even if in practice this responsibility is often token. This masculinity is linked to ideas of sacrifice, support, loyalty and permanence, and as such harmonizes with some of the values centred around femininity as motherhood. These two rather different sets of values surrounding masculinity have also been noted in a variety of ways for the Caribbean and, of course, are not unconnected to European and North American notions (Whitehead 1986). As Whitehead notes for the West Indies, constructing a powerful or strong masculinity depends largely on achieving a balance between these two sets of values (1986: 224).

The most central concept of femininity, in contrast, sees women as a stable force. In the Pacific region, for example, the mother is symbolized as the *guayacán de esquina*, a house corner post made from a very hard and durable tropical wood which supports the whole structure of the house (Maya 1987: 139). A woman is considered adult when she has had her first child and her basic responsibility is to her children. If she is unable to support them from her male partner's or her own income, she will find someone, usually a female relative, to look after and maintain them. A very important concept of femininity, then, is that of mother. There are also other concepts of femininity – *la puta* (the whore), *la solterona* (the old maid), among others, not to mention differences of race and class – but that of mother forms the basis for this analysis. The concept of mother itself is, however, also differentiated, since mothers can be young or old, with many or few children, and so on. Crucially, they can also be with or without a male partner, and married or unmarried. There is a major tension – corresponding to the tension between masculinities of *mujeriego/parrandero* and good father – between what we might call 'conjugal' and 'independent' motherhood: the mother who not only relies on her partner for material support, but is also involved in a conjugal relationship in which both partners identify themselves with the union and contribute to its stability; and she who tries to maintain a material and psychological independence which transcends the temporal boundaries of what may be an impermanent union.

As men and women constitute through their lives subjective positions of masculinity and femininity, they deal with these concepts as central defining forces – discourses and practices – which they know and recognize. But they relate to them, and hence to each other, very differently, and in ways strongly influenced by unequal gender relations of power. Men take a positive attitude towards the image of man as nomadic *parrandero* and *mujeriego*. Being, or claiming to be, like this is a strong basis on which to negotiate a masculine position which is seen as prestigious by other men, and to some extent by women as well. Being a 'good father' is also approved of by men, but if it undermines representing oneself, and being seen by others, as *parrandero* and/or *mujeriego*, then it can easily be seen as a sign of weakness. Whether or not women approve of masculinity as nomadic hunter, it is clear that in some sense they accept the man as polygynous, or even as womaniser. As mentioned above, rural women from the Chocó province of the Pacific region may simply say that polygyny is a man's 'right' by custom. One Chocoano woman observed to me that she would not mind her man having *mujeres en la calle* (women in the street, i.e. sexual liaisons outside the conjugal relation), as long as she was *la principal* (the main woman).

On the other hand, given the sexual division of labour and women's disadvantaged position in the labour market, the material basis with which they can constitute a feminine position as a central stable family focus is threatened by the possibility of male impermanence.[3] Clearly, a main source of support is the child's father and a woman generally expects and wants him to provide economic support. Men's actual tendency to change partners and their positive evaluation of being *mujeriego* means that their economic contributions to successive or contemporaneous female partners and their children can be irregular and subject to attenuation. Women therefore recognize their own need to construct a more independent position from which to pressure men into providing economic support and to make them fulfil obligations, using their own position as providers of domestic and sexual services and possibly using magical manipulations as means to this end. Therefore, while women may see man the nomadic hunter as a 'natural' aspect of masculinity, they also refer to a further concept of masculinity which sees men as *irresponsable* (irresponsible), a concept recognized by men and women alike, but which tends to be used more by women against men. In this, men pursue values of womanizing and *parranda* (partying) at the expense of the responsibilities of fatherhood.

The central feminine position of stability and support is viewed positively by both men and women, but there are significant differences. For women, it is a position the negotiation of which necessarily involves commitment and sacrifice, and which may have aspects which are forced onto her by her male partners' impermanence and the weakness of her own position within the labour market. The positive value that attaches to it is therefore closely connected to a sense of personal sacrifice for, and investment in, her family which may perforce have been created partly independently of male partners. Men, in contrast, may approach this feminine position from a different angle, viewing it for what it does for them as men. They may assert that they owe everything to their mothers who bore and raised them, rather than their father who was a more shadowy figure. Capitalizing on positive images of women as stable and domestic, men try to present a picture of women as people over whom they have control, and who will submit to men's demands. The *mujer conforme* (the acquiescent woman) is selfless and disinterested: she loves her man, provides him with domestic support, tries neither to control or exploit him, and does not interfere with his activities outside the home.

On the other hand, there is a further concept of femininity, again recognized by men and women, but represented differently by them. For women, there is the notion of an independence in motherhood which serves to protect them to some extent. Men tend to represent this in the concept of women as *materialista* (mercenary), that is, as grasping and trying to exploit men economically. Men may also assert that women try to ensnare them and even render them helpless by magical means. This concept of a dangerous femininity is also expressed in men's belief that sex with a woman is a weakening activity and hence that repeated sex can undermine a man. In this state of weakness his control and dominance are lessened and he becomes more susceptible to magical attack. Here it is not so much women who constitute a threat as the sexual relation itself. There is a fear that there are limits to how many women a man can encompass, that he might not be able to keep all his sexual liaisons active and all his women partners 'under his thumb' in a sexual sense.

Realms of conflict emerge, then, as men and women intersubjectively constitute positions of masculinity and femininity. A man, for example, can try to negotiate a masculinity based on being *parrandero* and *mujeriego*, and, at the same time, try to create and keep a family and avoid accusations of *irresponsable*. There may be a processual element here, as older men progressively invest more time and energy in defining themselves as 'family men' and refer back to a youth of *mujeriego* activities as a substratum of their personal masculinity – although other men may see them as having been 'tamed' by their female partners. A woman may try to constitute a personal femininity based on motherhood, and avoid being neglected by the father(s) of her children, or being sexually exploited, or, as I will discuss later, physically abused. Colombian women, as might be expected, see their strategies to this end as being undertaken in the context of unequal power relations between them and men. That is, men and women occupy different positions in the sexual division of labour which gives women less economic power (but see Note 3); and – obviously connected to this in a mutually empowering fashion – there is a dominant discourse of gender which hierarchizes the engendered positions which men and women constitute, subordinating and circumscribing femininities.

I will look more closely at men's and women's strategies in constituting their masculine and feminine positions in the next section. Here I want to explore some of the images I have described as they are portrayed in the lyrics of *vallenato*. While the representation of masculinity in this genre is couched in the dominant discourse of gender, there is recognition of different masculine and feminine positions and an attempt to reconcile these in a form which reproduces the dominant masculinity. The balancing of different masculine values of good fatherhood and being *mujeriego/parrandero* emerges in the lyrics, but it is men who define this balance, and in achieving it dominate women.

Vallenato came into its own in the 1940s, although its roots are in the traditional folk music of la Costa, a corpus heavily influenced by the presence of many black slaves. It is based on the accordion (which replaced earlier guitars), a single drum called a *caja* (box), and a *guacharaca* (scraper). In the last few decades it has become a nationally known form of pop music and is highly commercialized. In general there are various 'cultural themes' underlying *vallenato* (Llerena 1985: 102), although these are contained within a discourse of masculinity: life should be enjoyed in *parranda* (drinking, dancing, and music) and womanizing; men should have sexual relations with various women at one time; a man should be an honourable and loyal friend, son, and father; money is inferior to moral qualities; women should not begin a relationship with a man out of economic self-interest. It should be noted that the themes of women and *parranda* are not specific to la Costa and are characteristic of the Pacific too.[4]

The theme of womanizing is a popular one, usually linked with *parranda*, as in 'Los Gavilanes' (The Hawks) by Calixto Ochoa, where the theme of the predatory male is very clear.

Allá en la Costa hay dos gavilanes	In la Costa there are two hawks
Muy peligrosas con las muchachas	Very dangerous with the girls
Uno llama Manuel Lora	One is called Manuel Lora
El otro es el turco Aza	The other is the Turk Aza[5]
Esos muchachos sí pasan	Those boys sure have
Una vida muy sabrosa	A real good time
Ellos parecen dos gavilanes	They are like two hawks
Que cuando hay fiesta	That surround the house
Rodean la casa	When there's a party
Antes de acabarse el baile	Before the dance is finished
Se pierde alguna muchacha	Some girl is lost
Si no se la lleva Lora	If Lora doesn't get her
Se la lleva el turco Aza	Then the Turk Aza will

The imagery of predation is quite explicit: the men are 'dangerous' and they are compared to birds of prey with all the connotations of freedom,

unrestrained movement, dominance over their victims, cruelty and violence. The girls are portrayed simply as helpless victims, whose fate is
certain: they are 'lost', i.e. not only physically abducted but also robbed of
their virginity. The overall tenor of the lyrics is humorous and light-
hearted, rather than threatening or menacing, but this does not detract from
the portrayal of men as 'hunters' of women. Perhaps, also, the lightearted-
ness serves to belittle the implicit reference to the real violence men may
do to women: this belittling representation is something I refer to again in
discussing domestic violence.

Rather than portraying the man as switching partners in a series of
uniones libres, the songs tend to present the male in a steady relationship
with one woman, *la principal*, with whom he has a strong romantic attachment, while he carries on several sexual liaisons beyond the domestic
sphere. In several songs, the contradictory antagonisms and attractions
between men and women in this relationship are explored, but always from
the male point of view. The man's behaviour as a source of irritation to the
woman is recognized, but she is persuaded to believe that the man is
committed to her and will fulfil his obligations to her whatever his extra-
domestic activities. Rafael Escalona's 'La Maye' starts with the woman,
Maye, constantly checking up on her man in his *parrandas*. He tells her:

¡Ay! tranquilizate Maye	Oh! take it easy Maye
Deja a Rafael tranquilo	Let Rafael alone
Que no me gasto por la calle	For I don't waste myself in the street
Yo siempre te llego lo mismo	I always come to you in the same state

The last two lines are especially important. The most superficial reading is
that the man can take endless *parrandas* and not return home a drunken
wreck. Behind this is a hint that he avoids extra-marital sex (*no me gasto
por la calle*), but the real force of this remark is a denial that the sex he does
in fact have weakens him, that he is able to sexually dominate several
women at one time. The interesting undertone here is that the sex he has
with his *mujer principal* is in fact a *duty* he owes her, rather than an
expression of his sexual dominance. That is, in order to keep the domestic
sphere in order, the man has to fulfil certain obligations and one of these is
sexual. This leads into the third level of meaning of these lines which refers
to a man's domestic obligations as a whole. In effect, the man is claiming
that he can both lead the life of an *hombre parrandero* and *mujeriego*, and
maintain his domestic situation intact at the same time, recognizing the
legitimacy of and fulfilling his economic duties towards the household.

A distinction emerges here between a man's activities *en la calle* (in the
street) and his domestic activities. In the former domain he is *parrandero*

and *mujeriego*, and women are his victims; in the latter he is the husband/ father and his wife and children have certain rights. The point is, of course, that the two realms are intimately interdependent, since a man's success as party-goer and womanizer is partly dependent on him keeping his *mujer principal* happy, or, failing that, submissive in the domestic realm. Their interdependence is further strengthened, as I will discuss later, by the fact that *parrandas* are often brought into the home and a man's wife is expected to cooperate in and support his hospitality. This interdependence often means that conflict arises between men and women in conjugal relations over the man's extra-domestic activities: in this conflict men try to impose their authority on women.

As part of the exhortation of women to submit to men's interests, *vallenato* songs also emphasize that a woman should not marry for money or more generally have a relationship with a man for self-interested economic motives. In 'Amor Comprado' (Purchased Love) by Armando Zabaleta, the man says

Pero es triste que una mujer	It is sad that a woman
Se entregue a un hombre por interés	Gives herself to a man for self-interest
Porque ese hombre no la puede querer	For that man cannot love her
Pero ni ella puede quererlo a él	But neither can she love him
¡Ay! si yo tuviera pa' comprar tu amor	If I had enough to buy your love
Yo lo compraba	I would buy it
Cuando estuviéramos en lo mejor	When things were at their best
Yo te olvidaba	I would forget you

In effect, by asserting that mercenary self-interest cancels out the real love which brings with it the harmonious fulfilment of obligations, the man is denying the woman the right to *demand* that he do his duty by her: this should be left to his discretion. In 'La Maye' there was a recognition of a man's obligations to his principal *mujer*, and specifically that the man had a sexual duty to perform to her, and this was passed off as a minor obligation because the man had enough sexual energy to go around various women. Here there is a more forceful assertion that a woman should not demand too much. In the last verse of the song, it is the woman's transgression of this male-imposed norm which provokes the man to reassert his discretion by totally abandoning his obligations to her and leaving her. In this way, a man can justify leaving women who make demands on his economic resources that become over-burdening: he reserves the right to be

nomadic and change female partners, against the woman's economic interest in stability (not to mention questions of love), saying that only if she
does *not* demand will he love her and thus fulfil his obligations. The woman
should be *conforme* (acquiescent), as in the song of that title, 'La Mujer
Conforme' by Máximo Movil, which paints a picture of a patient loving
wife helping her man through hard times on the farm. In return he promises
to give her a good life by moving her to town if he can, *porque la mujer
conforme / se merece muchas cosas* (because *la mujer conforme /* deserves
many things). That is, if a woman is acquiescent and submissive she will
get her due – as deemed right and proper by the man. A clear contradiction
is revealed in these songs between a man's recognition of the legitimacy of
his woman's demands, connected with images of masculinity as being a
good male partner and father and corresponding to ideas of conjugal love;
and his rejection of the woman's demands which corresponds to a concept
of masculinity based on womanizing and going out on *parrandas*. In
striking a balance between these values and activities, the songs say, men
define what demands are acceptable from the woman.

Let us look more closely at the *parranda* itself. What I want to focus on
here is its importance in defining a certain aspect of masculinity. In being
parrandero, a Costeño man can adopt a certain masculine position *vis-à-vis*
other men as well as *vis-à-vis* women. Being *parrandero* is a source of
prestige among men. In ideal terms a man should be able to drink heavily
without getting incapacitated. Costeño men tell, amid laughter, of the
standard tricks perpetrated on incapacitated men, such as shaving their hair
off, or perhaps one eyebrow. Instead a man should hold his drink and feel
proud to say to his friends at dawn '*estoy amanecido*' (I've been up all
night, i.e. drinking). One *vallenato* song says *La parranda es pa' amanecer
/ Al que se duerma lo motilamos* (the party is till dawn / he who falls asleep
gets shaved). A man should also be an indefatigable and skilful dancer.
However, dancing is only part of *la parranda*. There is a strong sense in
which *parranda* is an expression of male solidarity: only by participating
in *parrandas* with other men can a man establish close relationships with
them. Part of this participation consists of being loyal, cooperative, and
generous, and of reciprocating within the male group. If a friend wants to
parrandear you should oblige him with your company. In 'La Excusa'
(The Excuse) by Diomedes Díaz, the man explains that he met his *compadre* (ritual co-parent) in the street and they bought a bottle of rum. Then
some other friends turned up and his *compadre* persuaded him to stay on:
me dio pena no complacerlo / porque así somos los hombres parranderos
(it made me sorry/ashamed not to oblige him / because that's how we
parrandero men are). The very form of drinking emphasizes the social
solidarity between men. At the beginning of a drinking session and often

all the way through it, small shots are poured into each man's glass and are drunk in one swallow in unison. If there is only one receptacle, then it goes round each man in turn, being filled by the man holding the bottle. Male solidarity exists, of course, within a particular network of friends, *primos* (cousins) and *compadres* (co-fathers, i.e. godfathers of one's child). It is not generalized to all men and, on the contrary, relationships with other men can be competitive, antagonistic, and violent. I will refer to this aspect again in the next section.

Before that, however, it is necessary to consider briefly the status of the songs and images I have been discussing, since they raise the issue of the relationship between representation and practice. *Vallenato* songs are not simply an idealized version of the activities of men and women produced by male subjects; nor are they simply autonomous representations, which shape 'males' and 'females' into 'men' and 'women'. They are not a precipitate or distillation of practice, nor yet a set of rules for practice. Rather they are part of a discourse, representations which create masculinities and femininities as (internally differentiated) objects of knowledge, partly in relation to which men and women intersubjectively constitute their own senses of gender identity. Part of that constitutive process is also reproducing *vallenato* itself, through writing, singing, dancing, and listening to it. Doing these things is not simply an 'expression' of a sense of gender identity, it is part of constituting that sense. Relevant here is the concrete context in which much of this activity is carried out. *Vallenato* dancing, for example, is a significant context of male–female interaction, of courtship and male–female friendship, of womanizing and *parranda* (see below where I discuss dancing). Men and women of different statuses and ages engage in this activity – young and old, married/cohabiting and single, *mujeres conformes* and *hombres parranderos*, although they do so in different ways and with different ends in view – and when they do so, the male–female relationships dramatized in the songs are part of, and may be actively reproduced by, the constitution of masculinity and femininity of which the practice of dancing forms a part. A slightly different instance is from a case-study which I detail in the next section concerning a man whose *parrandero* habits created conflict with his wife. He would actively use the lyrics of *vallenato* songs, especially during periods of conflict, in assertions to her of his dominance and masculinity. One of his favourites was the line, *Yo soy parrandero – ¿y qué? / A nadie le importa* (I'm a *parrandero* – so what? / It's nobody's business [but my own]). As this example shows, power and representation are clearly linked and the fact that men are in control of these particular representations is reflected not only in the images of men and women they portray, but in men's real economic and social dominance.

GENDER RELATIONS AND STRATEGIES: THE ROLE OF VIOLENCE

The previous section outlined some basic concepts of masculinity and femininity, drawn both from *vallenato* and from my own observations. I now wish to examine in more depth the actual relationships and strategies involved in men's and women's constitution of their gendered identities, looking at the role of violence and using a particular case-study of a marital relationship in which I know physical violence against the woman to have taken place with some regularity.

The basic idea underlying this section is that men and women have different and often conflicting strategies in constituting their gendered positions. Men may try to change partners and/or have several at one time. This takes various forms – e.g. serial polygyny, through ordinary polygyny to a wife-plus-mistresses arrangement – and depends partly upon circumstances. Both serial polygyny and ordinary polygyny may be connected to men's economic strategies as they move around exploiting different economic resources and niches (Whitten 1974). All forms are also connected to the high value placed by men on sexual conquest and the prestige accruing to the *hombre mujeriego*. Men are also involved in strong male bonding relationships which are powerfully affective and also loaded with ideas about solidarity and duty. Prestige is also involved here since a man's reputation among other men is heavily dependent on being seen to be reciprocative, generous, and loyal. Participation in male networks is closely bound up with *parranda*: as one Costeño friend put it, 'The man who doesn't *parrandear*, can't relate socially'. Further, a man's economic situation is linked to *parranda* because by socializing in this way he makes crucial contacts for economic favours, aid, loans, information, and so on. Obviously *parranda* can be a costly business and the outgoings may outweigh the potential benefits, but part of the usefulness of the male network is its flexibility: when one man is short, another may have a little to spare. Also the network acts so as to redistribute income from richer to poorer men within the circle of friendship. A man with a solid economic base can afford in economic terms to opt out of this network (which he may indeed find becomes demanding and one-sided), but he still risks censure and forfeits prestige. A man with a less solid economic situation often depends quite heavily on this network. In practice, of course, men actually also frequently default on each other's debts, hide money to avoid buying rum or being asked for a loan, and poke fun at each other for meanness, and so on: economic realities mean the ideal cannot always be attained. The clever man is he who times his moves strategically so that he keeps up the reputation of a good friend.

A woman's strategies are rather different. Clearly there are a number of feminine positions to which a woman can relate. For example, single childless women are generally at a stage in which they anticipate children sometime in the future. Increasingly a minority of women prolong this stage in the interests of education and career ambitions, and the position of femininity they enact usually privileges preserving their reputation and avoiding children. Resistance to men's attempts at conquest, discretion in the relationships they decide to embark on, and contraception are the basic tactics here. Single women with children may avoid relations with men, creating an independent position. Mercedes Maya (1987: 129) records asking a black woman miner with five children if she did not want a man, and she replied, 'What use would men be, if there are no women to cook for them?' (*¿Para qué varones, si no hay hembras que les cocinen?*). Maya interprets this as female approval of a division of labour in which women cook for men, but it sounds to me very much like a refusal by *this* woman to take on that role (cf. Moore, 1988: 64, on evidence for women's preference for independence). It remains the case, however, that the vast majority of women are in a conjugal relation and/or have children, and that, given economic inequalities, one fundamental strategy for their maintenance and that of their children is based on securing economic contributions from men. In this process, women constitute a gendered identity which responds to both 'conjugal' and independent notions of motherhood. In the first, a union with a man is seen as one in which both parties construct positions of mutually reinforcing stability and support, built around ideals of romantic love, fidelity, and loyalty. In the second, the man is impermanent or conflicts emerge which threaten stability. Women can therefore constitute a position, and a representation of themselves, as relatively independent – without, however, abandoning a notion of 'conjugal' motherhood as a definition of themselves, or as a claim on men.

For women there are various tactics in the overall strategy of getting, keeping, and obtaining contributions from a man which refer to both these notions of motherhood. They can attract men by offering them domestic services, and thus implicitly the possibility of sexual services. A woman may give a man cooked food, or offer to cook food he supplies; or she may offer to wash his clothes. This indicates her interest in a man and is a way of initiating a relationship that she may or may not wish to become more permanent, depending on her position and her motives. These offers of tokens of conjugal rights refer to the possibility of 'conjugal' motherhood. Logically, a woman can also retract services of this kind in an attempt to apply pressure to her partner, and denying a man sex is probably the simplest option. One Costeño woman neighbour of mine spoke quite openly about how she would *apretar los tornillos* (put the screws) on her partner to ensure economic contributions. Offering sexual and domestic services to other men is also a means of terminating one union and beginning another. I have no data on how common this tactic is, but my impression is that women's freedom to do this while in a conjugal relation is heavily policed by their male partner and by social opinion in general. The power that women can wield by offering domestic, and especially sexual, services can in certain situations be considerable: the story of the man infatuated by his mistress is one I came across more than once.

The retraction and manipulation of conjugal tokens refers to the notion of independent motherhood, and this is even clearer in the realm of magic. Magic, or 'popular religion', is used extensively in Colombia and its commonest targets of action are *amor, salud y dinero* (love, health, and money). In many areas of the country, women use magic to try and control men (Bohman 1984), while men may use magic to try to 'conquer' women or to enhance their own sexual powers. Men told me that female strategies can take various forms. A woman can attempt to *embobar* the man, make him stupid or fascinated or, more specifically, without a will of his own and thus subject to her control. She can do this in a number of ways; for example by leaving underwear stained with menstrual blood under the mattress, or by putting a drop or two of menstrual blood in food or drink. A man has to guard against these strategies by keeping alert, by avoiding food given to him cold when it is better suited to adulteration by magical substances, and also by not indulging in sex too frequently. Excessive sex can weaken a man and make him more susceptible to *brujería* (witchcraft). Thus womanizing carries within it the possibility of its opposite: submission to a woman's demands for stability. Other magical strategies for a woman consist of attacking other women who are competitors or attacking a man on whom she wants to take revenge. Women's magic, therefore, is seen by men as a threat in two ways: not only might it restrict his field of action in 'conquest', his mobility, and his free will, it might also overturn his dominance within the household making him subject to female control. This is a male view of female magic and as such has a paranoid ring about it: unfortunately, women did not talk to me about how they used magic to control men.

Just as for women the constitution of a certain identity as a woman is often dependent on the nature of their relationship with men, a relationship they may try to actively control and manipulate, so for men their relationship with women is critical in the negotiation of their masculine identity, particularly with respect to their prestige strategies.[6] Concentrating now on men as *mujeriego* and *parrandero*, with all the latter implies in terms of participation in a world of male solidarity, affect, economic reciprocity, and prestige, a man has to enforce his dominance over women in various ways.

At the most obvious level, this is implied in the 'conquest' of women in which men should be insistent and not take 'no' for an answer. Dominance is expressed in more than just 'conquest' here. Ideally, seduction should be thanks to a man's personal qualities: the man conquers the woman by virtue of his personality. However, men recognize that economic status and money are crucial assets in this game, since any 'conquest' of a woman involves expenditure and also because further economic obligations may be incurred if the relationship continues or results in a child. A man can assert his dominance here by accusing a woman of being *materialista* and then breaking off the relationship or restricting her demands. Whether he does this or not, of course, depends partly on how much of a drain this represents on his material assets (given other obligations) and how much he values that particular relationship. The image of the infatuated man arises again in this context.

Dominance is also expressed in *parranda*, again in a variety of ways. Men expect to dominate on the dance floor, generally initiating and leading the dance. They often also try and dance close with a woman, if she is a suitable partner, and in slow *vallenato* songs this may lead to an intimate dance style known as *covar*. In this style, the man and woman are effectively in an embrace in which their bodies are in a greater or lesser degree of contact, especially round the hip area. The man's thigh is between the woman's legs and her thigh is between his. If the man has an erection, for example, he can make this apparent to the woman with little effort, if he thinks he can get away with it in the context of the social relation that exists between them. On occasion the woman may push the man right away if she feels he is becoming too brazen. The word *covar* also occurs in a gold-mining context in which it means to excavate a hole with a large, iron-tipped pole in search of gold-bearing deposits: people recognize the, to them humorous, congruence of the two uses of the word and there are clear connotations of a passive, secretive 'gold-bearing' female and an active, searching, 'gold-seeking' male who tries to wrest the treasure from the other. Men also enact their control over women by offering their *mujer* to other men as dance partners in gestures of generosity in the network of male solidarity and prestige. Women's tactics here are more circumscribed. They can keep a man at bay while on the dance floor and they can also ask men to dance, especially if they are unaccompanied themselves. Nearly always, however, this is a man seated at their table and part of their immediate social circle. To ask a strange man to dance, or a man at another table, would be very unusual, whereas men commonly do this to women.

Parranda also requires a different form of dominance. A man who has a conjugal relationship often finds his *parranda* activities, and of course his womanizing, are at odds with his wife's interests. A woman is expected to

deal with the domestic sphere if her husband is always out with his friends
and this may interfere with her work and/or study if she does either. His
expenditures obviously affect the whole household budget. Moreover,
women within their own domestic domain are crucial to home-based
parrandas. They are expected to prepare food at short notice and at odd
hours, fetch and carry, wash up, sweep up, care for children woken by loud
music and, in addition, to act as dance partners. This is not to say that
women do not enjoy these parties, because often they do and they can also
arrange for their own friends and relatives to be there. Clearly, too, a
woman's prestige among men and women is affected by how she handles
these parties. The point is that many of these *parrandas* are aimed prin-
cipally at a world of male prestige and women often find themselves as
servants and adjuncts to this world. This requires male control of the
woman, but it is acknowledged that a man also has obligations towards the
domestic domain. In essence, the man should maintain the household
economically: a man whose children are known to be going hungry because
he spends too much money on *parrandas* and other women is liable to lose
prestige (although perhaps not as much as if he did not go out with his
friends).

In practice, of course, it becomes a question of balancing *parranda* and
all that it entails in the world of male prestige against demands from the
domestic sphere and it is here, I argue, that physical violence towards
women can emerge as part of a man's reaction to the protest and criticisms
of a wife/partner who is blocking the fulfilment of his desires and, especially,
his participation in the male prestige world. Whitehead (1986: 224) also
notes how West Indian notions of a 'strong man' depend on maintaining a
'social balance' between 'respectability traits' (e.g. domestic stability) and
'reputational traits' (e.g. sexual prowess, drinking).[7] Generally, then, being
unable to maintain this kind of balance can block the constitution of a
valued sense of masculinity, resulting in threat to personal identity and
feelings of frustration from which violence towards the domestic female
partner may emerge. This is my understanding of the wife-beating that took
place in the following case study, which illustrates these themes more
explicitly.

The family was originally from Turbo, a town in the Atlantic coast
region, but very close to the Chocó. They had migrated to Medellín some
ten years before and I lived with them there. The man, Alberto, was
well-educated to university level and held a primary school teaching post,
but his origins and social circle were mainly working class. The woman,
Nancy, had only primary education. She worked in a clothes factory during
the day and also did night-school classes in secondary education. His
beating of her was surreptitious and I only found out about it quite late on:

she colluded in keeping it hidden, feeling that it was a private and shameful business, although once she knew that I knew, she was willing to talk about it. He was generally defensive about it, saying that he knew he should not do it, but also saying that anyway he only 'gave her a few slaps' and did not really hurt her.

My interpretation of his violence sees it as an expression of the frustration he felt at not having things the way he wanted, a frustration he vented on her. More particularly, his frustration derived from the tension between the two central concepts of masculinity with which he concurrently tried to define himself as a man, and which were in conflict for him; and between these and his wife's attempts to define her own femininity in terms of a position of independence for herself via her education and her work, while still valuing the possibility of a 'conjugal' form of motherhood, which corresponded in some ways to the notion of 'good father' which he himself valued. What he wanted was for her to stay at home and look after the house and the children 'properly'. At that time, he worked only half days and some of the care of their two children fell to him, such as getting them ready for school and so on. He did not earn enough to really permit her not to work, however, so he was stuck. At the same time, he wanted to have enough money and time to go out drinking with his friends and *compadres*, to be able to invite them back to his house to eat, drink, listen to music, and dance. He also wanted to be able to take his wife out, along with his friends and their women/wives, so that she would enjoy herself too. His wife's activities in this respect were crucial since his absence while out with his friends meant that the children might be left alone, something that neither he nor she approved of, while her triple burden of factory work, night-school, and housework meant that she often had little time or patience for going out with him and his friends or for the hospitality and parties that he wanted to give since this meant demands on her for cooking and clearing up and also kept her up late.

Ideally for him, he would have had enough money to keep her at home, and be a good father/husband, while at the same time go out drinking, invite his friends back and give them hospitality, thus balancing his image as a good father/husband with his reputation as a good party-loving drinking companion among his friends. But his financial situation, combined with the need for his wife to work and her determination to do so and to go to night-school made this ideal hard to achieve and made attempts to achieve it very irritating to her, causing fights and disagreements which ended in him beating her. This physical violence was thus a venting of his frustration at life in general and specifically at her.[8] He would have liked her to be a 'good wife': submissive, pandering to his demands and those of his friends after an afternoon's drinking. To a remarkable extent she did all this and combined it with factory work and studying, but she also criticized him, put her foot down on certain issues, and insisted on trying to better herself through education and this departed from his view of how things should be. The question remains, however, of why his frustration should express itself in violence, and of why violence towards his wife rather than, say, his male friends.

This can be approached to a limited extent on an individual level. Alberto was in many ways a violent person who tended to resolve certain types of confrontation with violence. But this type of explanation is very partial and needs to be put in context. Colombia is a violent country and violence has been an endemic feature of its history. This is a vast and complex topic, which I cannot encompass here. Suffice it to say that the many conflicts of class, race, region and political allegiance in the country's history and still today have given it a particular social context in which violence is a major element in the management of social relations and conflicts. Against this background, in which violence is frequently resorted to in a conflict of interests, it is also the case that male identity is often asserted and protected with violence. A friend of mine, for example, was shot in the ankle for making a *piropo* (an amorous, flirtatious comment) to a woman whose man was in the vicinity; and in the newspapers accounts appear of shoot-outs in bars over similar incidents. Men here assume their right to control and possess a woman against attempts by another man to encroach on that right – and the reaction tends to be a violent one. This type of violence is not a male prerogative. Women also fight and I have seen women attack each other with fists, fingernails, knives and bottles. The most usual cause of violence is conflict over men, and most of the violence I witnessed was in Medellín where black women migrants outnumbered men, creating a situation of competition. Violence is thus also a tactic used by women as a means to their ends and, to this extent, women collude in a system in which violence is seen to be a legitimate reaction to a conflict of interests.

Men use violence against women in a number of ways. They use it to circumscribe women's freedom to initiate sexual liaisons outside a conjugal relation, whether these are transient affairs or the antecedent to breaking up a consensual union. If a woman is considered to be the *mujer* of a man and is cohabiting with him, infidelity of this kind is liable to lead to violence. Equally, violence may be meted out to women when they challenge a man's dominance or interfere with his preferences in how to balance out his different obligations and ambitions, as in the case of Alberto and Nancy. This, however, still begs the question of why violence towards women in a situation in which a man feels torn between two masculine positions which are in conflict for him. Part of the answer here must lie in the experience of violence in the home: the beating of children, as dependents who are clearly lower in the familial hierarchy than adults, is standard practice throughout Colombia as a punishment for misdeeds, and, of course, this is undertaken as much by women as by men. Beating children, however, is not a right generalized to the adult world: a parent may beat her or his own children, but beating another person's child is fraught with the risk of encroaching on that person's authority and rights. Violence, then, is considered normal within the home as a corrective measure, but it takes place within a definitely established framework of kinship (or quasi-kinship) seniority. In the violence of a man against his wife/woman, the same kind of rationale is at work: the woman is being seen as a social junior in the relationship and the man is asserting his social seniority and hence his dominance and the priority of his wishes within the household. Violence here has a different character from violence outside the home (just as conjugal relations are distinguished from transient sexual affairs in the *vallenato* songs): men locate it in the realm of punishment of juniors for misdemeanours, a type of violence that adults laugh about when they recall how they suffered as children, and often laugh about in relation to the beatings they themselves administer, once their anger has died down. Violence directed against men within the male circle of solidarity, for example, would have a very different and much more dangerous character, implying radical rupture and the possibility of retort and escalation.

This interpretation is supported by the way men sometimes talk about violence towards women, presenting it in benign light. From time to time women get refractory and difficult, they criticize and make demands. They are, so men say, 'asking for' a beating. When this is administered, so the story goes, the woman becomes happy, loving, compliant. That is, men portray this violence as a necessary corrective discipline to women, and they may go even further and say that women actually want a man to assert his authority by beating her. Men often recount these apocryphal morality tales with an air of slight amazement: incredulous, as it were, that women should actually be so perverse as to want to be beaten. This incredulity is also an indication that men know that their attempt to represent violence towards women in this light and assimilate it to the punishment meted out to naughty children is in fact highly contestable and that the reality is that women are being pressured by material dependence and dominant definitions of gender into playing a certain role, that of *la mujer conforme* (the obedient acquiescent woman), which suits men's strategies, whether these be directed towards changing households in patterns of serial polygyny, 'conquering' many women, or maintaining their reputations as good drinking and partying companions. Men have an ambivalent attitude to violence, on the one hand taking it as a right of quasi-parental dimensions and, on the other, recognizing it as an abuse, especially if it is brutal.

Women's reaction to violence places it in a very different light from the benign facade men sometimes attempt to draw over it. In my admittedly limited experience, they see it as an abuse of strength and power, as patently unjust and unfair, and as an experience which does more than anything else to alienate them from their partners. There is no doubt, however, that it instils fear as well as intense resentment and to this extent it may effectively act as a restraint on a woman's tendency to criticize her partner and make demands on him. Tactics for dealing with violence appear limited. Leaving a man is possible, but depends heavily on a woman's economic position, whether she is married or not, the age of her children and the possibility of moving in with kin. Violence to a wife or female partner, however, is also violence to another man's sister, daughter, mother or *comadre* (co-mother, i.e. godmother of one's child), and calling in an intermediary is perhaps more common than leaving the man. In my experience, however, men's intervention in violence towards women is limited. In Alberto's case, both his sister and a *comadre* of his used to be attacked occasionally by their husbands. Alberto would intervene here in a diplomatic way, but he never broke off relations with either man and would still socialize with them; neither did he censure them heavily. In these cases, then, male intervention took place strictly within the bounds of male solidarity, with *compadres* or relatives perhaps drawing the man aside and persuading him not to be too violent, rather than censuring him and thus endangering the relationship between them. Men's ambivalent attitude towards wife-beating is evident here.

CONCLUSION

I have argued that violence towards women in the domestic sphere is rooted in conflicts between men's and women's processes of constituting their own gendered subjectivities, processes which themselves involve contradictory concepts of masculinity and femininity. These gendered concepts, although familiar enough to a western observer, are nevertheless culturally specific elements in the constitution of a gendered subjectivity. Violence, then, does not emerge straightforwardly from some self-evident conflict between 'masculinity' and 'femininity' seen as univocal opposites in a relationship characterized simply by 'male dominance' or 'patriarchy'. It emerges rather from conflicts within and between different aspects of masculinities and femininities, various of which men and women recognize and may value in themselves and in others, male and female. This is not to deny gendered power differences, enacted in economics and representations; it is to qualify over-simplified and undifferentiated notions of gender and dominance. Gender inequalities are not differentiated and opposed in a simple way: not only are masculinity and femininity conflictive and ambivalent for both men and women, but in the case of Alberto and Nancy, the context of the violence was a working-class one in which money was scarce, and yet, for men at least, the values surrounding *parranda* more powerful in defining certain aspects of masculinity. Gender and class (not to mention region and race) intersect to differentiate still further masculinity and femininity.

Violence seems to take place towards the silent margins of different gendered subject positions. Alberto and Nancy colluded in keeping his domestic violence a secret and even when I found out it remained a silent, nocturnal and shameful activity. Similarly, in the images represented in *vallenato* lyrics there is no overt place for the wife-beating man or the physically abused woman. These are not positions which men or women generally care to make public. Instead they are tactics of the margin which men adopt and women endure (and perhaps reject) in their attempts to constitute themselves as valued 'men' and 'women'. This violence is given little voice, at best a whisper. But this is relative, since for the man it may be a means to a potentially valued end, albeit an unacknowledged one, while for the woman, although it may lead somewhere (e.g. 'the mother who has endured everything'), it is generally not a valued position. For men, it can be a release of anger and a hidden tactic in constituting the productive tension between contradictory aspects of their masculinity; for a woman it is more a moment of unproductive tension in which her own subjectivity is put in stalemate while she becomes an object violated in the constituting of masculinity.[9]

Representing Nancy's experience of violence is clearly problematic for me. I run the risk of representing her as an object and thus reproducing her objectification; or I run the risk of trying to represent her as a subject without sufficient knowledge of her experience. Moreover, as a third party, my own sense of masculinity was deeply involved in the conflict and my knowledge of the violence mediated by my relationships with Alberto and Nancy. Loyalty to Alberto, guide and mentor in *parranda* circles of ostentatious male solidarity and in my growing network of informants and friends, uneasily paralleled sympathy with, admiration for and also loyalty to Nancy, she and I both opposed (albeit from different points of view) to Alberto's treatment of her. As a man, I positioned myself with him, but also with her. The structure of this essay clearly reflects my position and my experience as much as it does theirs, but this in itself is not some kind of 'invalidation'. Situatedness cannot be avoided, nor its implications fully resolved: it can be recognized rather than masked.

136   *Sex and violence*

NOTES

1 My thanks to Cecilia McCallum and Penelope Harvey for commenting on an early draft of this chapter: the usual disclaimers apply. Fieldwork in Colombia was carried out 1982–3 with an SSRC grant, and 1986–7 with a Research Fellowship from Queen's College, Cambridge, and grants from the SSRC (USA) and the British Academy. Thanks are due to the following publishers for permission to reproduce the following song lyrics: 'Los Gavilanes' (Calixto Ochoa), PRODEMUS/Colombia; 'La Maye' (Rafael Escalona), EDIMUSICA/Colombia; 'Amor Comprado' (Armando Darío Zabaleta), EMI/Colombia; 'La Mujer Conforme' (Máximo Movil), EMI/Colombia; 'La Parranda es pa' Amanecer' (Lenín Bueno Suárez), PRODEMUS/Colombia; 'La Excusa' (Diomedes Díaz), Sony Music/Colombia; 'Yo Soy Parrandero y Qué' (Lenín Bueno Suárez), EMI/Colombia.
2 Costeño means pertaining to *la Costa* (the Atlantic coastal region).
3 There is a significant difference here between the Pacific region and the Atlantic in this respect. In the former, women form a much greater proportion of the economically active population, according to official statistics (Dane 1986: 541, 676), working in agriculture and mining. Therefore, there are indications that they are not as dependent economically on men. However, since gender relations and the sexual division of labour were not my main research concerns, I do not have enough data to know what the real differences in dependency are, or the impact of this, on gender relations.
4 Some of the lyrics which are examined here are taken from Llerena (1985) as follows: 'Los Gavilanes' p. 92; 'La Maye' p. 77; 'Amor Comprado' p. 88; 'La Mujer Conforme' p. 119. Of the other songs cited, 'La Excusa' is from the LP *Los Incontenibles*, 1987, CBS 142043.
5 *Turco* here refers to people of Sirio-Lebanese origins.
6 As Ortner and Whitehead (1981) discuss at length, the role women play in men's prestige strategies is of crucial importance in influencing gender constitution and relations. 'Prestige' as discussed by Ortner and Whitehead (1981: 14) includes command of material and human resources, political might, personal skills, and connectedness to the wealthy, mighty and skilled. Clearly, the role men play in women's strategies is also crucial.
7 See also Wilson (1973) who was one of the first to contrast reputation and respectability in a similar way.
8 Cf. Moore's idea of 'thwarting' (this volume).
9 In the context of *sati* (self-immolation of widows on the funeral pyre of their husbands), Spivak talks of a 'violent aporia between subject- and object-status' (cited in Young 1990: 164). In 'Can the Subaltern Speak? Speculations on widow sacrifice' (*Wedge* 1985, vols 7/8, pp. 120–30), Spivak suggests that the very assumption that an authentic voice corresponding to a fully constituted subjectivity is in principle recoverable for women involved in widow sacrifice is itself problematic (see Young 1990: Chapter 9 for a discussion). The same might apply to domestic violence, but such a conclusion would, I think, be subject to more investigation into how women like Nancy verbalize their experiences.

BIBLIOGRAPHY

Bohman, Kristina (1984) *Women of the Barrio: Class and gender in a Colombian city*, Stockholm: University of Stockholm.

Dane (1986) *Colombia Estadística, 1986*, Bogotá: Departamento Administrativo Nacional de Estadísticas.

Dussán de Reichel, Alicia (1958) 'La estructura de la familia en la costa caribe de Colombia', in *Minutes of the Thirty-Third International Congress of Americanists*, México: Universidad Nacional Autónoma de México.

Friedemann, Nina de (1974) 'Minería del oro y descendencia: Güelmambí, Nariño', *Revista Colombiana de Antropología* 16: 9–86.

Gutiérrez de Pineda, Virginia (1975) *Familia y Cultura en Colombia*, Bogotá: Colcultura.

Llerena Villalobos, Rito (1985) *Memoria Cultural en el Vallenato*, Medellín: Centro de Investigaciones, Facultad de Ciencias Humanas, Universidad de Antioquia.

Maya, Luz Mercedes (1987) 'Familia, parentesco y explotación minera desde el fin de la esclavitud hasta hoy', Unpublished field report, Ecole des Hautes Etudes en Sciences Sociales, Paris.

Moore, Henrietta (1988) *Feminism and Anthropology*, Cambridge: Polity Press.

Ortner, Sherry and Whitehead, Harriet (eds) (1981) *Sexual Meanings: The cultural construction of gender and sexuality*, Cambridge: Cambridge University Press.

Pleck, Joseph (1981) *The Myth of Masculinity*, Cambridge, Mass.: MIT Press.

Wade, Peter (1993) *Blackness and Race Mixture: The dynamics of racial identity in Colombia*, Baltimore, MD: Johns Hopkins University Press.

Whitehead, Tony (1986) 'Breakdown, Resolution and Coherence: The fieldwork experiences of a big, brown, pretty-talking man in a West Indian community' in Whitehead, Tony and Conaway, Mary (eds) *Self, Sex and Gender in Cross-Cultural Fieldwork*, Urbana: University of Illinois Press.

Whitten, Norman (1974) *Black Frontiersmen: A South American case*, New York: Wiley & Son.

Wilson, Peter (1973) *Crab Antics: The social anthropology of English-speaking Negro societies of the Caribbean*, New Haven: Yale University Press.

Young, Robert (1990) *White Mythologies: Writing history and the West*, London: Routledge.

6 The problem of explaining violence in the social sciences

Henrietta Moore

The papers presented in this volume raise a number of issues: does violence enter into the cultural construction of personhood in distinctive ways for women and men, and if so, how; is violence between the sexes instrumental in converting gender difference into gender hierarchy; are we to understand violence as a universal feature of male/female relations or should we be looking instead to the culturally specific forms which violence takes; is sexuality itself something which is inherently violent? When it comes to considering these and other related issues, we need to examine, of course, the theoretical and methodological tools available to us. The sociological, psychological and criminological theories about the origins and causes of interpersonal violence have been summarized elsewhere, and I do not have the space to review all these theories here, nor am I qualified to do so. Instead, I wish to work from two starting points. One is that in spite of a great mass of writing, research, and speculation, the concept of violence in the social sciences still seems remarkably undertheorized. This situation is exacerbated by the fact that the causes of violence are clearly multiple and cannot be explained using a single set of determinants. From an anthropological perspective, there is an obvious need to integrate the sociological and psychological theories of interpersonal violence with theories about meaning, representation and symbolism.

A second starting point is the way in which discourses about sexuality and gender construct women and men as different sorts of persons. One very obvious example of this in many western cultures is the way that male sexuality and persons of the male gender are portrayed as active, aggressive, thrusting and powerful; while female sexuality and persons of the female gender are seen as essentially passive, powerless, submissive and receptive. The interesting fact about such constructions is that they have only the most tangential relation to the behaviours, qualities, attributes and self-images of individual women and men. Discourses about gender are powerful precisely because, amongst other things, they engender women and men as persons who are defined by difference.

I should say that when I speak of women and men as different sorts of person, I have two interrelated, but very specific things in mind. First, I am not speaking of the differences between women and men which result from biology, and most particularly, I am not referring to those differences which according to various folk theories – including respectable ones like sociobiology – are thought to result from the naturalized differences imputed to biological difference, such as differences in levels of aggression, nurturance, propensity for emotion and so on. It follows therefore that I am not referring to the differences which can be said to exist between women and men as a result of socialization, which as a process so often works to miraculously reproduce those very naturalized differences whose origins the folklorists locate in biological difference. Thus, male children, in many societies, are encouraged to be more assertive, more aggressive, more thrusting and more powerful. I am instead talking of the differences which exist between women and men as a result of the workings of signification and discourse, the discursive effects which produce gender difference and which, therefore, produce the symbolic or culturally constructed category woman as different from that of man. Gender difference is not merely, however, an effect of signification or language. This brings me to the second sort of thing I have in mind when I speak of women and men as different sorts of person.

If we accept the idea that the concept of person is only intelligible with reference to a culturally specific set of categories, discourses and practices, then we have to acknowledge the different ways in which the categories woman and man, and the discourses which employ those categories, are involved in the production and reproduction of notions of personhood and agency. We have to recognize in addition the ways in which the categories, discourses and practices of gender are involved in the production and reproduction of engendered subjects who use them to produce both representations and self-representations, as part of the process of constructing themselves as persons and agents. It is for this reason that the symbolic categories woman and man, and the difference inscribed within and between them, have something to do with the representations, self-representations and day-to-day practices of individual women and men. It follows therefore that we need some way of theorizing how individuals become engendered subjects; that is, how they come to have representations of themselves as women and men, come to make representations of others, and come to organize their social practices in such a way as to reproduce dominant categories, discourses and practices. However, the interpellation of individuals as subjects within particular discourses and discursive practices is never fully determined and is always open to challenge and resistance. This means that any theory must account both for the reproduction of dominant categories and discourses, and for instances of non-reproduction, resistance and change. In order to theorize how persons become engendered subjects, we need, of course, a theory of the subject, and we need a theory which will allow us to construct the links between representation, power, knowledge and subject. I want to argue in this paper that without such a theory of the subject we will be unable to respond adequately to questions concerning the interrelations of gender difference, gender hierarchy, violence and sexuality.

One of the most difficult sets of processes or relationships to grasp when it comes to a discussion of the construction of engendered subjects is how the social representations of gender affect the subjective constructions of gender, and how the subjective representation or self-representation of gender affects its social construction. In any functionalist theory in the social sciences, including, of course, certain Marxist theories, this relationship is unproblematic because social representations simply determine subjective representations of gender which, in turn, reproduce the social representations. Apart from the impossibility of imagining how change comes about in this tidy circle of production and reproduction, there is the added difficulty that this is not actually an accurate description of the relationship between social and subjective representations of gender. In order to work towards some kind of accurate description of this relationship we need to maintain both an emphasis on meaning and signification, and an emphasis on practices and their effects.

THEORIZING THE ENGENDERED SUBJECT

Before going on to say something about the relationship between gender, violence, and sexuality, it is necessary to try and say something about how we might construct a theory of the subject which would allow us to look at the relationship between gender, violence, and sexuality, and to try and say something about what that subject would look like or what sort of a subject it might be.

Since the 1960s, work done by various scholars in a variety of disciplines has been concerned to undermine the western concept of the transcendental, unified, rational subject of Enlightenment thinking: Lacan's work in psychoanalysis, Barthes's semiotics, Derrida's work on deconstruction and Foucault's investigation into the historical production of knowledge and discourse – to mention only the more famous male figures. One of the cumulative effects of this type of work in the social sciences has been that it has forced us to question whether such concepts as the 'individual' and 'society' can stand as pre-givens around which we structure our questions, or whether they have to be regarded as the effects of discourses and practices which require analytical specification (see, for example, Strathern 1988).

There is clearly a relation between the concept of the individual in the social sciences and a specific material entity, but what has to be explained is how and why that physical entity is constructed in its specificity through particular discourses, and how that specificity is anchored to social practices. Using this kind of approach, it is a relatively straightforward matter, as others have so convincingly argued, to trace the historical genealogy of the western concept of the unified, rational subject – which is identified with or corresponds to an individual agent – and show it to be a specific historical and cultural construction, rather than a description of a fixed and pre-given entity in the world. Thus, the facticity and naturalness of the western concept of the post-Enlightenment subject is an imaginary facticity. It is only one way of representing and understanding the subject and subjectivity. The resulting conclusion is that subjects are not therefore pre-given entities which exist in the world, but effects of social discourses and social practices which have to be specified.

The post-structuralist concept of the subject which has emerged from this debate is quite different from the unified, transcendental subject which it seeks to deconstruct. The basic premise of post-structuralist thinking on the subject is that discursive practices provide subject positions, and individuals take up a variety of subject positions within different discourses. Amongst other things, this means that a single subject can no longer be equated with a single individual. Individuals are multiply constituted subjects, and they can, and do, take up multiple subject positions within a range of discourses and social practices. Some of these subject positions will be contradictory and will conflict with each other. Thus, the subject in post-structuralist thinking is composed of, or exists as, a set of multiple and contradictory positionings and subjectivities. What holds these multiple subjectivities together so that they constitute agents in the world are such things as the subjective experience of identity, the physical fact of being an embodied subject, and the historical continuity of the subject which means that past subject positions tend to overdetermine present subject positions. The notion of the subject as the site of multiple and potentially contradictory subjectivities is a very useful one. If subjectivity is seen as singular, fixed and coherent, it becomes very difficult to explain how it is that individuals constitute their sense of self – their self-representations as subjects – through several, often mutually contradictory subject positions, rather than through one singular subject position.

Anthropology as a discipline has been slow to recognize the potential of this approach to the study of subjectivity and, in particular, to the study of gender and gender identity. The symbolic analysis of gender in anthropology in the 1970s and 1980s emphasized that gender systems were culturally constructed and therefore variable. This meant, paradoxically, that this important research stressed inter-cultural at the expense of intra-cultural variation. The implication was that since all cultures defined, constructed and enacted gender in specific ways, each culture had its own distinctive gender system. However, recent work in anthropology has demonstrated that cultures do not have a single model of gender or a single gender system, but rather a multiplicity of discourses on gender which can vary both contextually and biographically (Sanday and Goodenough 1990; Strathern 1987). These different discourses on gender are frequently contradictory and conflicting. Anthropology, therefore, has begun to move away from a simplistic model of a single gender system into which individuals must be socialized, towards a more complex understanding of the way in which individuals come to take up gendered subject positions through engagement with multiple discourses on gender. This move has enabled researchers to focus on processes of failure, resistance and change in the acquisition of gender identity, as well as instances of compliance, acceptance and investment. An emphasis on resistance and failure – that is, on the partiality of the effects of discourse – helps to explain the evident disparity between the range of discourses on gender which exist in any particular context and the actual self-representations of individual women and men as engendered subjects.

It seems clear that individuals do constitute their self-representations as engendered subjects through several different subject positions on gender. It is equally certain that, at different times, most individuals will be asked to act out a variety of these subject positions and will have, therefore, to construct themselves and their social practices in terms of a competing set of discourses about what it is to be a woman or a man. These competing notions are not just ideas, because as discourses they have both material and social force. Thus, the enactment of subject positions based on gender provides the conditions for the experience of gender and of gender difference, even as those positions may be resisted or rejected.

Many women acknowledge the feeling of being a different person in different social situations which call for different qualities and modes of femininity. The range of ways of being a woman open to each of us at a particular time is extremely wide but we know or feel we ought to know what is expected of us in particular situations – in romantic encounters, when we are pandering to the boss, when we are dealing with children or posing for fashion photographers. We may embrace these ways of being, these subject positions whole-heartedly, we may reject them outright or we may offer resistance while complying to the letter with what is expected of us. Yet even when we resist a particular subject position and the mode of subjectivity which it brings with it, we do so from the position of an alternative social definition of femininity.

(Weedon, 1987: 86)

The experience of gender, of being an engendered subject, is given meaning in discourse and in the practices which those discourses inform. Discourses are structured through difference, and thus women and men take up different subject positions within the same discourse, or rather, the same discourse positions them as subjects in different ways. All the major axes of difference, race, class, ethnicity, sexuality, and religion intersect with gender in ways which proffer a multiplicity of subject positions within any discourse. This notion of the engendered subject as the site of multiple differences, and, therefore, of multiple subjectivities and competing identities is the result of the recent feminist critique of post-structuralist and deconstructionist theory. This work has been inspired, of course, by Lacan's notion of the subject in contradiction and process but, as de Lauretis points out, the feminist rethinking of the post-structuralist subject – what might be termed the post-post-structuralist subject – is crucially different. In particular, she argues that the notion of identity as multiple and even self-contradictory points to a more useful conception of the subject than the one proposed by neo-Freudian psychoanalysis and post-structuralist theories.

For it is not the fragmented, or intermittent, identity of a subject constructed in division by language alone, an 'I' continually prefigured and pre-empted in an unchangeable symbolic order. It is neither, in short, the imaginary identity of the individualist, bourgeois subject, which is male and white; nor the 'flickering' of the posthumanist Lacanian subject, which is too nearly white and at best (fe)male. What is emerging in feminist writing is, instead, the concept of a multiple, shifting, and often self-contradictory identity. . . . an identity made up of heterogeneous and heteronomous representations of gender, race and class, and often indeed across languages and cultures. . . .

(de Lauretis, 1986: 9)

This feminist post-post-structuralist view of the subject is, of course, radically different from the traditional subject of anthropological enquiry, the unitary, whole, rational individual which is prototypically male. The 'person' in anthropological discourse is not only male by default, but is also an individual whose identity is 'externally' guaranteed by difference. Thus, in its unitary nature, the anthropological individual is defined by difference from other individuals in the same culture, as well as by its difference from other individuals in other cultures. The post-post-structuralist subject, on the other hand, is the site of differences; differences which constitute the subject and are 'internal' to it. This notion of an 'internally' differentiated subject, constituted in and through discourse, is analytically powerful. It is of particular value in analysing the question of how individuals become engendered and acquire a gender identity in the context of several co-existent discourses on gender, which may contradict and conflict with each other. In order to demonstrate this point, it is necessary to discuss the relationship between multiple gender discourses within a single social setting.

DISCOURSE AND DOMINATION

Gender discourses are variable cross-culturally. It is clear that many gender discourses are oppositional, that is they are constructed around the idea that gender has two forms one female and one male, and that the categories woman and man which are produced from and through this discourse on difference are mutually exclusive. However, not all gender discourses are premised on the mutual exclusivity of the categories woman and man. In many cultures, gender is conceived of processually, and femininity and masculinity are qualities of persons, rather than categories (e.g. Meigs 1990). But, inter-cultural variation has to be understood in the context of intra-cultural variation, and the fact that within each social setting a number of discourses on gender will exist. The existence of multiple gender discourses means that in many situations, a discourse which emphasizes the oppositional and mutually exclusive nature of gender categories can exist alongside other discourses which emphasize the processual, mutable and temporary nature of gender assignment. The co-existence of multiple discourses, however, produces a situation in which the different discourses on gender are hierarchically ordered. This ordering may be both contextually and biographically variable, as well as being subject to historical change. The result is that some discourses overdetermine others, and various sub-dominant discourses develop in opposition to dominant ones.

In many cultures, oppositional gender discourses which emphasize the mutual exclusivity of the categories female and male are structurally and hierarchically dominant. It is a peculiar feature of gender discourses of this kind that the categories woman and man are not just mutually exclusive, but that the relationship between them is defined as one of hierarchical difference. Woman is man's other, what man is not, the lack and the object of man's desire and knowledge. What is important here is that relations of difference are frequently hierarchically ordered both within the dominant discourse, and between discourses. This gives rise to a situation in which gender difference can come to stand for other forms of hierarchically organized difference, as, for example, in contexts where people who are deemed inferior for whatever reason are represented as feminized, controlled, and subordinate. It is a feature of the power of dominant discourses that they operate through the overdetermination of relations of difference within sub-dominant discourses, rather than through the total suppression of alternatives.

However, in those contexts, as, for example, many western cultures, where a hierarchical and mutually exclusive relation between the categories of difference defines the dominant discourse on gender, it is clear that this discourse should not be understood as an accurate reflection of what women and men actually do in social life. This is partly because the relations established between the categories woman and man in such instances are themselves ideal and naturalized relations, the broad outlines of a discursive schema which operates at a certain remove from variability in gender relations at a day-to-day level, and at some remove from the self-representations of engendered individuals. This gives rise, as Denise Riley points out, to a specific difficulty which is that women, *qua* individuals in specific historical circumstances, have a complex and shifting relation to the category 'woman'. They are both defined by it and simultaneously exceed it, in the sense that the gap between the categorical definition of woman and individual understandings of femininity is rather large (Riley 1988). The same difficulty pertains, to a certain extent, to the relationship established in specific circumstances between men and the category 'man'. However, there are a number of notable differences, one of which is that since the characteristics or attributes associated with the category 'man' are frequently predominantly positive, it is possible for male individuals – or, at least, some of them – to identify with the dominant cultural ideals which cluster around that category. The situation for women is far more problematic since the attributes associated with the category 'woman' are often predominantly negative, making identification not only risky, but potentially pathologizing.

Anthropologists recognize this difficulty in so far as they note the disparity between the cultural definitions or attributes of the categories 'woman' and 'man' and the actual context of gender relations and roles (Ortner and Whitehead 1981). However, anthropology has made little attempt to analyse the 'gap' which exists between dominant cultural categories and the actualities of day-to-day gender relations. This gap is filled with or inhabited by a whole variety of discourses and practices, all of which are informed in some way or other by the dominant cultural discourse on gender. It is through engagement with and investment in the subject positions offered by discourses at this level that individual women and men succeed in reproducing the dominant cultural discourse, whilst simultaneously standing at some remove from the categories of that discourse. It is at this level that the multiple subject is positioned and constituted. It is also at this level that we can properly speak of the existence of multiple femininities and masculinities, multiple ways of being feminine or masculine, within the same context.

Bob Connell, for example, argues for the existence of a number of femininities and masculinities within the same social setting, and he provides a number of interesting examples from Australian and British life which illustrate the hierarchical relations between dominant and sub-dominant discourses. He describes one Australian school where two identifiable groups of boys are in conflict. One group is the 'Bloods', the traditional, sporting, physically active group who bully the members of the second group known as the 'Cyrils', who are described as 'quite clever little boys who are socially totally inadequate, and yet who have got very good brains. They've all got glasses, short, very fat and that sort of thing' (Connell 1987: 177). It would be wrong to represent the difference between these masculinities as one of simple choice. For one thing, this pattern of difference, as Connell points out, is a product of the possible subject positions offered to individuals in the school as part of a tension within school policy between success based on sporting achievement and success based on academic excellence. This tension reflects wider social and cultural dynamics about how to succeed in the world, and about what kind of successful masculine self one can be. The school, in order to be attractive to parents and pupils, needs both kinds of masculinity and rewards both as forms of achievement, albeit in very different ways. However, what is more interesting is the way gender difference is inscribed into this difference between masculinities. In this case, the perpetrators of violence, the bullies, are the Bloods, and they persecute the Cyrils because of their effeminacy, their lack of physical prowess, and their general passivity and weakness (Connell 1987: 177–8).

The inscription of gender difference onto the difference between or within multiple femininities and masculinities within the same social setting is of particular interest. One of the things revealed through an investigation of this point is the extraordinary variety in the type of social practices, discourses, and institutions which proffer and work over these multiple femininities and masculinities. The degree to which individuals recognize the alternatives which are available to them is obviously very variable, and the lack of any conscious reflection on the possibility of choosing alternatives does not mean, of course, that individuals do not 'select' from amongst possible alternatives, this is something they can do through practice, and is not something they have to be consciously or intellectually aware of. However, the recognition of possible alternative femininities and masculinities is facilitated, to a certain degree, by the fact that competing discourses are constructed in counterpoint with one another. This oppositional relation is emphasized by the constant reinscription of hierarchical difference between the genders, and thus by the constant reference to the mutually exclusive categories woman and man.

Connell provides an example drawn from British advertising, in which he describes two posters. On one, which is an advert for a perfume, a woman strides out boldly in trousers, and this image is clearly intended to depict various things about activity, professionalism, self-determination and so on. In a second poster – and it is worth bearing in mind how often these posters might occur in the same magazine or on the same hoarding – a company advertises its sheer stockings, accompanied by the caption 'For girls who don't want to wear the trousers' (Connell 1987: 179). In the case of both posters, the images of femininity they convey are only comprehensible within wider gender discourses, but their comprehensibility is crucially dependent on the overt reference to the mutually exclusive nature of dominant gender categories. However, in the case of the advert for perfume, it is precisely that gap between dominant gender categories and the actualities of individual women's experience of gender identity and gender roles which the poster seeks to play with. It is this element of play which makes the advertisement, and hence the product it promotes, seductive. The poster which advertises stockings plays with the same gap, but from the opposite perspective, and engages subtly with anxieties about changing definitions of gender and gender roles. In a sense, both posters play with each other, interrupt and continue each other's narratives. This parodic play is a noticeable feature of much contemporary advertising. What is interesting about it, of course, is that it continually reinscribes dominant categories and discourses through reference to a fixed relationship of difference, whilst appearing to embody challenge, resistance, and change.

Connell's argument is that in western societies, and perhaps globally, a particular type of hegemonic masculinity orders the structural relationship between alternative femininities and masculinities. This is the masculinity which is associated with global capitalism and the domination of the west in economic and political life, and it is also the masculinity which constructs the self-representations of those men who actually do rule the world – of which, perhaps, the most blatant recent example is Ronald Reagan. Connell also argues that through the workings of this hegemonic form of masculinity, the dominant constructions of gender are strongly implicated, if not actually inscribed within, other social relationships. Thus, hegemonic masculinity penetrates political and economic relationships in a way which guarantees that domination itself is gendered. Groups or cabals of powerful heterosexual – that is represented as heterosexual – men dominate both the running of modern states and relations between states, and they thus control the means of public force and violence. These means are not simply, of course, military, but also economic and political. As a result, it is not usually necessary to reinforce their domination through the use of actual physical force, unless – as in the recent Gulf War – there is a breakdown of economic and political control. The current treatment of Iraq by the west shows the importance not just of dominating, but of feminizing and passifying that which is dominated, in order, at least in part, to establish a hierarchical relationship of domination which appears as natural as gender difference itself. The result is that violence at the national and international level is strongly sexualized, and the distinction between perpetrators and victims of violence is a genderized difference. This means, of course, as Penelope Harvey points out in Chapter 3, that gender or rather genderized difference represents, or comes to stand for, very real differences in power between groups of people and between individuals. Gender idioms are frequently used to order differences in power and/or prestige, with the result that power itself is represented in many contexts as sexualized. This is evident both in western discourse and in much ethnographic material.

The hegemonic masculinity described by Connell is recognizably western. However, it is worth pointing out that this particular form of hegemonic masculinity is now global, and it is significant that it has found resonances with a number of local or indigenous masculinities. It is not possible to analyse discourses on gender, wherever they occur, without recognizing the ways in which they are implicated in larger processes of economic and political change well beyond the control of local communities. This is a point which Peter Wade makes in Chapter 5. The personal experience of gender and gender relations is thus bound up with power and political relations on a number of different levels. One consequence of this is that fantasies of power are fantasies of identity. This point is made very forcefully by a number of chapters in this volume, and it is a point from which it is possible to begin to make sense of the connections between gender, violence, and sexuality.

THEORIZING INTERPERSONAL VIOLENCE

The discussion in the previous section emphasized that there is no single femininity or masculinity for individual women and men to identify with in their social settings, but a variety of possible femininities and masculinities which are provided by the contradictory and competing discourses which exist, and which produce and are reproduced by social practices and institutions. However, sexuality is intimately connected with power in such a way that power and force are themselves sexualized, that is they are inscribed with gender difference and gender hierarchy. This connection does not have to be confined to a discussion of dominant forms of western masculinity or discourses on gender, although it does presuppose the existence of a dominant discourse on gender, which can in theory be an indigenous one. There are two points which arise from this argument. First, femininity and masculinity cannot be taken as singular fixed features which are exclusively located in women and men. We must agree to this if we recognize that subjectivity is non-unitary and multiple, and that it is the product, amongst other things, of the variable discourses and practices concerning gender and gender difference. Women and men come to have different understandings of themselves as engendered persons because they are differentially positioned with regard to discourses concerning gender and sexuality, and they take up different positions within those discourses.

The advantage of a theory which stresses that at any one time there exist competing, potentially contradictory discourses on gender and sexuality rather than a single discourse, is that we can ask the question, how is it that people take up a position in one discourse as opposed to another? If becoming an engendered person is not just a question of acquiescing to or identifying with a single femininity or masculinity, then what is it that makes people take up particular subject positions as opposed to others? What accounts for the differences between people with regard to their self-representations as engendered individuals? Why do men differ from each other with regard to their understanding of masculinity, and why do women differ with regard to their understandings and representations of femininity, of what it is to be a woman?

Wendy Holloway has suggested that we can come to an understanding of what makes people take up certain subject positions by developing a notion of 'investment'. If, at any one time, there exist several competing, possibly contradictory, discourses on femininity and masculinity, then what motivates individuals to take up one subjective position as opposed to another is their degree of 'investment' in a particular subject position. Holloway conceives of an investment as something between an emotional commitment and a vested interest. (Her use of the term has a strong connotation of cathexis.) Such interest or commitment resides in the relative power, conceived of in terms of the satisfaction, reward, or payoff, which a particular subject position promises, but does not necessarily provide (Holloway 1984: 238). It is clear that the term 'investment' could be problematic here because of its economistic overtones. However, it is useful precisely because it allows us to retain a link between questions of power and questions of identity. If we imagine that individuals take up certain subject positions because of the way in which those positions provide pleasure, satisfaction, or reward on the individual or personal level, we must also recognize that such individual satisfactions only have power and meaning in the context of various institutionalized discourses and practices, that is, in the context of certain sanctioned modes of subjectivity. Holloway emphasizes the very important point that taking up a position or variety of positions within competing discourses is not just about the construction of self-identity and subjectivity. She argues that to be positioned is always to be positioned in relation to others, and thus, one's inter-relations with other individuals – intersubjectivity – will also determine what positions one takes up. In addition, there is the question of the institutional power of dominant or hegemonic discourses, where there are very tangible benefits to be gained from constructing oneself as a particular sort of person and interacting with others in specific sorts of ways. It is important to recognize that investment is not just a matter of emotional satisfaction, but of the very real material, social, and economic benefits which are the reward of the senior man, the good wife, the powerful mother, or the dutiful daughter in many social situations. It is for this reason that modes of subjectivity and questions of identity are bound up with issues of power, and with the material benefits which may be consequent on the exercise of that power.

It would be a mistake, however, to represent the process of taking up a subject position as one of simple choice. For one thing, the historical contextualization of discourses means that not all subject positions are equal: some positions carry much more social reward than others, and some are negatively sanctioned. The role of dominant or hegemonic discourses on gender and gender identity are crucial here. The reason being that, while non-dominant discourses certainly provide subject positions and modes of subjectivity which might be individually satisfying and which might challenge or resist dominant modes, those individuals who do challenge or resist the dominant discourses on gender and gender identity frequently find that this is at the expense of such things as social power, social approval, and even material benefits. The same argument may also explain why those in power are so vulnerable to accusations about their sexuality and sexual behaviour. The second reason why the taking-up of a subject position cannot be seen as a matter of choice is linked to the multiple and contradictory nature of subjectivity. The fact that individuals take up multiple subject positions, some of which may contradict each other, obviously cannot be explained in terms of a theory of rational choice. Holloway's notion of investment reminds us of the emotional and sub-conscious motivations for taking up various subject positions. In this context, fantasy, in the sense of ideas about the kind of person one would like to be and the sort of person one would like to be seen to be by others, clearly has a role to play. Such fantasies of identity are linked to fantasies of power and agency in the world. This explains why concepts, such as reputation, are connected not just to self-representations and social evaluations of self, but to the potential for power and agency which a good reputation proffers. The loss of reputation could mean a loss of livelihood, and the lack of good social standing can render individuals incapable of pursuing various strategies or courses of action. The use of the term fantasy is crucial here because it emphasizes the often affective and subconscious nature of investment in various subject positions, and in the social strategies necessary to maintain that investment.

Holloway herself does not discuss the relationship between identity, subjectivity, power, and violence. However, a close reading of a number of papers in this volume suggests a link between the thwarting of investments in various subject positions based on gender and interpersonal violence. Thwarting can be understood as the inability to sustain or properly take up a gendered subject position, resulting in a crisis, real or imagined, of self-representation and/or social evaluation. Such crises can be of various degrees of seriousness and of variable duration. Thwarting can also be the result of contradictions arising from the taking-up of multiple subject positions, and the pressure of multiple expectations about self-identity or social presentation. It may also come about as the result of other persons refusing to take up or sustain their subject positions *vis-à-vis* oneself and thereby calling one's self-identity into question. A phrase such as 'she/he wasn't a proper wife/husband to me' emphasizes the intersubjective nature of questions of gender and gender identity. It is equally a phrase which can cover everything from a failure of sexual relations to the failure of economic provisions. Thus, thwarting can characterize the inability to receive the expected satisfactions or rewards from the taking-up of a particular gendered subject position or mode of subjectivity. It is, of course, not necessary for an individual to have a specific conscious view of what the satisfactions or rewards ought to be for them to experience thwarting.

Many writers in this volume report that violence is often the outcome of an inability to control other people's sexual behaviour, that is other people's management of themselves as engendered individuals. This explains not only violence between women and men, but also between mothers and daughters, between sisters-in-law, and between men themselves. In all such situations, what is crucial is the way in which the behaviour of others threatens the self-representations and social evaluations of oneself. Thus, it is the perpetrator of violence who is threatened and experiences thwarting.

Interestinglyenough, many of the violent events described in this volume occur in situations where the thwarted party is likely to suffer direct material loss, whether in terms of social status or access to economic resources, as a result of the insufficiencies – so perceived – of the victim of the violence. Once again, fantasies of identity are linked to fantasies of power, which helps to explain why violence is so often the result of a perceived, rather than a real, threat. As Christina Toren notes in Chapter 1, wives are frequently beaten for imagined infidelities; a fact which makes violence and the threat of violence so much more effective as a means of social control.

In Chapter 5, Peter Wade's discussion of gender relations and violence in Colombia demonstrates the existence of multiple and contradictory discourses on gender, and the way in which the dominant discourse on gender emphasizes that the differences between women and men are categorical. This chapter is particularly useful because it shows extremely clearly how the goals of identity and personhood are different for women and men, and how engaged individuals are in strategies which invest in and maintain particular self-representations and social evaluations. Dominant discourses, and the differential subject positions which those discourses proffer women and men, work to limit the strategies which individuals can pursue. The clear satisfactions and rewards, many of them actually economic, which follow on the successful management of modes of gendered subjectivity – most particularly for men – are directly demonstrated. The relationship between fantasies of masculine identity and fantasies of power is especially volatile. Men have a clear investment in two competing discourses, one the providing husband/father and the other the *hombre parrandero*. The fantasy of masculine identity is predicated on the ability to balance these two modes. Men, therefore, have to pursue strategies to get their wives to submit to their interests, with the result that there is often conflict between spouses over the man's extra-domestic commitments. Discourses on gender identity, as Wade points out, not only structure relations with women, but also with other men. To be an *hombre parrandero* is a source of prestige among men, as well as an expression of male solidarity. Participation in *parrandas* not only establishes close and affective relations with other men, but it provides a man with a crucial economic network. Thus, successful economic strategies involve successful management of gender identity. The volatile relationship between fantasies of identity and fantasies of power frequently gives rise to violence both between women and men, and between men. The successful man is a man who manages the relationship between the role of husband/father and the *hombre parrandero*, and thus contains and controls his domestic situation, while at the same time keeping up his reputation as a good friend.

The crucial point here is representation and others' interpretation of that representation. The perfect husband and the perfect friend do not exist, but their images and effects must be kept constantly in play. In this sense, violence, when it occurs, is the result of a crisis of representation, as well as the result of conflict between social strategies which are intimately connected to those modes of representation.

Wade's paper emphasizes, as do many others in the volume, that the experience of identity is bound up with the experience of power, and that challenges to the exercise of power, or to its effects in terms of status, strategies, and interests, are perceived as threats to identity. The obverse appears equally true, so that challenges levelled at an individual's gender identity and gender management, specifically as these are reflected in the behaviour of others to whom that individual is closely connected, may be perceived of as a threat to power, position, control, and even assets. Penelope Harvey provides two interesting examples in her paper. The first is of a woman regularly beaten by her husband, who reported that his behaviour could be attributed to the fact that he was seeing another woman, and that this always makes men vicious towards their wives, especially when their lovers are not really under their control. It was significant in this case that the man's lover was also the lover of one of the local policemen. The second is the example of a woman who was severely beaten by her husband, who had allegedly beaten her for all the faults of his other lovers, calling them by name as he did so. In both cases, the violence is explicable as the thwarting of the expected outcome of particular modes of gendered subjectivity. In both cases, the self-representations of the individual men as gendered persons includes the right and the power to have extra-marital relations, as part of a definition of masculinity as active and aggressive, and hierarchically defined in relation to femininity. The wider Andean cultural understanding of complementarity as predicated on hierarchical difference is particularly relevant here, as Harvey points out. However, the ability to pursue extra-marital relations is both a consequence of gender discourses and the hierarchical nature of gender difference, and a confirmation of a gender identity, as well as a particular set of gender relations, which are intimately bound up with those discourses. However, the reality of the situation, as the ethnography makes clear, is that in the context of these specific extra-marital relations, attributes of desirable masculinity far from being confirmed are challenged, perhaps even denied. The men cannot control their lovers as they would wish, they cannot control other men's access to these women, and therefore they cannot control the definition of their own masculinity because they cannot control the definition of or the social practices surrounding the femininity of their lovers. The only women they can control are their wives, and it is they who confirm their husbands' masculinity, by their proper adoption of the opposite feminine subject position, and so their husbands hit them. Once again, violence is the consequence of a crisis in representation, both individual and social. The inability to maintain the fantasy of power triggers a crisis in the fantasy of identity, and violence is a means of resolving this crisis because it acts to reconfirm the nature of a masculinity otherwise denied.

In those social settings, where dominant discourses on gender construct the categories woman and man as mutually exclusive and hierarchically related, the representation of violence itself is highly sexualized, and is inseparable from the notion of gender, and, in particular, from the notion of gender difference. However, gender difference is not the only form of difference employed in the representation of violence. Other forms of difference, notably class and race, are crucial in the formation of discourses on social identity, and will thus be constitutive of modes of subjectivity in the same way as gender. It follows, therefore, that these forms of difference will be strongly implicated in the relationship established between fantasies of power and fantasies of identity. Whenever that relationship is called into question, violence, or the threat of violence, may result. In making this argument, I do not want to fall into the trap of suggesting that all violence is of similar origin, and/or that there is no difference between the forms and degrees of violence, or in terms of its incidence. However, I do want to suggest that in terms of interpersonal violence, and with regard to the relationship between violence and particular forms of difference – gender, race, class – we might come closer to an understanding of the phenomenon if we shift our gaze and move from imagining violence as a breakdown in the social order – something gone wrong – to seeing it as the sign of a struggle for the maintenance of certain fantasies of identity and power. When we come to a final consideration of the relationship between violence and gender, it is clear that violence of all kinds is engendered in its representation, in the way it is thought about and constituted as a social fact. In its enactment as a social practice, therefore, it is part of a discourse, albeit a contradictory and fragmented discourse, about gender difference. The difficult thing to explain is not why gender relations are so violent, but why violence is so gendered, so sexualized.

BIBLIOGRAPHY

Connell, R. (1987) *Gender and Power*, Cambridge: Polity Press.
de Lauretis, T. (1986) *Feminist Studies/Critical Studies*, London: Macmillan.
de Lauretis, T. (1987) *Technologies of Gender: Essays on Theory, Film and Fiction*, London: Macmillan.
Holloway, W. (1984) 'Gender Difference and the Production of Subjectivity', in

Henriques, J. (ed.) *Changing the Subject: Psychology, social regulation and subjectivity*, London: Methuen.

Meigs, A. (1990) 'Multiple Gender Ideologies and Statuses' in Sanday, P. and Goodenough, R. (eds) *Beyond the Second Sex: New directions in the anthropology of gender*, Philadelphia: University of Pennsylvania Press.

Ortner, S. and Whitehead, H. (eds) (1981) *Sexual Meanings*, Cambridge: Cambridge University Press.

Riley, D. (1988) *'Am I that Name?': Feminism and the category of 'women' in history*, London: Macmillan.

Sanday, P. and Goodenough, R. (1990) *Beyond the Second Sex: New directions in the anthropology of gender*, Philadelphia: University of Pennsylvania Press.

Strathern, M. (1987) *Understanding Inequality*, Cambridge: Cambridge University Press.

Strathern, M. (1988) *The Gender of the Gift*, Stanford: Stanford University Press.

Weedon, C. (1987) *Feminist Practice and Poststructuralist Theory*, Oxford: Basil Blackwell.

7   Cultural difference and the lust to kill

Deborah Cameron and Elizabeth Frazer

INTRODUCTION

Henrietta Moore (in this volume) makes a number of important theoretical proposals about violence: that it is engendered in its representation, and that it signifies not a breakdown in the social order but 'a power struggle for the maintenance of (a certain kind of) social order'. It is not therefore surprising, she suggests, if gender relations – which are most often hierarchical and unequal relations – are frequently violent; what is more surprising is the gendered and sexualized nature of violence itself.

We are in broad agreement with Moore on these points, and in the following discussion we examine a type of violence – mass and sexual murder in which the victim is a representative object of desire – which is a particularly apt demonstration of her argument that violence is 'engendered in its representation'. Further, in this instance the discursive process by which a particular form of violence is gendered and eroticized can be traced with some precision; as can the specific power-struggles of which sexual murder is a sign.

In addition, we will consider the question of cultural and historical variation and change. Like other contributors to this volume, we take the social realities of gender and violence to be socially constructed, which entails that our definitions, interpretations, and representations of these phenomena can and do shift; the fact of cultural difference leaves them always open to contestation and challenge. In any society at a given moment, there is a range – though not an unlimited range – of possibilities for gender identity; similarly there might be a contested set of meanings available to deal with violence. Tracing the complex interrelations of these multiple and shifting possibilities is, we argue, a crucial dimension of any satisfactory analysis of any particular social practice.

To illustrate this argument, we consider the emergence of two novel representations of sex murder and mass murder in the late 1980s and early

1990s, one in Britain and one in Japan. In the British case a new stereotype, the murderer as 'body builder', has been elaborated to deal with anxieties about the definition of gender. We see this discursive shift as part of a struggle now going on around the meaning of masculinity. In the Japanese case: a mass murderer (whom in British or US society would be assumed to be a sex murderer in the sense we use that term) is understood to be the product of westernization. Here the struggle is around notions of cultural identity.

Before we turn to these novel representations, it is necessary to place them in the historical context of previous discourse. There has not always and everywhere been sexual murder: we trace it back to discourses emerging out of the cultural and political changes of the European Enlightenment, discourses of violence, masculinity, gender relations, subjectivity, and sexuality. During the nineteenth and twentieth centuries, sex murder has been understood, explained, talked about and indeed experienced in a variety of different ways which we will sketch in the following section.

THE LUST TO KILL[1]

In contemporary society in Britain, the United States and other areas of the modern 'west' all members take for granted the fact that some people kill for sexual gratification. The existence of sex murder and the sex murderer is as unproblematic, for the mundane purposes of social life, as the exis- tence of bushes and trees. We recognize – because it happens all the time – that some people kill compulsively and without having any specific grudge against the particular individuals who become their victims. These individuals are often selected because they are of a certain type: prostitutes, young girls or boys, elderly people, blondes. The killings are not for gain, or jealousy, or revenge; they are animated by desire for a particular type of sexual object. Killings are frequently accompanied by some of a range of associated acts – mutilation, torture, ritualistic treatment of the body.

The canon of clear cases includes a number of famous mass-killings: those of Jack the Ripper, Kürten, the Boston Strangler, Christie, Brady, Sutcliffe, Ted Bundy and Dennis Nilsen, to which we were able to add a large number of equally well-documented cases which are not quite such familiar household names: Ronald Frank Cooper, Ed Kemper, Henry Lee Lucas, John Straffen, Vincent Verzeni and many more. Three things are striking about this list. In the first place it contains not a single woman. Second, none of the cases on it occurred any earlier than 1888. Third, all these men are white, European, North American, South African. It implies that the category 'sexual murder' is distinctively modern, distinctively 'western', and exclusively male.

Our investigation largely bore this out. We made one major theoretical adjustment – we concluded that sex murder is 'masculine', not male, and that it cannot be understood straightforwardly as violence against women because many victims are men or boys. Empirically, we failed to find a single account of a woman killing in a way that could conceivably be construed as sex murder – that is as killing, and often mutilating, a representative object of desire for sexual gratification. Women have killed cruelly, they have killed repeatedly; but they have not done what Peter Sutcliffe did, or John Christie, or Denis Nilsen. The obvious possible counter-example is Myra Hindley: but she acted not alone but as her boyfriend's accomplice, she herself was the masochistic partner of a sadist lover and was photographed by him with the marks of his whip on her back.

We did come across some (recent) incidents of sex murder from outside of the culture of Europe and its white settler descendants – in India, for example, feminists insisted that the showing of Hollywood thrillers in Delhi must have been material in a spate of prostitute murders.[2] The Japanese mass-murder case we consider below is the latest candidate, and the most striking. It seems clear that members of other cultures cannot 'own' sex murder as part of their culture. Of course, our society also denies that sex murder has a social or cultural origin; but, as we shall see, commentators lay the blame on individual sickness, and even supernatural sin – they do not see this form of violence as an import from an alien culture.

Our argument that sex murder is modern has so far not been empirically challenged – we have discussed our thesis with medievalists, historians of the Elizabethan period, and classicists, and have not learned of any account (factual or fictional) of a killing which could be construed as sex murder in those periods. There is an obvious objection to this empirical historical and anthropological thesis: that the 'empirical facts' are themselves theoretical constructs. Just because in the past, and in other contemporary cultures, people didn't, and now don't, describe any killings as sexual murders, doesn't rule out the possibility that the same thing was, or is, going on under a different description. It might equally be that women do the same kind of thing, but when a woman does it it is not understood or interpreted in the same way. Our response to this is that not only the 'empirical facts', but also the empirical *reality* itself, are a theoretical construct. A proper description of a human action includes the meaning of the action for the actor him or herself, and this subjective meaning of an action is itself inter-subjective, or cultural, in origin. Between the Elizabethans and ourselves lie a number of highly influential discourses – psychiatry, sexology, criminology – which have redefined our notions of sexuality and crime. It is these ways of conceptualizing and understanding that enable us to think of murders as sexual, enables murder *to be* sexual, and enables men to commit sexual murder, to take on the role of sex murderer, while such a role and such a desire is effectively debarred to women.

FEMINIST CRITIQUE OF SEX MURDER

In our research for *The Lust to Kill* we set out to investigate sex murder from a feminist perspective. We initially saw it as a particular and extreme form of male violence against women, a phenomenon which functions materially and symbolically to maintain women's subordination to men. We wanted to expose its misrepresentation in journalism, popular culture, and social and medical science, where, like rape, it is presented as a matter of individual pathology and never as having any systematic political effect, where disproportionate attention is paid to the victims' behaviour rather than the perpetrators', and where the possibility that norms and ideals of masculinity might invite criticism is never addressed.

Our research strategy, and our strategy for organizing our argument in the book, was to submit extant explanations and accounts of sex murder to feminist critique. Our reading of popular culture and journalism, art, philosophy, social, medical and biological science, sexology, psychiatry and psycho-analysis exposed two broad accounts of what sex murder is and why sex murderers do it – either the sex murderer is a pathological deviant committing lamentable crimes, or he is a celebrated hero flouting social convention and the forces of law and order. In most discourses both of these accounts co-exist. Popular journalism, for example, tends to harp endlessly on the murderer's heroic status – giving him names like 'The Ripper' or 'The Beast', emphasizing his uniqueness and isolation in his contest with the police and society, putting him at the centre of a narrative and inviting readers (read: masculine readers) to, to some degree, identify with him, to thrill to his exploits. At the same time journalists have to condemn the horrible crimes, and have to introduce psychological or criminological theories of deviance and pathology in readiness for the day when a perfectly ordinary and uninspiring man of decidedly *un*heroic proportions appears between two police officers. Other discourses, for example biological science and existentialist philosophy, emphasize one account to the exclusion of the other.

From a feminist point of view, these two accounts – seemingly logically opposed or at least in severe tension with one another – can be deconstructed. They can be shown to share a refusal to engage with the gender systematicity of sexual murder – the fact that the murderer is a man is at one and the same time presupposed (not deemed worthy of comment) and yet obscured. They also share an assumption that the roots of this kind of violence lie in individual pathology, not in the social–cultural context. It is sex murder's rootedness in cultural context, its roots deep in modern patriarchal society, that we want to expose.

SEX MURDER AND ENLIGHTENMENT THOUGHT

Our argument is that the category, the idea, and the act of 'sex murder' is only possible by virtue of the existence and influence of a series of discourses – psychiatry, sexology, and criminology among them. The discourses in question have their roots in the European Enlightenment, and are underpinned by Enlightenment philosophy and its derivatives: a gendered philosophy of the subject, focused on the dilemma of Man who finds himself the object of science at the same moment that he finds himself master of the universe. The man who knows that he is subject to social forces and conditioning knows that being the subject of his own life and destiny, being an actor (rather than a behaver), is problematic. Enlightenment and post-Enlightenment philosophy's endless preoccupation with freedom is explained thus: no sooner had men shaken off the yoke of political subjection by displacing God and the divinely ordained king, no sooner had they asserted the moral and metaphysical pre-eminence of the individual over the collectivity, than they found their shoulders bowed by the weight of subjection to social forces.

In *The Lust to Kill* we trace connections between responses to this problem of freedom and individualism, and redefinitions of the sexual and the erotic. This is not hard to do: in the work of de Sade, the Romantics, and the twentieth-century Existentialists, the link is quite explicitly spelled out. The human condition is one of miserable subjection to political and social forces; the morally brave and authentic will strive to transcend their situation and act freely; transcendence involves transgression – of social norms, conventions – against authority and expectations; it also involves mastery over oneself and others (making oneself a true Subject); the most cherished social conventions are those governing sexuality; so acting freely on sexual desire is transgressive, and to act freely on sexual desire is to unleash the sexual master in oneself – 'Do not all passions require victims?' asks de Sade rhetorically. Another cherished social convention is the taboo on murder: so to murder can be to violate the ultimate taboo and thus, by definition, to act freely. In these writings there is a twist in the reasoning which moves from the erotic being transgressive, to all transgression being erotic and beautiful. We see here how the powerful link between violence, murder, and eroticism is forged. The Romantics developed this into a full-blown aesthetics.

We argue that the nineteenth and twentieth-century 'scientific' discourses, and lay understandings and experience of sexuality in this culture, carry traces of this complex link between individual freedom, domination, transgression, the erotic, and the beautiful. We may be appalled at the acts of Peter Sutcliffe, we may shrink from the thought of acting so ourselves, but they do make sense.

This 'we', though, needs unpacking. The Enlightenment understanding of freedom as inhering in transcendence of social and bodily conditions has effectively made freedom a masculine project; and Enlightenment philosophy articulated the subjectivity–objectivity dichotomy along with the dichotomies of freedom and boundedness, culture and nature, rationality and emotion, in terms of masculinity and femininity.[3] Men's and women's fit with their culture's conceptions of masculinity and femininity is clearly never perfect. But as a matter of philosophy as well as a matter of fact women have not been likely to unleash the sexual master in themselves, to act on their passions by subjugating victims, or to understand and enact subjectivity by transgressing and transcending the social. In this particular human drama the role of sex murderer is always taken by a man. It means that men in our culture have the option (which some of them take up) of taking the sex murderer role. It means that men have the option of identifying with the sex murderer (during the time of the Yorkshire Ripper football crowds chanted 'There's only one Yorkshire Ripper', and 'Ripper eleven, Police nil'). (This is, of course, a matter of social relationships as well as a matter of philosophy.)

DISCOURSE AND SEX MURDER

We have argued that a particular set of modern themes underpin a commonsensical intertwining of transgression, murder, mastery or subjectivity, and eroticism. These themes are systematically (at the most basic philosophical level) connected with masculinity. We want to make it clear that we do not intend to suggest that this be understood as the hegemonic conception of masculinity or the erotic – modern western culture is highly complex and differentiated; gender, eroticism and freedom are all contested concepts. Nevertheless, it is a powerful conception, and one which chimes with dominant codes of masculinity. Its traces can be read in all sorts of cultural products, surface in all sorts of discourses, and shape, at least partially, much of our experience. It is particularly interesting that the concepts we are discussing surface in the understandings, accounts and explanations of sex murderers themselves.

Clearly the accounts of their actions elicited from sex murderers in court, or by journalists, have to be read extremely carefully, and cannot be understood as a perspicuous and straightforward story of how things really were with them. When Peter Sutcliffe says he was cleaning up the streets, or when a wife-killer says 'I really loved her', he is employing an already encoded formula, a generic convention, learned in society, with a social origin. Our attention cannot focus on the causal connections which brought about the set of bodily perturbations we understand as sex murder; it must perforce focus on the codes, conventions, understandings and discourses, which organize an action, and which organize also an actor's understanding of his own action, his account of it to others, and our understanding of him. That Norman Collins, killer of seven women in Michigan, wrote a college essay on the theme of the individual's duty to make his own choices 'regardless of what society thinks may be right or wrong' (and his professor later said that Collins had always seemed 'completely normal'); that Denis Nilsen said that he 'worshipped the art and the act of death over and over' (in true Romantic style); that Ian Brady has expanded at length on the significance of Dostoevsky's Raskolnikov in his life and career as a sadistic murderer – these instances tell us a great deal about our culture, and a great deal about the cultural nature of persons and their acts. In this sense, sex murder is a discursive phenomenon.

But discourse and representation and sex murder are linked in another way too: it is notable that sex murderers seem to have a powerful urge to render their deeds in representation and discourse. Ted Bundy, recently executed in the United States, rounded off his account of his murderous career prior to his death, achieving 'narrative closure'. Denis Nilsen also wrote and wrote, and drew, obsessively, while he was on remand, trying to make a satisfactory account of what he had done. Ronald Frank Cooper kept several diaries in which he fantasized about and planned his murders, and in which he made numerous accounts of the events. Think of Brady's photographs and tapes of his victims' deaths. Denis Nilsen took photos of the corpses with a polaroid camera. In our view this urge to authorship is also connected with Enlightenment individualism – the construction of self as a narrative persona, as the hero of a text, as the author of an authorized version of one's life, is a distinctively modern and western cultural phenomenon, closely connected with modern forms of subjectivity, with transcendence and mastery.

We are now going to discuss two distinct examples in which the discourses surrounding sex murder have been taken up in historically and culturally specific ways. We first discuss a development in journalistic and courtroom discourses of sex murder which has occurred since *The Lust to Kill* was published. A link has been made between sexual crime and body building, martial arts and other ways of working out. Second, we discuss reports of a series of murders in Japan which demonstrate the understanding of sex murder as of specifically western origin, and also show how (as with other imports) it can take on a specifically local form.

THE BODY BUILDER: A NEW SEX CRIMINAL?

On 14 April 1989 *The Guardian* reported that Tony Maclean, the 'Notting Hill Rapist', is the most recent in a lengthening line of sex criminals who are also martial arts experts or, as in his case, body builders. The list includes Peter Chmilowskyj whose conviction for kidnapping and rape in 1987 was headlined 'Life for Bodybuilder who Repeatedly Raped Women' by *The Guardian*.

If journalists are anything to go by, recent years in Britain have seen a startling increase in crimes of sexual violence committed by body builders. The phenomenon was prefigured in the case of Peter Sutcliffe, who used weights to improve his 'soft' physique. But body building really came into its own in the reporting of the 'M4 Rapist' John Steed, convicted of rape and murder in November 1986. At Steed's trial much was made of his 'fanatical' body building and use of anabolic steroids. From then on, journalists' research has frequently uncovered a connection between pumping iron and sex crime. Quality papers often mention rapists' and killers' body building in their reports, while the more popular tabloid papers use phrases like 'the crazed body builder', the 'body building psychopath' and 'the muscleman'.

The body builder is a new addition to the gallery of familiar characters who have been evoked in crime reporting since the days of the broadside and the penny dreadful: the 'beast', the 'monster', the 'fiend' and the 'maniac' (the 'psychopath' is a more recent 'scientific' addition). The invocation of these stock figures – whose most important shared characteristic is that they are sub- or extra-human, like animals and demons – has always perpetuated the comforting illusion that sex crimes are not committed by ordinary 'normal' people like ourselves, our boyfriends, fathers and brothers (for although it is seldom explicitly pointed out, the 'beast' and the 'monster' are invariably *male*). These representations are important for the mythical causal relations they evoke: sex crime is understood as an animal impulse periodically 'breaking out'. Or, it is even seen as an incomprehensible, inexorable madness, with supernatural origins. This rhetoric of 'the sex beast' obviously precludes any real understanding, since it directs our attention away from the social relations of gender inequality which are the context for all sex crime.

In the light of this the body builder might seem to be an improvement on these traditional fiends and monsters. Body building, after all, is a human activity; more precisely, an activity connected with a certain version of masculinity – part of an obsession with the body, with proving one's manhood through endurance, strength, and power. Making a connection between this culturally constructed masculine image and sexual violence is, on the face of it, a step in the right direction; it seems to offer a *social* and cultural explanation of sexual violence. In the event, however, this new representation still does not entail real critique of our culture's standards of masculinity. This is because there is a twist in the story: in many *causes célèbres* as reported by the press, the body building superman, apparently the acme of self-assured masculinity, turns out to be a wimp or a pansy in disguise. This account not only consigns sex criminals once again to the realm of the abnormal; it asserts that their abnormality consists in a failure to be truly or properly masculine.

Sutcliffe, for instance, allegedly took to body building not as an expression of his confident masculinity, but because he was extremely anxious about it. He had reason to be anxious, in the opinion of his family: as his father put it, 'he was a right mother's boy from the word go', the sort of oversensitive weakling who gets sand kicked in his face. John Steed was also obsessed with a stereotypical masculine image, and it is even hinted in some reports that his crimes were caused by the steroids he took (the old 'rampaging hormones' explanation of sex crime). Body building in these instances is treated as a symptom of a deep and well-founded insecurity about whether one is a 'real man'. The multiple killer (and 'fanatical body builder') Michele Lupo, convicted in 1987, was said to be 'obsessed with his looks'. Even Michael Ryan, the Hungerford mass killer who modelled himself on the character of Rambo, was thoroughly scrutinized for effeminate tendencies; commentators dwelt on his lack of a girlfriend, and his unhealthy relationship with his mother.

This discourse implies that crimes of sexual and other extreme violence are committed by men who are not really men: weaklings, mothers' boys, perverts, and queers. They are also obsessive, fanatical. The problem, in other words, lies not in our culture's definitions of masculinity – what cultural critics might see as crass hero-worship of violent macho bullies, and an endless conflation of sex, power and death. Instead, the problem is the failure of some men to measure up to those definitions. Instead of clarifying issues of male violence, the 'body builder' stereotype clouds them further. Worse, it casts suspicion on 'new men' and gay men who pose a challenge to cherished notions of manhood.

In addition this fixation directs our attention away from what we might consider to be the really extraordinary fact about Tony Maclean – that he was a very ordinary looking married man and father of two, socially and psychologically indistinguishable from thousands of others. His obsessiveness and fanaticism and his psychological abnormality are only seen with hindsight. In reality scientists have not found that rapists and other sex criminals are different in any particular or systematic way from the mass of ordinary men – apart, that is, from the massive fact of what they do.

'JAPAN BLAMES CHILD KILLINGS ON AFFLUENCE'

The news item reproduced overleaf reports an horrific series of murders, rapes and violent attacks against children. The liberal daily newspaper *Asahi Shimbun* received grotesque letters graphically describing the murder of a four-year-old (presumably from her killer, who also took polaroid photographs of the little girl's body and sent them to her parents) and wrote that Japan's recent affluence has been accompanied by 'some sort of distortion or imbalance in the minds of some people'. A social scientist claimed that the killings pointed to the 'Americanization' of Japanese society.

It is clear from this that the fact that people do commit this kind of violence is not part of Japanese common sense. In Britain, by contrast, this kind of bafflement and outrage would hardly be expressed by a news editor – the familiar combination of rapes and multiple murders would obviously be taken to be the acts of a Sex Beast. Here, then, an explicit link between a particular form of violence and western culture is made. We would argue, though, that this account is still mystificatory, as it focuses on urbanization, affluence, and presumably individualism, while ignoring gender. Here also is a notable example of the urge to discourse that we have already mentioned – the urge to narrative, to authorship – by the murderer who also, interestingly, adopts what is clearly a persona, the (female) pseudonym itself also signifying authorship.

It is notable that the *Asahi Shimbun* leader writer put forward a social and cultural account of how these appalling crimes have come to be committed. This is practically unknown in western journalism – although feminist protests and analysis during the Yorkshire Ripper era did have some effect on some papers. Nevertheless, there are two things to notice. First, social analysis seemingly is acceptable if it is not *one's own* cherished cultural ideals and social arrangements which are being vitiated. As we have seen, western journalists (and experts) invariably have recourse to explanations in terms of the individual's pathology, to concepts like Beast, Fiend, and Monster, which strongly suggest that sex murderers are the manifestation of supernatural forces (and in no way the product of modern western culture itself). Second, however, it is, in the end, individual pathology which is invoked in this editorial: irritation, dissatisfaction with no outlet, distortion and imbalance 'in the minds of some people'.

Japan blames child killings on affluence

Lisa Martineau in Tokyo

A man was arrested in Tokyo yesterday for killing an 11-year-old girl, the latest in a series of murders, rapes and violent attacks on children that has left the country stunned and horrified.

Japan considers itself "child-centred" and this fourth murder of a child this week has provoked much soul-searching.

Japan's affluence had been accompanied by "some sort of distortion or imbalance in the minds of some people," the liberal daily Asahi Shimbun wrote in an impassioned editorial. "These crimes represent the dark side [of our modern society] . . . where irritation and dissatisfaction has no outlet."

The paper probably had in mind Tokyo's overcrowded but affluent suburbs in which recently two four-year-old girls have been murdered, two others are missing presumed murdered, 15 toddlers have been stabbed and seriously wounded by a knife-wielding assailant on a bicycle, and almost 40 attempted abductions of children have been reported to the police.

The National Police Agency (NPA) has declared it is in "a state of emergency" over the crimes, which one social scientist claims point to the "Americanisation" of Japanese society.

The case that has won the most attention is that of Mari Konno, the four-year-old girl whose burnt remains were dumped in a cardboard box outside her parents' front door last month. She had been abducted six months earlier.

Inside the box there were also two polaroid photographs of the girl, taken after she had been murdered.

The murderer, writing as a woman called "Yuko Imada", sent two grotesque letters to the parents with copies to the Asahi.

In the first letter the murderer – whose name can be read as a pun on the words "I am telling the story now" – claims to have lost her own child in an accident. As she, due to "complications following a caesarean", was unable to have another child she took Mari and then felt an overwhelming urge to kill her – which she graphically describes.

In the second letter, which arrived on the day of Mari's funeral, the murderer told the parents that the remains of her own child, whom she had also burnt, were mixed up with Mari's in the cardboard box, and that she was glad both would now "have a proper funeral".

Although the letter is written in "women's language" – a politer and more stylised form of Japanese – neither the police nor the parents believe that Mari's killer is a woman.

The Guardian, 24 March 1989

It is also striking that gender is erased from this analysis. Even though the female variety of Japanese is used in the letters, the police believe that Mari's killer is a man; a man has been arrested for killing an eleven-year-old girl; and yet the paper uses sex-neutral language and refers to 'people'. Is it possible that the 'knife-wielding assailant on a bicycle' is a woman? – surely if this were the case we would be told. The obvious question, the question that cries out for explanation, is Why? Why do *men* turn to this form of violence? Why only men? Why not women? This is still not a question whose salience is widely accepted. The gender of these killers is both assumed, taken for granted, and glossed over.

The photographs, the letters, the killer's pseudonym which signifies 'I am telling the story now', the taking up of a literary persona, strike us forcefully as fitting in the most extraordinary way with our analysis of authorship and mastery. But this begs the questions of the place and meaning of writing, discourse and representation in Japanese culture. For clearly here we have a meeting of two cultures, and the emergence of a specific form of this kind of killing. In this connection – what is the significance of the writer of the letters posing as a woman who has an overwhelming urge to kill a child after her own is lost in an accident? Is this the invocation of a culturally familiar and perfectly understandable motivation given a grotesque twist? Has Japan now imported from the west the lust to kill?

WHY IS VIOLENCE GENDERED AND SEXUALIZED?

Particularly during the 1980s, feminists have grappled with the theoretical question whether sex and violence are linked in some necessary, trans-cultural, and transhistorical relation. The claim that they are is, of course, present in many common-sense discourses, and it has been elaborated 'scientifically', most notoriously by sociobiology. We will have little to say here about discourses that ground the sex-violence link in biology, since anthropologists (and almost all feminists) agree in rejecting purely biological accounts. Instead we will consider the more interesting argument that while the sex-violence link is culturally constructed it is still necessary, and perhaps even a cultural universal.

The most influential non-biological argument for a necessary sex/violence connection is the psychoanalytic argument that love and rage, desire and hatred become entwined at a deep psychic level through the infantile experience of absolute dependence on the mother (this also explains, or purports to explain, why women are the prototypical objects of both desire and violence). It is, of course, a matter of dispute whether this psychoanalytic account should be regarded as universally valid for all times and places, or whether the claim that sex and violence are linked must be taken as specific to the social and family structures that are typical of or normative for the people of the modern west.

Even if we concentrate on the more modest claim, the non-universal version of the psychoanalytic argument that violence is necessarily erotic, our own analysis of the lust to kill leads us to reject it. We would want to reject any analysis of violence that suggests it is an undifferentiated phenomenon: there are different forms of violence with differing histories and meanings, and the assumption that all of them have the same ultimate source in the infant's contradictory impulses towards her mother seems to us hopelessly reductive and unrevealing.

For example, as we traced the history and elucidated the meaning of sexual murder, we were compelled to acknowledge – despite our deep, politically-motivated resistance to the idea – that the lust to kill cannot even be bracketed in any simple way with other forms of 'male violence' such as rape or the beating and killing of wives. Certainly there are points of resemblance, and they are important ones for feminist political organizing. But in the final analysis, the lust to kill is distinctive, the product of a highly specific historical/discursive conjuncture.

Although this point is more obvious with regard to sex murder than it is in a case like wife-beating (which is so widespread as to appear almost universal) we would argue that it holds in principle for all forms of violence. And this begs the question: In what sense is it useful to explain this complexity, this specificity, in terms of some single factor or universal narrative? Even if, for the sake of argument, we were to take it as axiomatic that violence and sexuality are inescapably conflated in the construction of human subjects, this would still tell us nothing whatever about the processes whereby the potential for eroticized violence is taken up in specific cultural practices. Conversely, if we pay close attention to the processes and practices themselves, there does not appear to be a major gap which the psychoanalyst's axiom is needed to fill.

To sum up, then, we would regard the project of explaining 'violence in general' as inherently misguided; and we would claim that theories which assert a necessary connection between violence and the erotic, such as psychoanalysis, are not capable of explaining violence in more specific terms.

It is also very often true that general accounts of violence as erotic, again including psychoanalytic accounts, neglect the equally important point that many forms of eroticized violence are also gendered. In psychoanalytic theory, all of us harbour both desire for our mothers and murderous impulses towards them. In practice, however, it is only men who kill for sexual pleasure; and we have yet to read a psychoanalytic account addressing this point seriously. For example, Flora Rheta Schreiber's Freudian reading of the 'Shoemaker' Joseph Kallinger is very convincing in its detailed treatment of Kallinger's childhood experiences shaping his fantasies and shaping his killings,[4] but it depends on our agreeing *not* to ask the question 'Would a girl in the same position have become a sexual killer?' In fact, Schreiber herself has given the world a famous account of a girl – 'Sybil' – who was in a somewhat similar position, and who became not a sexual killer but a multiple personality.[5] Psychoanalysis is not, of course, in the business of prediction, but it surely does owe us some account of the overwhelming gender asymmetry in the ranks of sexual murderers.

What the case of Kallinger indicates to us, once again, is that forms of violence are produced within discursive *conjunctures*. The lust to kill, for instance, is constituted by an interaction of discourses of subjectivity, sexuality, and gender (and also, as the Japanese press was partly right to point out, urbanization and industrialization – a classic 'stalker' or 'serial killer' cannot operate within social spaces where everyone knows everyone and there is no mobility). Only by considering all the discourses in play (and as we have noted already, they are liable to shift and change) can we arrive at a satisfactory account. It is a serious problem with applying 'grand theories' like psychoanalysis, or for that matter sociobiology, to phenomena like sex murder that they fail to capture this interplay of different factors.

It is obviously possible, within the framework we have outlined here, that shifts in the discourses of gender and subjectivity might permit the emergence of a female sex killer. We would however predict that the behaviour of such a murderer would be constrained by the historical gendered form of the subject–object relation: in other words, that women sexual murderers will choose children or other women, rather than men, as their victims. There is an interplay not only of different discourses, but of discursive representations, with actual social relations, to which we must also pay attention.

Finally, just as we cannot assume that all forms of violence are gendered and sexualized in exactly the same way, so we also cannot assume that similar instances of violence in different cultures have the exact same constitution – the same history, the same meaning, the same social function and effect. The Japanese sex murders discussed above are a case in point. How far they are a local form drawing on 'indigenous masculinities' and how far they are an imported western form is a question that cannot be answered without thorough historical and anthropological investigation of the discourses and practices in circulation in Japan.

In our view, the Japanese case does show some evidence of cultural diffusion. The lust to kill depends on a particular conception of the individual and of his (*sic*) relation to society which is the dominant conception of personhood in western societies; given the dynamism and the hegemonizing tendency of western ideas, it is unsurprising if this notion of individual personhood is making inroads in non-western cultures. On the other hand, the case of 'Yuko Imada' has features which may be culturally specific, and which are certainly untypical of western cases. The murderer's use of a female person who tells a story about the loss of her own child is especially striking because in the western heartlands of the lust to kill it would make no sense. In Japan it might not make sense for the murderer to *be* a woman, but it does apparently make sense for him to be *represented* as one; whereas no western sexual killer since Jack the Ripper has been represented as female, and the only western woman ever to be tried for sexual killing, Myra Hindley, was represented either as Brady's dupe, a woman but not a killer, or else as his evil genius, the killer who abdicated her womanhood.

It seems then that 'Yuko Imada' is both similar to and different from his western counterparts. It is to historical and discursive processes that we must look in order to account for both the similarities and the differences. More broadly, while feminists must continue to make abstract theoretical and practical political links, we must understand the relation between sexuality and violence as one mediated by cultural difference.

NOTES

1 The analysis of this chapter is worked out in more detail in Cameron and Frazer (1987).
2 Gothoskat (1986).
3 For elaboration of this argument see *inter alia*: Jaggar (1983), Lloyd (1984), Pateman (1989).
4 Schreiber (1984).
5 Schreiber (1975).

BIBLIOGRAPHY

Cameron, Deborah and Frazer, Elizabeth (1987) *The Lust to Kill: a feminist investigation of sexual murder*, Cambridge: Polity Press.
Gothoskat, Sujata (1986) 'An Interview on Feminist Action against Violence in India', *Trouble and Strife* 8.
Jaggar, Alison M. (1983) *Feminist Politics and Human Reason*, Brighton: Harvester Press.
Lloyd, Genevieve (1984) *The Man of Reason: 'Male' and 'Female' in western philosophy*, London: Methuen.
Pateman, Carole (1989) *The Disorder of Women*, Cambridge: Polity Press.

Schreiber, Flora Rheta (1975) *Sybil: The True Story of a Woman Possessed by Sixteen Separate Personalities*, Harmondsworth: Penguin.

Schreiber, Flora Rheta (1984) *The Shoemaker: Anatomy of a Psychotic*, Harmondsworth: Penguin.

8 What counts as rape?

Physical assault and broken contracts: contrasting views of rape among London sex workers

Sophie Day

INTRODUCTION

Talk of sexual violence is topical. Harassment at work is mentioned along-side marital rape and the abuse of children. Rape, the topic of this chapter, is generally seen as a moral as well as a physical assault, particularly by feminist scholars advocating legal change. Thus:

> We are saying that our rape laws should reflect the perspective of women – the victims of rape. They experience rape as an *assault, as an unprovoked attack on their physical person and as a transgression of their assumed right to the exclusive ownership and control of their own bodies* . . . .
>
> (Clark and Lewis 1977: 166–7)

The law reform commission of Canada reads:

> The concept of sexual assault more appropriately characterizes the actual nature of the offence of rape because the primary focus is on the assault or the *violation of the integrity of the person* rather than the sexual intercourse.
>
> (Law Reform Commission of Canada, Sexual Offences, p.16, quoted in Temkin 1986) [my emphasis]

Rape is commonly understood to refer to non-consensual sex and, more narrowly, non-consensual intercourse. At the same time, the nature of this lack of consensus is disputed. Prostitute women in London operate a definition of rape at work which is much broader than the majority view and broader, too, than their own view of rape outside work. These two kinds of rape have different effects on a prostitute's person.

Prostitute women in London distinguish working sex from personal sexual relationships. It is suggested that work involves a broad 'inclusive' definition of rape which is documented below by reference to the 'broken contract'. This refers equally to physical assaults, cheques that bounce, and the duplicity involved when a client deliberately removes a condom. In contrast, prostitutes' personal relationships involve a more 'exclusive' view which is similar to other common ideas about rape. By 'exclusive', I intend to refer to a naturalistic understanding of sexual violence which is seen in the use or threat of force that will be visible in the body of a victim. Rape is seen or anticipated in the physical marks left after the event. This view 'excludes' (other) 'broken contracts' and may be related to general ideas about sex, which are embraced by prostitutes too in their personal relationships. Sex is often seen precisely as that which is not rational, nor explicitly negotiated. The difficulties of negotiating terms for sex have been amply documented in recent studies of condom use: numerous reports suggest that men and women find it very difficult to discuss the terms of their relationship.[1] Generally, sexual relations are seen to unfold or happen; notions of consensus remain implicit and assumed. Therefore, it may be difficult to attach legalistic notions of consensus retrospectively to a context in which, at the time, they were irrelevant. Since the basis for consensual sex was never explicitly negotiated, its breach must be sought in some incontrovertible evidence; in physical nature; that is, in the body, and in a form that permits no argument.

While the use of the single term to describe sexual violence suggests continuities, this chapter explores these contrasting senses of rape. Rape outside work is constructed differently from rape at work: it is also generally seen to constitute a more extreme violation. A second point of contrast is not explored at length below: rape involving physical violence in whatever context is likewise seen as a worse kind of rape than other forms.

The data in this chapter derive from interviews and conversations with sex workers during a research project on lifestyles and sexually transmitted infections from 1986–91. This research was based largely in a medical setting where a medical service, counselling, and a drop-in centre were also provided.[2] In what follows, I describe individual episodes and cite verbatim accounts in the manner of much ethnographic writing. I had thought of excluding these examples because they can be seen to confirm common representations of prostitutes as victims and marginals. However, I decided to preserve this detail because it is through such accounts that I reached the conclusions presented and because, hopefully, the examples allow prostitutes to speak for themselves.

DIFFERENT KINDS OF SEX

In order to understand ideas about rape, it is necessary first to elucidate distinctions between various sexual activities. Prostitutes I have met associate certain types of sex with work and others with their personal lives.

London prostitutes constantly reiterate that they are doing business; they are working. These claims suggest that sex can be sold through a process that constitutes legitimate work. At the same time, women distinguish certain sexual activities associated with a public domain of work from others which are not sold and which belong instead to the private domain of women's personal relationships.[3] Sex work, like other kinds of work, is demarcated in a complex and variable fashion but, for the purposes of this section, I emphasize the radical separation between different sexual activities. First of all, working sex is almost invariably framed by reference to price, a price that is negotiated by reference to units of time and particular services. Second, work tends to be restricted to a 'workplace', be this a particular street, sauna, or rented flat. Sometimes, women work at home, but they make sure to distinguish the place of work within their home by using separate rooms or beds or even covers. Jean,[4] for example, marks work through an apparently minor change involving three towels:

> My boyfriend hates it. He says he don't want no punter in his bed. *But, it's not my bed.* I have three towels. I put one over the pillow, one over the mattress and there's one for him to wash with. Nobody except for clients ever touches those towels and they're even washed separately.

Third, working sex is almost always distanced further from any personal involvement by means of physical barriers. Condoms are the most important of these barriers but they are frequently combined with lubricants and spermicides, caps, sponges and purely contraceptive devices, namely, the coil (IUD) or pill (OCP). While these barriers are seen to offer protection from sexually transmitted infections and related problems of infertility, they equally create a distance between the self and a stranger. As Jane says:

> I don't want strangers' semen inside. I only drop the barrier with someone I really love.

Fourth, the type of sex sold is generally restricted. Some women prefer to sell vaginal sex because 'it requires no effort'. Others prefer to sell oral sex because it is quicker. A few do not sell intercourse[5] at all. Many women who work in saunas offer only 'hand relief' or masturbation. Others, often working by telephone or privately, refuse all physical contact with their customers to sell fantasies of various kinds. While the restrictions on working activities vary, two very general types of discrimination might be noted. First, the body often has its 'private' and 'public' parts so that the mouth, for example, comes to be aligned with an upper and private part of the body that is kept out of the work process as far as possible. Some women say that they have oral sex with their boyfriends but never at work. Interestingly, this is described as the only type of private sex for a few women in the study. The back is also private and vulnerable. Some prostitutes report passive anal sex at home but never at work. They say boyfriends can be trusted; clients would hurt you. Second, what is sold is divested of any nurturing qualities. Thus, women will not kiss or cuddle their clients. In this way, penetration at work is distinguished from sexual intimacy in other relationships. This intimacy might be seen in terms of an inner person that is separated from the exterior working body.

Fifth, sexual pleasure is avoided. Women describe arousal with some embarrassment, referring perhaps to that one exception involving the client who became a boyfriend, even a husband.

Sixth, working sex is a non-reproductive sex. Logically, this must be the result of activities that are clothed in latex and which, for some women, exclude vaginal intercourse. However, sex workers frequently describe their personal relationships in terms that suggest reproduction is a natural consequence of sex at home and they draw a contrast with the work process, which must never lead to children.

Working sex is demarcated in further ways. The women I know seem particularly skilled at juggling a variety of personal names together with different looks – wigs, colouring, wardrobes, make-up. Orgasms, personal biographies, likes and dislikes are fabricated just like the detailed fantasies that are so often constructed for sale. Other distinctions include contrasts based on colour and gender. For example, some women describe them-selves as lesbians; they have sex with men at work and with women for pleasure.

These are the criteria most commonly used to define work. Sex is priced and circumscribed in place and time. Activities are restricted, protected by latex, and dissociated from pleasure and reproduction. These processes may create such a gulf between working and other types of sex that the former come to be known purely as work and the term sex is reserved for other personal relationships.

Personal sexual activities are contrasted with working practices along all the dimensions I have mentioned. Sex takes place at home, it is rarely restricted to particular parts of the body and physical barriers are avoided. There is no talk of time or money. Sexual pleasure is important and may be associated with a usually potential or future motherhood. Some form of contraception, other than condoms, is often used in private relationships but it is anticipated that sex will eventually lead to reproduction. What happens at home is the opposite of what happens at work and vice versa. These differences do not merely provide points of contrast. All the con-trasts described, such as the use of condoms at work but not at home, the absence of oral contact at work and its presence at home, the type of partner seen at work as opposed to private partners and so forth, are ideally constitutive of two distinct types of sex. This point is illustrated in the following two examples. The first concerns condom use. A woman expressed horror at the thought of using barriers with her boyfriend:

> How could I? He would be like a client. It's different for people who don't work [i.e. sell sex].[6]

The second concerns a woman's behaviour from the perspective of one key personal relationship. Anna had separated from her boyfriend and returned to the project after a visit to the USA. She said that she had not been behaving like herself. She had been drinking a lot and, on one occasion, lost her temper and forgot what happened next. She described a number of unprotected sexual contacts on holiday with men who were neither clearly 'clients' nor 'boyfriends'. Her visit to the project suggested that things would change. Anna asked about the risks (in the context, this referred to risks of HIV infection) from oral sex without condoms and then decided once more to insist on condom use for oral sex. It was at this point that we learned of the reappearance of the boyfriend and Anna explained:

> Most working girls take to drink or drugs. They haven't got anything to keep themselves for. I've got him.

This comment might be interpreted in relation to Anna's recent experiences. Distance and safety at work have become important once more in relation to Anna's private life, which has just been re-established.

It is beyond the scope of this chapter to describe the difficulties women experience in separating working and personal sexual relationships. Most women, however, worry that private sexual partners may be drawn into the work domain. In particular, an underlying dynamic suggests that women may be paid for sex by customers only to pay their personal partners in turn. Comments suggest that this logic is only explicitly formulated with respect to unsuccessful and past relationships. Thus, one woman describes a past boyfriend:

> My pimp had at least three other women. It's like having company [i.e., having a pimp]. While you're on call [from an agency], it's like turning you into a client.

This woman is saying that, in the past, she paid her 'pimp', implicitly, for his company just as clients paid her. This relationship developed through her work – it was boring to be 'on call', to wait for work from an agency at the end of a telephone. Others claim that boyfriends get paid twice when they enjoy sex for free and a living from prostitutes' earnings. Because of these difficulties, a minority of women embrace 'celibacy', at least in the short-term. At times, however, some women point to the positive aspects of these generally unwelcome continuities between different sexual activities. One woman, for example, described how she won back her boyfriend simply because she was good at sex. Another, who enjoyed role-play in her private life with women, explained how her experiences enabled her to develop a particular working style in domination, which she enjoyed.

These examples illustrate great diversity in the construction of sex work. However, for the purposes of this chapter, I have emphasized the mutual construction of working and private sex through a sense of opposition and contrast. This division shows that sexual activity is not all of one piece. It seems that constantly shifting boundaries are negotiated between those aspects of the sexual which can be alienated from the person and those which remain integral to a sense of self. Ideally, the two types of sex should remain quite distinct although, in practice, this separation is hard to achieve. Ideas about rape are best understood in the context of this emphatic demarcation of sexual activities.

RAPE AND WORK

The broad or inclusive view of rape that I have mentioned, which inheres in the broken contract, can be illustrated initially by contrasting different types of condom failure. The following examples suggest both similarities and differences in women's reactions to accidents, on the one hand, and client duplicity, on the other. Sometimes, physical barriers fail. The condom falls off, it breaks or it leaks. In most accounts, clients' semen is associated with contamination. Women say they wash immediately and repeatedly. Some douche with various mixtures. Most visit the clinic for check-ups. A number report confusion and anxiety. Reactions may be relatively mild or vehement, as shown in the following two accounts:

> If the condom breaks, I start swearing and have a quick wash, inside, with the shower. I have a check-up the next day if possible . . .

> I saw my . . . regular. The durex was left inside . . . . They don't ever leak but this one came off inside. Condoms aren't small enough for [some men], they get lost inside. I had in a sponge and three orthoforms but some spilt. I was so upset. It was horrifying.

The speaker goes on to describe how many times she washed and bathed that day, not just inside but all over and, especially, her hands. This careful hygiene characterizes relations with her boyfriend as well during the next few days.

Alternatively, semen enters the body as clients consciously remove or break condoms. Note:

Last night, I had a twit. There was two hundred on the go for it and the twit doesn't want to wear a condom. I say the usual, 'it's not worth my while', so, in the end, he puts it on. Somehow or other it came off . . . . They are crafty. Thing is, you could be doing the business and, you check every so often, but, keeping your hand there, you can't do it. It came off inside. You're tired, all you want to do is get home and then there's this.

Gail was talking about difficult clients. One, she said, refused to have sex with a condom:

I didn't feel able to get up and go because we had been playing around for 20 minutes and I wanted my money – he's rich. So, he promised to withdraw and I was stupid enough to believe him. What happened was that he withdrew as he came. I was very upset and very angry but I couldn't make a fuss, or I felt I couldn't, because I was in a hotel. The only retaliation I had was – later, when he phoned, I simply didn't turn up.

Sometimes women describe condom failure that is caused by clients as rape:

That was the time when one of [them] conveniently lost the condom. He'd obviously just pulled it off – I checked with my hand. I'd just finished my period . . . . I washed with soap and water under the hotel tap. I felt like I'd been raped . . . . I nearly had to walk out. We argued, because of the condoms.

Reactions to these two types of condom failure are similar in many respects. Women deal with uninvited physical contamination in a number of ways which range from cursory to extensive hygiene and mild annoyance to great anxiety. In both situations, women report washing, douching and other types of cleansing, such as meticulous house cleaning. Some women find it difficult to work. In both situations, the boundaries I have described between two ideally distinct kinds of sexual activity are threatened. Substances associated with work penetrate the person. Often, worries about 'polluting' private sexual partners are reported and condoms may be used at home for several days. Condoms will protect a partner from possible infection. They may also be seen to perform a larger symbolic role, insulating a boyfriend from the work environment and thus re-instituting the differences so important to prostitute women, between private partners and clients, between two kinds of sex. Indeed, my earlier point about the mutual construction of working and personal sex is confirmed further in this context, as things go wrong. It can be seen that the relationship of difference or contrast is more important than the content of any particular sexual activity. When working sex is not associated with condoms, then private sex is.

However, there is a key difference between the two kinds of condom failure described above. In the latter situation, when clients intentionally cause condom failure, women may say that they have been raped. The use of the term, rape, describes sex to which the woman did not agree. It describes non-consensual sex in contrast to the accidental penetration of substance. It suggests that the conscious infraction of an agreement violates the prostitute's person in a more dramatic way than an unfortunate accident. And it constitutes a protest. The use of the term registers a woman's opposition to the behaviour of her customers and her refusal to accommodate this behaviour in the normal work process.

Rape more commonly describes other kinds of broken contracts at work, namely non-payment. Women who work indoors often accept cheques. A price is agreed, sex takes place, and then the cheque bounces. The client has failed to keep to his agreement and has had sex for free. Alternatively, and equally commonly, a client attempts to change the agreement and, when this fails, he refuses to pay. Rachel comments:

> I've been ripped off a couple of times. There's nothing you can do. Last time, I had to walk home at 3.00 in the morning. Normally, if they're people I don't know, I get the money up front. But he had been referred on a personal recommendation. What happens is, they probably weren't going to pay anyway, but they keep asking for sex without [a condom] or whatever, and then they refuse to pay you. It's rape and you can't do anything but walk away. I was really angry, especially, when you've done your work well . . . .

The duplicity of clients who remove or break condoms, who introduce new terms to the agreement previously negotiated, and who refuse to pay for services received is central to concepts of rape in sex work. This duplicity describes a form of violence in which an agreement is apparently negotiated and accepted, only to be broken. In the introduction, it was suggested that prostitutes construct an inclusive view of rape at work. Physical violence or the threat of violence is classified together with broken contracts through the use of the one term, rape. Indeed, in some situations, physical violence is no worse than non-payment or other breaches of contract, as shown by the following example. Claire told me how she was locked up by a client and forced to have sex. She initially described this as rape though she described another rape, by an acquaintance outside work, with much more horror. Later, she accommodated the episode to the business of sex work largely, it seems, because she got her money in the end. While the client was out shopping, she managed to steal his money and jump from the window of the first floor flat.

The above examples suggest the importance of a unitary, inclusive view of rape at work. However, this focus requires certain qualifications. On the whole, as noted in the introduction, prostitutes consider rape with physical violence an especially extreme violation (despite the above example). Client duplicity is countered but it is likewise predictable and expected. Rape, through condom failure or non-payment, might be described as 'rape at a distance'. It is, for example, distanced by time: rape defined through a cheque that bounces is only identified retrospectively. I suggest that prostitutes often use the term rape self-consciously, perhaps even rhetorically, to register a protest that has as much to do with work conditions and social stigma as with violation of their persons. Rapes that include physical assault are generally evaluated differently; they are seen to constitute an immediate and direct attack on a prostitute's sense of self. In this way, the physical nature of the violence may elicit the same response, regardless of the wider context. Thus, distinctions between working and personal sexual relationships may be modified by a second point of contrast, between physical and other forms of violence.

Of course, prostitutes are vulnerable to physical violence. They often describe sex work under the threat or exercise of physical force as well as robberies and muggings. A woman might agree to sex, to one kind of rape, through fear of worse physical violence:

> I was told not to take the case to court 'cos they'd make out I was the criminal. They [the police] knew I worked the streets. It was this client I had in a hotel. I got him to wear a contraceptive. He took the kit off and had sex with me two or three times. I didn't fight. Then I escaped . . . and called the police . . . .

It is not my intention to minimize the degree of physical violence to which sex workers are exposed. It is perhaps obvious from what has already been said that prostitutes are often unable to enforce the agreements they have made and have little redress against any form of rape. As Rachel said when she was not paid, 'you can't do anything but walk away' (quoted above) and, as the woman says above, 'they'd make out I was the criminal'. However, a focus upon the physical aspects of violence alone distorts the wider context in which different forms of violence are grouped together. This inclusive view of rape is not apparent in prostitutes' descriptions of their personal relationships outside work.

RAPE OUTSIDE WORK

While working sex involves contracts, prostitutes make use of the wider imagery of love, sexual desire and romance in describing their personal relationships. In general, a different view of rape is offered along with this imagery. Most of the information that I have on the rape of prostitutes outside work concerns either past relationships with boyfriends or casual encounters. As shown by the following examples, women report a range of attitudes.

Maureen reported a sex assault in answer to my question. She said that her then boyfriend had raped her in 1983:

> I couldn't make a huge fuss because my son was asleep upstairs. Then, he stole my car when I wouldn't go out with him any more. I never got it back. I didn't report any of this. Who would have believed me?
>
> (Maureen had a previous conviction related to her work.)

This account illustrates a typical response: prostitutes cannot complain about rape, no-one would believe them.

Occasionally, this kind of rape is accommodated to work experiences. Karen, for example, told me how she had been raped by an acquaintance, outside work:

> 'It was a one-off', she said. 'I didn't bring charges because I had seen a rape case going though the courts with a prostitute. She had such a hard time.' Karen then told me that she got over her experience a lot quicker than other people would because, 'when a cheque bounces or whatever, it's the same – it's a rape.'

Karen refers first to general ideas about prostitutes, in order to explain that there would have been no point in taking this case to court, but Karen then explains that the rape was not particularly traumatic because of her previous experiences at work. In other words, she builds upon the continuities between different sexual activities in a positive way.

In other contexts, these continuities are unwelcome. Kay, who is pregnant, says that she wants to live on her own, with her child:

> I don't want no man around me. I'm alright but not really because I know what men can do to me and I don't want it to happen to my child
> .... I don't care who the father is. I know who the mother is.... Don't worry, I'll never hold it against my child. It doesn't bother me – as far as I'm concerned, he hasn't got a father, he'll never have one. He may as well not have one anyway. The way I am, I never stay in relationships too long, so I'd never intend this man to be his father. It wouldn't be like that. I'll say, 'I'm sorry that you haven't got one; you have me and that's

it'. . . . He doesn't know anything about it. Do you realize my baby was made in a BMW car? I can tell you a story about how it happened. Big problems, I mean mega-suicidal, and if he knew I was having his child, my life would be finished. I'd never want this man to know I'm having his child. I was with him two years ago and he gave me grief and he made me lose that baby and now he's put one there now. He caught me on the beat, I was working on the beat, and we went out dancing and, by the end of the evening, he said I had to fuck him or he'd smash my face in . . . . And, I'm not into having my face smashed in so I've fucked him before, I fucked him again. It was only two minutes, but I never knew it was going to lead to all this.

Interviewer (SD):   So, in a way, you were raped?

Kay: Yeah, I was, because it was against my will but, as well, I may as well let it happen as I'd have been beaten up anyway. Hit him, hit me, but there's no point in getting your face smashed in, especially on the beat, because no one cares anyway. So what, I thought. I done it and I got out of the car, but I never knew it was going to lead to all this problem of getting pregnant and that. But, right now, I'm happy that I'm pregnant . . . .

Kay had split up with this man, with whom she had become pregnant previously. However, because of her work on the streets, he was able to find her again. Kay does not describe the man as a boyfriend, nor as a client, but simply as a violent man. This time she agreed to sex for fear of worse violence. Once more she becomes pregnant. Kay now seems to invest her sense of self in motherhood instead of a private sexuality. She seems to give up on the idea of a separate private sex life; sexuality as a whole is 'lost' to work.

A final example implicates the boyfriend in work rather differently. He is gradually redefined as a pimp. He comes to be seen as a man closely involved in the business of prostitution, indeed, as a man who makes his living from sex work. Caroline had described a man, S., as her boyfriend but other girls' pimp. Later, during their separation, she saw that he was her pimp too. This final move was prompted by extreme physical violence, including rape. Parts of Caroline's account are presented below, beginning with threats by S., who asks:

'Who the hell do you think you are?' I said, 'I don't think I'm anybody'. And he got this stun gun and he kept hitting me with it and giving me electric shocks. And then he said, 'Oh, sorry, please don't leave me. I need you for the future, I love you' and all this rot. And, I thought, 'Oh, so everything's alright now', you know what I mean. He came back home on Tuesday. . . . We found out that this girl in Yorkshire, she's got all the money that me and this other girl have earned and given to him. The girl in Yorkshire's got it all. And, if anything happens to him, she gets everything . . . . [7] Well, after he'd stunned me, you know, with this stun gun thing, he went with me. I said, 'I don't want to go with you', I said, 'cos I was really crying. And he started going with me, and I kept saying, 'No, no, no', and he kept saying 'sshh', like this, 'it's gonna be alright', and he was going with me. And I think it turned him on, you know, that I was so upset and everything. And I felt really sickened by it all, because I was just crying the whole way through. I just couldn't join in. He kept saying, 'Please stop crying, join in' and everything. But, I couldn't, just couldn't. And that was the only time we went with each other while I was up there . . . . I told [my friend] that I'm leaving him. The money that I earn from now on, I'm keeping it . . . .

This account does not describe a broken contract at work, nor has it much in common with accounts of comparable physical violence at work. Caroline describes an assault on her personal integrity and her moral being.

The examples in this section of rape outside work illustrate a range of attitudes and events in prostitutes' personal lives. None involves reports of prior negotiations about sex and none involves reference to broken contracts. However, some are clearly more upsetting than others and extreme physical violence seems to cause the greatest distress and anger. The first two examples, involving Maureen and Karen, are described at a distance – the rape happened long ago or it involved an acquaintance. But, the second two examples, involving Kay and Caroline, are more immediate and Caroline's account focuses almost exclusively on the attack on her personal integrity through physical violence.

The examples in this section illustrate the contrast between views of rape at work and outside. The last two examples, at least, suggest a narrower definition of rape, involving physical coercion. These examples also illustrate the disabling effects of social stigma upon prostitutes. It has been shown that work involves an impersonal sex, surrounded by a work rationality and calculation. This is sex 'at a distance' which contrasts with an ideal closeness in personal relations. Distance at work is constructed through the contract, the condom, the division and fragmentation of the body and of personal identities captured in a particular name and look. The accidents and violations discussed subsequently threaten to dissolve that distance as semen penetrates the person, wages/profit disappear, and clients break the rules of the market. Minimally, they breach prostitutes' own ideas about appropriate 'occupational health and safety'. More seriously, such problems at work impinge upon a sense of self. In general, rape at work poses a threat to part of the person, to the working persona, while rape outside work constitutes an immediate and more acute assault on the 'real' person, in which a woman invests her moral and personal integrity, and which is constructed outside work. Accordingly, 'rape at a distance' might be contrasted to rape 'close up'. However, in both contexts, rape threatens the boundaries that are so important between one kind of sexual relationship and another. And, it is in women's personal relationships that these problems are felt most acutely. When prostitutes accommodate personal sexual violence to prostitution, they self-consciously dismantle the boundaries so carefully constructed between ideally different types of sex. In the first two accounts, reference is made to the total silence surrounding the rape of prostitutes. In the third, Kay notes her vulnerability to violence. In the fourth, Caroline comes to see her boyfriend as an unwelcome partner in her business rather than a separate romance.

These reactions should be understood in the context of general attitudes towards prostitution. Common stereotypes suggest that women who sell sex cannot be raped because they have already agreed to give sex away, albeit for money.[8] Problems associated with the exchange of sexual services for money are part of the generally unsavoury character of prostitution. While prostitutes may construct an alternative view, as I have suggested, this view carries little legitimacy in a wider context that involves police, courts and so forth. As noted above, prostitutes have little redress against rape at work.

Commonly, prostitution describes a type of person rather than a type of work and consent is written into all sexual encounters. And so the same common attitudes apply equally to prostitutes' private lives: women cannot be raped by their boyfriends any more than by their clients for they are typified by the liberal manner in which they give sex away. I suggest that dominant views of prostitution, which imply that prostitutes cannot be raped, hit women hardest in this context. Prostitutes may identify rape in physical violence only to find, once more, that they have no public voice through which to obtain redress. They are, as it were, triply disadvantaged. First, there is the general imagery of intimacy and romance which excludes explicit negotiations in personal sexual encounters. Second, prostitution may be associated with a particular fixity in this imagery owing to the ideal contrast between types of sex, where romance in one context is identified by reference to work rationality in another. Third, in the event of any kind of rape, prostitutes expect, and frequently encounter, negative public attitudes.

In some cases, women then give up on a personal sex life altogether and some, like Kay, try to build an alternative sense of themselves through pregnancy and motherhood. In this way, women may be forced to follow the majority view of prostitution in a limited sense: private sexual relationships cannot be separated from working sex. Sexuality, as a whole, is lost to work, at least in the short term. Thus, the experience of rape outside work constitutes an acute assault on the moral person. Consequently, women often remain silent about rape in the public arena.

Similar points have been made by others. Walkowitz, for example, writes of the operation of the Contagious Diseases Acts in the late nineteenth century:

> At the local level, they [Contagious Diseases Acts] were used to clarify the relationship between the unrespectable and respectable poor, and specifically to force prostitutes to accept their status as public women by destroying their private associations with the poor working-class community.
>
> (Walkowitz 1980: 192)

> Streetwalking at night was one thing; being forced to attend examinations during the day . . . was another. . . . The domiciliary visitation by the police and the central location of the examination house made it impossible for a subject woman to keep her private and public worlds apart. This is what destroyed her 'self-respect'.
>
> (ibid.: 202)

CONCLUSION

The use of the term 'rape' to describe sexual violence suggests similarities among the different episodes described. In all of them, rape might be said to violate a sense of self. However, it has been suggested that what counts as rape differs in prostitutes' working and personal sexual relationships and rape, in the latter context, violates this sense of self more extensively.

The sale of sexual services involves a working rationality that makes explicit what precisely will take place. Agreements are made for the exchange of particular sexual services for money. It is then relatively clear when agreements have been breached for whatever reason, be it non-payment, non-use of condoms, the attempt to practise particular forms of sex, or the use of physical force.[9] Broken contracts are labelled rape. Prostitutes might be said to construct an oppositional view, which rejects a distinction between physical and other forms of violence.[10] Sexual encounters at work are framed by a rationality that has much in common with debates about consent in the public and, especially, legal arena. Through appeals to a similar language, prostitutes are able to construct an alternative image of rape: the idiom of the broken contract unites different forms of violence and renders them all equally visible. This visibility has remained largely internal to the world of sex work.[11] My concern, in this chapter, is to show that the conduct of commercial sexual relationships provides a particularly cogent critique of the dominant naturalism. Contracts for sex specify the grounds for consent. This work rationality anticipates potential conflict about what exactly counts as consent, a question at the centre of public debates about rape. Prostitutes are consequently enabled to construct an alternative and broader conceptualization of rape. In sex work, the image of the contract is seen to be as much an objective fact as the physical damage a woman may sustain through rape. The contract rescues an agreement for sex between two consenting adults from the realm of subjective and retrospective points of view.

Outside work, prostitutes' ideas about rape are much closer to the dominant naturalism. The similarities have been related to common ideas about romance and intimacy.[12] Commercial sexual relationships contrast with others. In dogma, at least, most sexual encounters unfold. It may not be clear what is legitimate and what is illegitimate, what is consensual and what is non-consensual. Only afterwards, may partners to the act conclude that this was not what they wanted. From the woman's perspective, which is the topic of this chapter, it may then be clear that she had sex to which she did not agree. Her disagreement may be silenced by the wider imagery of romance, passion, and desire that surrounds sex. For, in this context, it is hard to argue that one thing does not lead to another, that the body does not take over from the conscious will, that foreplay does not 'naturally' culminate in intercourse, that condoms do not impede intimacy. The woman may be left with just one context in which it is clear to herself and to the world at large that she did not agree to the encounter. She may be left with an image of rape characterized by the illegitimate use of physical force that is visible after the event. A woman's damaged body bears witness to a private encounter that went wrong; police, doctors, and lawyers can therefore construct a public argument of rape by reference to 'objective' facts rather than 'subjective' opinion. As noted, prostitutes may be particularly restricted by this process insofar as general assumptions suggest that consent is written into all sexual relationships involving prostitutes.

Thus, prostitutes' inclusive view of rape at work has wider implications. The image of the broken contract in sex work throws light on general ideas about rape. It illuminates a paradoxical situation involving different notions of consent. Public and legal debates imply that parties to sex know what they have agreed. However, widespread attitudes to most sexual encounters imply, to the contrary, that relationships are not anticipated in explicit detail. Lack of consensus is hard to specify for consent is normally implied, assumed or, simply, irrelevant. Disagreements and differing evaluations of the encounter may therefore remain unspoken. It is only in the limited and demarcated area of illegitimate physical coercion that publicly acceptable definitions of rape can be made to fit, retrospectively, the private and generally insulated domain of sexual encounters.

It has been shown that representations of rape depend upon the context of sexual relationships. Alternative views may be offered by the same person in different situations. In conclusion, the obvious might be emphasized. To label a sexual encounter 'rape' is to resist the violence or, at least, to register an objection. It is important, therefore, to distinguish one account of rape from another: as shown, a prostitute's use of the label, rape, has particular implications for her view of the world and her future behaviour. The use of the term is not a disinterested one; it brings with it different forms of resistance and different views of social order. While the inclusive view of rape remains largely internal to prostitution, it seems to provide, in itself, some means of dealing with sexual violence. The use of the label 'rape' to describe broken contracts of all kinds belongs to a minority view according to which prostitutes assert the legitimacy of their work in the face of general disapproval. It belongs to a discourse in which prostitutes object to the lack of normal safeguards relating to the contracts that are made, personal safety, occupational health, and so forth. When rape in a prostitute's private life is accommodated to work, this discourse provides, at once, a form of resistance and a defensive reaction to social stigma. Working ideology constitutes a means of resisting common stereotypes but only at the cost of identifying sexual activities that are ideally kept apart.

This chapter has attempted an ethnography of sex work in London and described how prostitutes operate two views of rape, which are associated with two different types of sexual activity. This ethnography may illuminate more general issues. It perhaps highlights the way in which the use of the term 'rape' by a survivor constitutes a specific action as well as a linguistic usage. And the explicitly oppositional view of rape at work illuminates a paradoxical situation in other sexual relationships where women agree to apply particular ideas about consent retrospectively to a situation in which they were absent, only to find themselves restricted by this process to identify their lack of consent with physical injury or the threat of injury.

GLOSSARY

beat	street area where prostitutes work
hand relief	masturbation
orthoform	spermicide pessary
pimp	a man seen to be making a living from a prostitute's work
punter	client

ACKNOWLEDGEMENTS

With thanks to the women who have participated in the research, to staff in the project and to AVERT and North West Thames Regional Health Authority who have funded the research. I should also like to thank Maria Phylactou and Louise Perrotta who made helpful comments on an earlier draft as well as those who contributed to the 1989 seminar in Oxford.

NOTES

1   See, for example, J. Holland *et al.* (1990).

2   See Day and Ward (1990) for further details.

3   See Day (1990) for a discussion of this point and a more extensive description of the distinctions between sexual activities that are summarized below.

4   Personal names are pseudonyms.

5   That is, oral, anal or vaginal sex; frequently glossed as penetrative sex in health education literature of the AIDS era.

6   In some quotations, I have inserted comments in brackets for the purposes of clarification. An ellipsis . . . represents passages which have been omitted from the quotation.

7   Caroline is describing the difference in these relationships. While she and her friend work as prostitutes in London and give their money to S., a third girlfriend in Yorkshire is not working. She is receiving all their earnings, via S. Should S. die, she would be the beneficiary.

8   Parallels might be drawn with other common stereotypes that have been challenged, regarding the rape of married women by their husbands. In law, women have found previously that they could not be raped by their husbands, as they had already given themselves away.

9   This chapter presents women's perspectives on sex work and on the sale of sex. However, clients also complain about broken contracts, in particular, about money. They worry about being 'ripped off' and, occasionally, complain of theft.

10   This rejection has some continuities with other views of rape for many non-prostitutes have 'agreed' to sex for fear of worse violence. Prostitutes and non-prostitutes alike have fought against the assumption that they have to agree to physical injuries in order to prove that they did not consent to sex. However, the more general context of working sex suggests important differences.

11   As Peter Gow has suggested, in editing this chapter, the metaphor of visibility involves a number of strands. For prostitutes, it is legitimate and acceptable to describe broken contracts as rape, on the evidence of the woman involved. However, this claim is not legitimate in the more public arena, in court. First, prostitutes are more or less excluded from court. They cannot appear and bear witness to broken contracts. Second, evidence of rape generally involves a specific kind of visibility, concerning evidence in the body rather than in speech. Evidence is to be seen by investigators such as physicians. This seen evidence is apparently 'objective' while that which is heard constitutes a point of view.

12   See, for example, Holland and Eisenhart (1990) on US women students' imagery of romance.

BIBLIOGRAPHY

Clark, L. and Lewis, D. (1977) *Rape: The price of coercive sexuality*, Toronto: Women's Press.

Day, S. (1990) 'Prostitute Women and the Ideology of Work in London', in Feldman, D. A. (ed.) *AIDS and Culture: the global pandemic*, New York: Praeger, 93–109.

Day, S. and Ward, H. (1990) 'The Praed Street Project: a cohort of prostitute women in London', in Plant, M. (ed.) *AIDS, Drugs and Prostitution*, London: Routledge, 61–75.

Holland, D. and Eisenhart, M. (1990) *Educated in Romance: Women, achievement and college culture*, Chicago: University of Chicago Press.

Holland, J., Ramazanoglu, C., Scott, S., Sharpe, S. and Thomson, R. (1990) *'Don't Die of Ignorance – I Nearly Died of Embarrassment': Condoms in context*, London: Tufnell Press.

Temkin, J. (1986) 'Women, Rape and Law Reform', in Tomaselli, S. and Porter, R. (eds) *Rape: an historical and social enquiry*, Oxford: Basil Blackwell, 16–40.

Walkowitz, J. (1980) *Prostitution and Victorian Society: women, class and the state*, Cambridge: Cambridge University Press.

Index